WITHDRAWN
NDSU

EUROPE AND AFRICA

SAIS African Studies Library

General Editor
I. William Zartman

EUROPE AND AFRICA

The New Phase

edited by
I. William Zartman

Lynne Rienner Publishers   •   Boulder & London

A project of the European Community Studies Association

Published in the United States of America in 1993 by
Lynne Rienner Publishers, Inc.
1800 30th Street, Boulder, Colorado 80301

and in the United Kingdom by
Lynne Rienner Publishers, Inc.
3 Henrietta Street, Covent Garden, London WC2E 8LU

© 1993 by Lynne Rienner Publishers, Inc. All rights reserved

Library of Congress Cataloging-in-Publication Data
Europe and Africa : the new phase / edited by I. William Zartman.
   (SAIS African studies library)
   Includes bibliographical references and index.
   ISBN 1-55587-280-8
   1. Europe—Foreign relations—Africa.   2. Africa—Foreign relations
—Europe.   3. Europe—Foreign relations—1989-.   I. Zartman, I.
William.   II. Series.
D1065.A35E87   1992   1993
327.406—dc20   92-7118
                                                                                            CIP

British Cataloguing in Publication Data
A Cataloguing in Publication record for this book
is available from the British Library.

Printed and bound in the United States of America

The paper used in this publication meets the requirements
of the American National Standard for Permanence of
Paper for Printed Library Materials Z39.48-1984.

*To Boutros Boutros-Ghali,
a friend of Europe and Africa
and a leader of the world*

Contents

List of Tables and Figures   ix

1   Introduction
    I. William Zartman   1
2   Looking South After the End of the Cold War
    Winrich Kühne   7
3   The Impact of Reduced European Security Roles on African Relations
    Edmond Kwam Kouassi and John White   27
4   When Weakness Is Strength: The Lomé IV Negotiations
    John Ravenhill   41
5   The Impact of 1992 on EC-ACP Trade and Investment
    Carol Cosgrove   63
6   The Common Agricultural Policy and African Countries
    Ousmane Badiane   75
7   Europe 1992 and Foreign Direct Investment in Africa
    Persephone Economou, Michelle Gittelman, and Mulatu Wubneh   95
8   Relative Performance of CFA Franc Zone Members and Other Countries
    Shantayanan Devarajan and Jaime de Melo   121
9   Aid Performance and Prospects
    Roger C. Riddell   139
10   Prospects for North-South Negotiations in a Changing International Political Economy
    Eve N. Sandberg and George E. Shambaugh IV   159
11   The Need for an African Response
    General Olusegun Obasanjo   179

Bibliography   187
About the Contributors   201
Index   203
About the Book   213

Tables and Figures

■ **Tables**

6.1	Sources of EC Imports of Selected Agricultural Commodities	81
6.2	Estimates of CAP Effects on International Price Changes	83
6.3	Impact of National Food Policies on the Stability of World Agricultural Prices	85
6.4	Long-Term Effects of Agricultural Trade Liberalization	90
6.5	Stabilization Effect of STABEX on African Export Earnings	93
7.1	Inflow of Foreign Direct Investment, 1970–1988	97
7.2	FDI Inflow to Selected African Countries	98
7.3	Distribution of Foreign Affiliates in Sub-Saharan Africa by OECD Country of Origin	99
7.4	Industrial Distribution of Sub-Saharan Affiliates of EC Transnational Corporations	103
7.5	Industrial Distribution of FDI Stock to Africa from Selected EC Members	104
7.6	Number of Affiliates and Share in Sub-Saharan Africa	110
8.1	Comparison of Indicators for CFA Countries and Comparator Groups	124
8.2	Breakdown of 1980s Indicators for CFA Countries and Comparator Groups	127
8.3	Estimated CFA and Comparator-Group Growth Rates from Error-Components Model	128
8.4	Comparator-Group Growth Comparisons by Subperiod	129
8.5	Comparative Performance in the CFA Zone and Comparator Groups	131
8.6	Changes in Resource Balance, Investment, and the Real Exchange Rate Between 1978–1979 and 1987–1988	134
10.1	Defining Successful Southern Bargaining with Northern States	161
10.2	Conditions Needed for Successful North-South Bargaining	170

10.3 Characteristics of Bargaining in a Changing International
    Political Economy   177

■ Figures

6.1 Ratio of Cereal Imports to Domestic Cereal Production
    in Africa   79
6.2 Degree of Trade Intensity with the EC   79
6.3 Index of Real Agricultural Unit Export in Africa   86
6.4 Efficiency Effects of Liberalizing Agricultural Trade   89
6.5 EC Shares in African Exports of Selected Agricultural
    Commodities   92
10.1 Total EC-ACP Trade as a Percentage of Total EC-LDC
    Trade   163
10.2 ACP-EC X and M as a Percentage of LDC-EC X and M 163
10.3 EC and Japanese Aid to ASEAN   166

1

Introduction

I. William Zartman

With the 1990s, Africa enters its fourth decade of independence from Europe. Twice as many people live on the continent as at the end of colonial rule; their per capita income is about the same, in constant terms. Two-thirds of them have been born since independence; with the exception of a few states in southern Africa, their nationalist struggle is the previous generation's history. To the European metropoles, colonialism is history too, a burden removed and now being repaid by a Third World immigration of new arrivals to perform the menial jobs of the economy and challenge the homogeneity of the society. In the 1960s, it was Africa that was proclaiming unity, to cover the weakness of separate independences; in the 1990s, it is Europe that is constructing unity, to combine the strengths of separate development.

During the past three decades, a debate arose over whether Euro-African relations were a case of decolonization or dependency—whether European presence and influence were gradually declining, leaving Africa increasingly on its own as a part of a multilateralized interdependent world, or were merely ebbing to a more subtle plateau of dominance, leaving Africa locked and co-opted in a class-society world (Zartman 1976; Shaw 1982; Shaw and Aluko 1985). Both were plausible scenarios in the 1970s, although the first was dynamic and more optimistic and the second static and pessimistic. What has happened another fifteen years later, as Europe and Africa stand on the verge of a new phase in their relations?

Two institutional developments give a formal structure to the new phase of relations. One factor is internal to Europe: the completion of economic integration within the European Community (EC) of twelve states in 1992, as a consequence of the Single Europe Act of 1985 (Lodge 1986; Lodge 1987; Church and Keogh 1991; Zysman and Sandholtz 1989; Moravcsik 1991). The other links Europe and Africa: the fourth edition of the Lomé Convention covering aid, trade, and other largely economic relations in the decade of the 1990s (Brüne 1990; Stevens and Faber 1990). The first development consecrates European economic efforts at consolidation and growth within the EC, turning attention inward and in certain areas building a wall of uniform height around the EC that keeps outsiders out. Because Africans have enjoyed some preferential access to Europe, any measure that either restricts access or that equalizes it for all outsiders worsens Africa's condition. The second institutional turning point establishes a regime, twice the duration of its predecessors, covering Euro-African exchanges (along with those of select Caribbean and Pacific countries as well), the thrust of which is to reduce some formerly preferential aspects and to concentrate essentially on a necessary but eroding aid relationship. It is significant that there is not yet any similar institutional turning point in relations among African states to complete the pattern.

The new relations are not simply a product of their own evolution, however. They respond to a third development that has left Europe and Africa free to deal with each other on their own terms, free of external impositions. This salient event of the turn of the decade is the end of the Cold War. Previously neither the United States nor the former Soviet Union had any direct and compelling interest in Africa that approached the historic dimensions or intensity accorded it by the former European metropoles. The superpowers' interest was largely preemptive, in making sure the other did not gain a position on the continent and in responding to perceived changes in advantage (Zartman 1989, ch. 1). For the first decade and a half of independence, Cold War relations were governed by the Congo Conventions, an implicit code of conduct evolving from the first Congo crisis of the early 1960s that stipulated that the United States and the then-USSR could have friendly political relations but not governments in their image in Africa and that the continent was to be a nonaligned part of the free world. This understanding was overturned in the mid-1970s by the Soviet-Cuban interventions in Angola and Ethiopia and the establishment of Afro-Marxist regimes having Soviet friendship treaties, but this second era ended at the same time as the Cold War. Whatever it does with its freedom, Africa is now free of any Cold War constraint to choose its own options, and any importance it may have had to the United States, the former Soviet Union, or Europe is no longer justified in terms of global strategic interests.

As the authors of the following chapters analyze in detail, the new phase is one of mixed characteristics. It is itself dynamic and is the product of a dynamic evolution; that is, it results from and continues a gradual diminution of privileged ties between the continent of the former colonies and that of the former metropoles. Between the two continents, relations have multilateralized, so that unilateral dependency on a former metropole is replaced by the presence of a number of EC members in each

African country's economy. This multilateralization began as early as 1957 with the inclusion of then-colonial Africa in part IV of the Rome Treaty instituting the European Community, and the process has continued unabated. Outside of the continents, relations have also multilateralized, as other countries (notably the United States) and other multilateral agencies (notably the World Bank) take their place as suppliers of aid, trade, and services; as consumers of debt and trade; and as new homes to immigrants.

Furthermore, the dynamic of Euro-African relations, as originally described in the earlier debate, continues to be one of "peeling an onion"—whereby the removal of each form of postcolonial presence uncovers and renders vulnerable and unnecessary the next level of Euro-African relations. Thus, the removal of sovereign control occasioned the withdrawal of military forces, leading to the exodus of expatriate populations and then to the reduction of educational ties, the reorientation of trade, the elimination of budgetary support, and the removal of other components of formerly dependent ties. To be sure, this has been and will continue to be a bumpy process rather than the smooth, paced set of steps the onion-peels image suggests. Indeed, it is even a reversible process in some of its details, as the increase in expatriate populations in some French-speaking countries in the 1970s attested. But the general trend is incontestable: African ties to Europe are multilateralized and diluted.

There are fewer Europeans, more non-European northerners (North Americans and Japanese), but fewer northerners of all types in Africa at the beginning of the 1990s than at any other time since World War I. Among them, there are fewer foreign military personnel. Both the civilian and the military figures were temporarily swollen in the mid-1970s, the former by a growth of the French expatriate colony in core countries of the active zone of French influence and the latter by the sudden influx of Soviet and Cuban troops into Angola and Ethiopia. Declining economic opportunity and waning Cold War competition account for the weakened "pull" factor drawing in these populations, but the "push" factor of increased national competence and assertion is also an element in their decrease.

With expatriate population decline also comes reduced security interventions, often justified as protection of foreign populations. As the 1990s began, African governments long dependent on external support for their security—for example, Chad, Liberia, and Ethiopia—fell to externally supported internal opposition movements, without the state's former supporters' lifting a finger to save them. At the same time, as pressures rose for democratization—for a greater participation of African populations in the control of their own governance—came also a sudden rise in the recourse to outside intervention to keep the process on track. In Rwanda, Zaire, and Togo, military forces from the metropole provided stability by supporting various sides during various forms of democratization. More broadly, in Angola, Mozambique, Ethiopia, and the western Sahara, foreign—if nonmilitary—intervention from Western countries or the United Nations was needed to mediate a peaceful governmental transition to a more democratic system. Alongside these contradictory signals from external sources of intervention was the transitional military operation of the Monitoring Group (ECOMOG) of the Economic Community of West African States (ECOWAS) in the Liberian civil war. Both cooperative great-power intervention to mediate conflict resolution and collective security intervention by an African regional group led by a dominant regional power are signs of the new times of the 1990s. The rising demand for democratization and the gradual government responses to it may work to remove some of the justification for foreign security interventions in the future, but they did not apply in the cases of the early 1990s. Africa had simply, finally, awkwardly, taken its security into its own hands, even though external help was still needed to manage outstanding conflicts.

Economic ties and effects are more complex and occupy the attention of most of the authors in the chapters here. Like the security relations, some of the economic ties are breaking down as they become less functional, while internal EC needs impose new restrictions on European states. A prime example is the last of the monetary links with Europe, the franc zone, which has outlasted its rival in Africa, the sterling zone, by a quarter of a century. Fixed-rate convertibility and shared monetary reserves provided stability and contributed to economic growth in franc zone countries in their first quarter century of independence, above the fortunes of other African countries. But when devaluation and economic flexibility became the requirements of structural adjustment, other African countries developed a stronger economic performance in the latter half of the 1980s.

At the same time, the gradual establishment of a European Monetary System (EMS) makes an African extension of the French monetary system difficult, if not impossible. The historic response would be an African franc (or all-currency) zone attached to the emerging European currency in some fashion, just as a French African colonial zone had its aid and preferential trade relations multilateralized thirty-five years earlier in the Rome Treaty. The more contemporary response, modeled on the ECOMOG analogy, would be the replacement of a colonial economic zone with an African regional economic zone within each of the economic communities established under the impetus of the UN Economic Commission for Africa (ECA), ECOWAS, the Economic Community of the Central African States (CEEAC), and the Preferential Trade Area (PTA) of east and southern Africa. The choice is between multilateralization with Europe and collective—or individual—delinking from Europe.

Like the EMS, other internal policies of economic harmonization reduce the trade flows and access of African products to Europe. Harmonization of standards, for example, raises barriers for African exports that better technologies from competing Third World countries can meet more easily. The Common Agricultural Policy (CAP), a kingpin in the trade-offs through which the Rome Treaty basis of European integration was put together, has a depressing effect on African agricultural exports to Europe and indirectly to the rest of the world.

In other aspects of economic relations, global multilateralization has been fostered from the European side, as privileges and preferences are gradually removed, leaving Africa to compete with the rest of the Third World. The General System of Preferences (GSP) has eliminated much of the edge the Lomé conventions have given to African tropical products, and if 95 percent of African exports enter the EC duty-free, it is precisely the structure of preferences that has kept the other 5 percent from expanding. Mechanisms in the Lomé system to cushion African economies against hard shocks, such as the fund for the stabilization of export earnings (STABEX and SYSMIN), have contributed to avoiding worst outcomes but have not produced effective stabilization. Indeed, after thirty-five years of debate, critics and defenders of the Lomé (and preceding Yaoundé) systems have finally joined in a consensual judgment that the arrangements have been beneficial to African trade and economies and that Africa would have been worse off without them, but even these systems have not enabled the continent to match its Third World competitors' growth, development, and commercial expansion.

Against these indications of ever-increasing decolonization and multilateralization remain some apparent dependencies, perhaps stronger in their effects for their isolated nature. Nothing suggests that they are permanent, but nothing promises their early replacement. For the major inputs to development and security—capital, capital goods, arms, technology—Africa depends on external sources. All such dependencies are African: There are mutually beneficial exchanges but no reverse dependencies. Europe's needs for African products can generally be met from other sources, often with no greater increase in price. However, African dependencies are not just on Europe alone. Africa's total reliance on outside sources for aid or arms draws on a wide range of sources, both private and public, bilateral and (for aid, not arms) multilateral as well. Thus, Africa's dependencies, like its other ties northward, are multilateralized. The problem is that they are not reduced.

If Africa is to maintain only a slightly positive per capita growth rate (1–2 percent), it needs half again as much foreign aid at constant prices over the 1990s as it received in the 1980s (World Bank 1989a, 176–179), between 50 percent and 60 percent of which came from Europe. The result is a rising condition beyond "aid-dependent," known as "aid-driven," and this condition stems from several factors: African exports have dropped by more than 10 percent and the thirty-two low-income African countries' exports by nearly a third in constant values throughout the decade of the 1980s (while other low-income countries held steady) (World Bank 1989a, 240); terms of trade for African products fell nearly 20 percent over the 1980s alone and African trade with Europe ran a constant deficit; and investment is down and decreasing as well and total (mainly public) African debt at the turn of the decade was ten times the total Lomé III aid budget. For these reasons, the only source of pump-priming resources is aid. Unfortunately, the notion of pump priming has faded in the daze of developmentalism, and aid has taken on a more permanent position in North-South relations. That sense of obligation remains on the part of the European North, and the experience of Lomé and other negotiations shows that African states' most powerful bargaining tool is an appeal to the sense of *richesse oblige* of the Europeans and a use of coercive deficiency by the Africans. This is ultimately an argument that is still colonial, not one between aspiring equals.

In sum, Europe and Africa in the new phase of their relations are increasingly more strongly separated from each other in many ways, although basic elements of the previous relationship remain, often in accentuated importance—a "contradictory juxtaposition of selective world market integration and selective disassociation" (Brüne 1990, 201). Partly, this results from a normal process of decolonization, the peeling of the onion. Partly, it results from the removal of external interferences and impositions derived from the Cold War. Partly, it is the by-product of Europe's own inward turning and rediscovery of new opportunities and priorities nearby.

The consequence of these causes is to lay a challenge before the African states themselves, to match these "pull-back" pressures with an internal "push-together" thrust of their own. This effort has begun in security affairs; it needs to be matched in other areas of activity, in developing meaningful solidarity and cooperation. Europe has picked its challenge out of the new phase of North-South relations; it is up to Africa to redefine its position on the other side. Gen. Olusegun Obasanjo, in the last chapter, has identified the ingredients of the challenge to institutionalize the elements of Southern cooperation and developments. The African response remains to be written.

2

Looking South After the End of the Cold War

Winrich Kühne

The Cold War has come to an end. Orthodox Marxism-Leninism has failed and lost its legitimacy for most people who lived under its rule. Through popular pressure, centralistic Marxist-Leninist one-party systems disintegrated almost overnight. On January 7, 1990, the Central Committee of the Communist Party of the Soviet Union (CPSU) renounced its claim for the party's monopoly of power, and in late 1990 a much-debated plan to introduce the market economy was adopted. Yet these and other measures came too late to stop the disintegration of the Soviet empire. The failed coup in August 1991 by conservative party and military leaders, intended to turn history back and save the centralized leadership of the CPSU, was the final blow. On December 21, 1991, the red flag was officially lowered from the Kremlin. There is no more Soviet Union!

In Africa and in the Third World in general, East-West rivalry of past decades dissolved as well (e.g., Halliday 1990; E. Thompson 1991, 139; Kalder 1990; Lowenkopf 1989; Katz 1990; Casteneda 1990). The agreements on the withdrawal of Soviet troops from Afghanistan and of Cuban troops from Angola, the achievement of Namibia's independence and peace in Angola, and the collapse of the Marxist regime in Ethiopia are well-known results of this change. Although other conflicts are still not solved, such as those in South Africa and in Mozambique, no significant differences on the issues remain between Washington and Moscow. Third World conflicts, once a field of fierce competition between the superpowers, changed dramatically: They were a hindrance for Soviet-U.S. cooperation even in more important fields, and then simply became irrelevant to Moscow as regional conflict took over the Soviet Union.

This rough overview may suffice to demonstrate the changed environment of African politics. It raises a number of difficult questions. Only a few of them are treated in this chapter, notably Eastern bloc disengagement from Africa, the failure of Marxism-Leninism and the future ideological debate, and finally the implications of European reconstruction and disarmament for development assistance to the African countries.

■ Moscow's Disengagement from Africa and Superpower Rapprochement

Within a short period, former Soviet President Mikhail Gorbachev's perestroika fundamentally changed the role of regional conflicts in the relations between Washington and Moscow. In the past, national liberation wars and armed conflicts in the Third World were perceived as an opportunity to shift the ideological and military balance of power between East and West, but they also became an obstacle to close cooperation in fields of vital mutual interests, such as arms control and economic cooperation. Furthermore, because of painful experiences one or the other country had in Vietnam, Afghanistan, Ethiopia, and Angola, each superpower had to realize the limits of its military power in directly fighting or assisting to fight popular indigenous uprisings. Their huge military machine was more efficient in perpetuating regional conflicts than bringing them to an end. Local factors proved to be too persistent.

During the 1985 summit meeting with Ronald Reagan in Reykjavik, Gorbachev therefore indicated a strong Soviet interest in cooperating with Washington for solving these conflicts. The Reagan administration responded positively. In 1988, Soviet troops started to withdraw from Afghanistan. At the same time, U.S.-Soviet cooperation to end the conflict in Namibia intensified. In May 1988, U.S. Undersecretary of State for African Affairs Chester A. Crocker and his Soviet counterpart, Deputy Foreign Minister Anatoly Adamishin, agreed on a framework for implementing UN Resolution 435. In this resolution the Security Council in September 1978 had laid down the terms and procedure for Namibia's independence. For a decade, its implementation had been stalled by, among other things, the global confrontation. Ten years later, on December 22, 1988, when the treaties for implementing Resolution 435 and for withdrawing Cuban forces from Angola were signed, U.S. Secretary of State George Shultz and Soviet Deputy Foreign Minister Adamishin congratulated each other on the constructive cooperation of the two superpowers in solving the Namibia conflict. In March 1990, Namibia gained independence.

In 1989, Soviet and Mozambican officials announced the departure of about 800 Soviet military advisers from Mozambique during the period 1990–1991. On July 31, 1990, President Joaquim Chissano announced that the political bureau of Frelimo, the ruling party, had decided unanimously that the conditions for the creation of a multiparty system had been achieved. He had presented in January a liberal draft constitution that (inter alia) stipulated basic individual freedoms, including the right to strike and to own property. Yet the first official talks between the Renamo insurgents and the Frelimo government in Rome in August 1990—facilitated by the Italian government together with the Catholic Santo Edigio community—and nine additional meetings into 1992 have not produced a breakthrough and an end to the war in Mozambique. In November, Portugal and the United States agreed to have representatives at the future meetings.

In Angola, Cuban units were out of the country even before the July 1, 1991, deadline agreed upon in the New York treaty that gave Namibia independence. After more than a decade of heavy military involvement in Angola, Havana concluded its "internationalist" phase in Africa. In late May the same year, Soviet diplomats for the first time had already met with representatives of the Uniao Nacional para a Independência Total de Angola (UNITA) in Miami (*Monitor-Dienst*, July 6, 1990). Moscow then supported U.S. efforts to establish "peace corridors" for saving Angolans from the hunger crisis created by the long war and a drought. Finally, Portugal, supported by Washington as well as Moscow, arranged for direct talks between UNITA and the Movimento Popular de Libertação de Angola (MPLA), which controlled the government. De facto, this put Lisbon into the position of chief mediator. Yet it felt compelled to call for the United States and the Soviet Union to support the process more vigorously in a later phase. Both superpowers agreed to assist in monitoring and implementing a cease-fire and peace agreement. On May 31, 1991, the government of Angola and UNITA in Estoril (Portugal) signed the "Peace Accords for Angola," four documents containing a comprehensive political settlement to end the sixteen-year-old civil war. The implementation of the agreements is to be supervised by UNAVEM II (UN Angola Verification Mission).

With respect to Ethiopia, the most important Soviet ally in Africa after the late 1970s, Moscow in 1989 started to put stronger pressure on Mengistu Haile Mariam to end the war in Eritrea, Tigre, and other parts of the country, as well as the mistaken "barracks-communism" of his junta. Arms supplies to the Ethiopian army decreased, and Gorbachev apparently threatened to stop deliveries altogether. Soviet military advisers were withdrawn from the battlefield in March 1990. One month before, Eritrean rebels captured the port of Massawa. The military and political weakness of the Mengistu regime became more and more apparent. In a desperate but belated move, Mengistu in March turned to reform politics, dropped Marxism-Leninism, and announced the setting up of a "mixed economy." De facto, his regime was already defeated, in military terms as well as in political. In a process brokered by U.S. diplomats, Mengistu was persuaded to resign and to leave the country on May 21; otherwise, heavy fighting and a bloodbath in Addis Ababa was to be feared. On May 28, rebel troops of the EPRDF (Ethiopian People's Revolutionary Democratic Front), with U.S. encouragement, entered Addis Ababa and took power. They committed themselves to a pluralist democracy and agreed that Eritrea should be allowed to determine its future in a UN-supervised referendum in 1993.

With respect to South Africa, meetings of Soviet and white South African experts, journalists, and diplomats became almost routine (Kühne 1988).[1] The ice was broken in October 1988 during a first meeting of more than twenty predominantly Afrikaans-speaking white South Africans with a delegation from Moscow and leading members of the African National Congress (ANC) and the South African Communist Party (SACP) in the Federal Republic of Germany (Leverkusen). The Soviet government already had stressed its preference of a negotiated solution instead of a continuation or even intensification of the armed struggle; "dialogue" was to be the new bottom line. The visit of Neil van Heerden, the director general of foreign affairs in Pretoria, to Moscow in summer 1990 marked the first contact on such a high diplomatic level since the breakup of consular relations between South Africa and the Soviet Union in 1956. On November 27, for the first time an official Soviet delegation was visiting South Africa, not only with the aim of discussing South African aid to clean up the Chernobyl disaster but also with the apparent purpose of improving economic links between the two countries. The delegation also met President F. W. de Klerk. At the end of the visit, the leader of the Soviet delegation stated his conviction that a "new era of good relations between the two countries had started" (*Monitor-Dienst*, December 6, 1990). A few months later, the first South African trade delegation visited the Soviet Union, and in Pretoria, a section to promote future Soviet–South African trade relations was established in the Austrian embassy, headed by Soviet diplomat Alexej Makarov. This section was planned to be the first step toward full diplomatic relations between the two countries. The plan after the demise of the Soviet Union is that the Russian federation will take over this initiative and establish full diplomatic relations with South Africa in 1992. The ANC, the government, and twenty other South African organizations began official talks on a new constitution and related issues on December 21 and thereby removed a major obstacle for withholding diplomatic recognition.

In August 1991 the failed coup d'état against President Gorbachev delivered the final blow to the Soviet empire. There will be no Soviet African policy; the Russian Federation has taken over the diplomatic facilities of the Soviet Union in Africa. The independent countries that have emerged from the former Soviet republic have little interest in African countries except that they will be competing with them for investment, market access in the industrialized countries, development aid, and so on. Even the Russian Federation, huge in terms of territory and population, will be an actor with less importance for Africa than the Scandinavian countries or Brazil, for instance. Mainly for economic reasons, Russia's future policy will focus on one country in particular: South Africa.

The change of relationship between most of the former socialist countries in Central and Eastern Europe and Pretoria is no less impressive. In February 1990, South Africa's Foreign Minister Pik Botha paid his first official visit to Hungary, on invitation of the Hungarian government. It was the first official visit of a member of the South African cabinet to a Warsaw Pact country. Half a year later, in August, the two countries signed their first trade agreement. Trade agreements followed with Poland and Romania in October and November and with Czechoslovakia in February 1991. Agreements to establish consular relationships with the four countries have also been concluded. They are urgently needed for more than 50,000 Poles, Yugoslavs, Hungarians, Soviets, and other groups that have applied for immigration to South Africa (*Star,* September 15, 1990; *General Anzeiger,* November 24, 1990; *Süddeutsche Zeitung,* July 23, 1990). Relations with Yugoslavia were improving along the same lines. In April 1991, Yugoslavia's deputy foreign minister, Branko Lukovac, went to South Africa in the first official mission since 1953, when Yugoslavia broke off relations because of apartheid. Yet there seems to be no future for Yugoslav–South African relations because Yugoslavia also is torn apart by the fight between its different nationalities.

With the end of the East-West conflict, not only the bipolar global military confrontation but also the long era of the "antiimperialist international struggle" (programmatically set up by Lenin in his work on "Imperialism as the Highest State of Capitalism") has ended. In Soviet textbooks and orthodox Marxist-Leninist writings, it was depicted as the most decisive factor in shaping the international system. For decades it served as the ideological rationale for Soviet policy in the Third World, above all in Africa, and facilitated close alliances with "progressive" forces and national liberation movements. Yet in 1989, Adamishin stated (1989, p. 14): "I do not see convincing evidence for the fact that the confrontation between socialism and capitalism is still the decisive factor for the developments in our world."[2] As early as 1988, two Soviet academics, Nikolai Volkov and Vladimir Popov, went even one step further. They opposed the argument that neocolonialism and neoimperialism still existed. In their opinion, "non-equivalent exchange" as a systematic element in the relations between Western industrial states and the developing countries was not evident: "By the 1980s there were practically no traces of colonialism left in the world capitalist economic relations. Consequently, there also vanished the real foundation to which one could add the prefix 'neo'" (Volkov and Popov 1988, 109).

One may not agree with this argument, but the West certainly will not be "buried in the Third World," as Nikita Khrushchev boasted in the early 1960s. Instead, the Soviet Union was torn apart by its internal contradictions; a bipolar world no longer exists. In the future, the United States, France, Great Britain, Japan, Germany, Italy, probably even the Scandinavian countries, and Third World powers such as India and Brazil may be more important actors than Russia and other former republics of the Soviet Union. The outlook for a return to some kind of a unified foreign policy of the former Soviet republic is remote.

■ Has Socialism Failed?

Liberated of all dogmatic ties by Gorbachev's glasnost, a rising number of Soviet authors in the mid-1980s initiated an impressive discussion of fundamental errors in Marxism-Leninism and past Soviet Third World policy. Georgy Mirsky, for instance (1987, 53), admits that "a sober assessment of the present-day situation shows that today there is less evidence than a quarter of a century ago that the newly independent states are abandoning the capitalist road of development and shifting to the noncapitalist course." W. Shejnis (1987, 398) goes one step further and concludes that the "profound contradictions which occur in a capitalist development are not merely a hindrance, but also a source of development." A. Kiva, a leading Soviet author on the developing countries for more than a decade, has stated (1989, 59): "As regards the administrative command-bureaucratic model, I suppose we have every reason to take a most negative view on it. Fettered from the outside by elements of social retrogression, it is historically doomed to reach an impasse." He castigates himself and his colleagues by asking: "But why did we fail to see in time what was obvious?" One can only agree with the answer Kiva himself gives (1989, 57): "For decades, our social science was hopelessly shackled by dogmatism and subjectivism." Boris Asoyan, deputy director of the Africa Department in the former Soviet Foreign Ministry, discards the hope for the possibility of a noncapitalist development with a socialist orientation (1989, 34): "We have realized that a voluntaristic shortcut from one social formation to another or a leap over development phases are utopian."

In Africa, there is not much reason for capitalism to triumph either. The developments under capitalist banners or, more precisely, state capitalist banners in Kenya, Zaire, Ivory Coast, and other countries are not at all impressive. The differences between Benin and the Congo, for instance, both of which officially pursued a socialist Marxist-Leninist orientation for many years, are marginal. The Congo, because of its oil reserves, even belongs to the few African countries with a continuous economic growth rate, though it is moderate.[3] And the performance of Mozambique, Angola, and Ethiopia would not have been so bleak had these countries not been in a state of war for decades. Their economic disaster resulted from several factors: war and destabilization from outside, a misguided economic policy, and natural disasters (Smirnov 1989). The Soviet economist Gleb V. Smirnov from the Institute for Africa in Moscow correctly emphasized that the grim economic results in Africa are not confined to countries with a socialist orientation but are a general phenomenon.

The controversy between capitalism and socialism is less relevant to African development than many observers assume, although the issue fills numerous books and articles. The overwhelming dominance of the state—more precisely, the more or less centralist, authoritarian-bureaucratic state and party structures that are a common feature of most African states—is much more important than this ideological controversy. On the one hand, authoritarian bureaucratic structures, inherited from colonialism, and on the other the authoritarian style of government of the new urban elites, partly based on African traditions, have joined in a repressive symbiosis, unanticipated at independence. The lack of indigenous African capital reinforced this tendency because for Africans the state became the main—if not the only—access route for the accumulation of capital.

It would be hypocritical unilaterally to castigate African elites for taking this direction. Mainstream thinking in development theory in the 1960s and early 1970s all over the world held that the state would have to act as the main "agent of development" and accumulator of capital to compensate for the lack of internal private capital. In practice, a more or less corrupt, more or less repressive, and more or less socialist- or capitalist-oriented "state class" evolved and became a widely discussed phenomenon in the development literature of the 1970s and 1980s. The results, however, were almost always the same: mismanagement, patronism, severe human rights violations, and ultimately the paralysis of private initiative and human creativity in the economic area, especially in the rural sector.

☐ *The Indispensable Market*

A thorough examination of the reasons for the economic failure of the centrally planned economies all over the world leads to the conclusion that the failure stemmed mainly from the dogmatic negation of the market and private initiative. Most orthodox Marxists (and similar schools of thought) made the mistake of perceiving these capitalistic notions merely as forms of exploitation. Although this is one aspect of the market and of private initiative, these forces also have vital functions for economic growth: information (through prices) on the low-cost allocation of resources, creativity, flexibility, and the ability to innovate (among others). These functions were strangled by the centrally planned command economies.

In fact, attempts to enact an all-encompassing system of planning did not lead to more but often to less rationality, freedom, and humanity, in addition to economic failure. In other words, Marxist socialism does not have a workable, refined theory and program for the construction of a socialist political and economic order and has been unable to develop one since the 1917 Russian Revolution. This is not surprising—Marx's writing is mostly about capitalism and its contradictions, and his few remarks on what a socialist society should be like are not very enlightening or definite. The same holds true for Friedrich Engels. "Naive organizational formulas like the withering away of the state [are used]," as Dieter Senghaas has noted (1990, 71). Recently a Marxist from the former German Democratic Republic (GDR) labeled the systems in the old Soviet Union and Eastern Europe as "feudal absolutist socialism" (Robbe 1990).

In Africa the negation of the market and of private initiative had negative effects particularly on the rural areas, where the majority of Africans live and work. Rural communities and peasants lost interest in producing for the private market or were prohibited from doing so. Consequently, they remained in or withdrew to a subsistence economy. Food production in Africa has shown a minimal increase of only 1.5 percent since the 1960s. In relation to the population growth of 3 percent, this is a de facto decrease. Exacerbated by protracted wars, natural disasters (in the mid-1980s, about thirty African countries suffered severe droughts), and other problems, poverty and famine are now endemic in several parts of Africa. In the Horn of Africa, about 25 million people are near starvation; in Angola, about 1 million; in Mozambique, several hundred thousand.

The nationalization of trade, implemented especially in countries with a socialist orientation, was disastrous. The interchange between urban and rural areas—which despite great difficulties small tradesmen had maintained in colonial times—broke down. Farmers could not sell their products or saw no logic in offering them in national buyouts at fixed prices. In the cities, markets and shops became empty.

The urban elites had a facile explanation: Because of the social and economic backwardness of African small farmers and peasants, they could not be expected to achieve quick and extensive production growth and supply the cities sufficiently. Because of their attachment to traditional cultural values, African farmers were deemed unable to modernize. Therefore, the state had to promote development, either through nationalized farms, collectivization, and nationally operated collectives (in countries with socialist orientation) or through agrobusiness, jointly managed by state and multinational companies (in countries with a so-called capitalist orientation). Nationalized farms turned into unproductive capital mongers, and agrobusiness did not care the least for the needs of the indigenous population. Urban elites in Africa were not the only ones to articulate prejudices about African peasants, however. Western agrotechnocrats and Soviet experts on developing countries as well as many orthodox Marxists were equally convinced of the peasants' inability to modernize (e.g., Andreyev 1977).[4] The negative attitude of Soviets toward the peasants is not surprising considering Stalin's liquidation of millions of Soviet farmers in the 1930s and Marxism's primary orientation toward urban industrial societies.[5]

This one-sided perception of the African peasants' ability to modernize has proved to be a crude prejudice. Agricultural production rose by several percent in countries that did not force peasants into the tutelage of bureaucratic structures and rigid pricing systems or that have stopped the practice. Zimbabwe, Tanzania, Mali, and Ghana are telling examples since they enacted reforms. Thus, traditional values do not keep African peasants from increasing their production and from modernization if prices are adequate and the political framework supportive. In Ethiopia, a land reform that benefited the peasants immediately after Haile Selassie's overthrow resulted in continuous production growth until Mengistu stopped it with his policies of forced collectivization and nationalization. After a decade of failure, Mengistu capitulated. In March 1990, he announced reforms favoring private peasant farming, although they were not enough to save his regime.

The significance of shadow economies and black markets in several countries—especially those with a socialist orientation—highlights the creative entrepreneurial potential of the African population. In Luanda, for instance, black markets (called "candongas") are more important than official markets. Acknowledging this fact, the government has labeled black markets "parallel markets" (though they are still only hesitantly shown to foreigners). A study on Zaire found that "unofficial sectors" were maintaining the economy of the country. Actual economic activities are three times as high as stated in official statistics, especially in the wide field of "informal foreign trade" or "smuggling" (MacGaffey 1989). Similar observations can be made in many other African countries.

☐ *What Kind of Market Economy?*
  The Debate about Economic and Social Justice

The revival of the market and of private initiative is not the remedy for all problems, as free marketeers maintain (encouraged by events in Eastern Europe). As German economist Meinhard Niegel (1990) has noted: "The market economy is not a plant which prospers always and everywhere. It is rather, especially its social variant (the social market economy), a cultivated (cultural?) plant, which needs ... intensive nursing." The fact that all economically prosperous states have a market economy should not mislead one to conclude that the introduction of a market economy is a guarantee for economic growth and prosperity. In fact, the majority of market economies are failures. Possibly Zaki Laidi (1988) is correct that the rapid conversion of Africa to the neoliberal model seems as illusory today as was its widespread Sovietization ten years ago.

As noted, the market is a multifunctional and multidimensional phenomenon. Exploitation—the focus of Marxist class analysis—is just one dimension. However, to ignore or underestimate the relevance of this dimension and its potentially inhuman and dangerous sociopolitical effects would be a mistake. Exploitation and social antagonism are possible in market economies; they may be called class struggle, social stratification, or whatever. The extremely uneven distribution of wealth in developing countries is one strong case in point. The immense and widening gap between rich and poor on the North-South axis, which is in danger of becoming irreversible, is another dimension of this problem. On the one side are the three industrial powerhouses—North America (and potentially Mexico), Europe, and Japan (and the four small tigers of Hong Kong, Singapore, South Korea, and Taiwan, whose economic productivity continues to rise with amazing speed); on the other side is the rest of the world, which faces unchecked population growth but is falling behind economically.

Just a few figures may suffice to underline this deepening division of the world: From 1980 to 1987, the share of the developing countries in the global gross national product (GNP) decreased to 16.8 percent, although two-thirds of the world's people live in these countries. The World Bank (1990, p. 28) stated that more than a billion people in developing countries are condemned to live on an annual income of less than $370. Africa's share of global foreign investment has fallen below 2 percent from 5.5 percent in 1960, and its share of global trade is down to about 1.4 percent (*Handelsblatt,* September 30, 1990). The fact that recently even French business is disinvesting from the continent at a rate of about 20 percent annually is alarming. It is estimated that in the coming years one thousand small- and medium-sized French companies will leave Africa. "Would you rent an apartment in a building which is on fire?" was the dry comment of a French businessman about this trend (quoted in Brüne 1990, 68). The Third World's share of German direct investments in developing countries has decreased from 20 percent in 1976 to 12 percent in 1987 and 2.7 percent in 1989.

This difference in productivity growth (because of accelerated technological innovation and social modernization) may render ineffective all structural adjustment policies to lead Africa out of its economic decay. There are few (possibly too few) pockets left for Africans to compete successfully on the world market or—even worse—in Africa itself. In most business sectors, cheap labor is no longer a very relevant cost factor. Good infrastructure, administration, and technical education are much more relevant. The marginalization of raw materials and cheap labor will prove to be a more decisive reason for the marginalization of Africa than will the end of the Cold War and the competition with Eastern Europe. Past debates and theories about imperialism and imperialist exploitation seem to be of little value for explaining this partition or for supplying practical advice to overcome it.

A sociopolitical discussion of the limits and risks of the market and private initiative will therefore be as important in the future as it was in the past. The fact that the controversy between socialism and capitalism is outdated does not mean the problems that generated it have been resolved. The debate on social and economic justice will go on—indeed, must go on. Unlike the past debate, which was little concerned with the real mechanism of economic productivity and focused in the abstract and almost religiously on "the masses," the new debate will have to be based on the realities of market economies and the forces functioning therein. As Richard L. Sklar (1988, 15) noted: "Plainly stated, there is no substitute for capital; it is the driving force of economic development."

☐ *The New Consensus on the Mixed Economy*

The "mixed economy," a combination of state intervention and the private sector, has already become the new catchword for the debate on economic and social justice. In South Africa, the ANC and most other liberation forces, including the SACP, have postulated this model as the basis for a postapartheid economy. Similarly, in Mozambique, Angola, Zimbabwe, Benin, the Congo, and Ethiopia, this notion has become the centerpiece of new economic policies.

In South Africa, leading social and political forces like the ANC and the Congress of South African Trade Unions (COSATU) are looking for a new balance between state intervention and private initiative. They also now have a much more differentiated view on the merits and dangers of nationalization. Sweeping, old-style socialist nationalization is no longer their policy. The consultative workshop organized by the ANC and COSATU in Harare, Zimbabwe, in April–May 1990 produced a document (ANC/COSATU 1990) containing interesting suggestions concerning the future organization of the South African economy. Although the necessity for overall macroeconomic planning was reaffirmed, both organizations are aware of the need to avoid an overcentralized state-command approach to economic policy.

The role of independent trade unions is also an issue not yet sufficiently discussed in Africa, with the exception of South Africa. Mixed economies have no built-in guarantee for social justice and redistribution. Therefore, they need trade unions and other social groups to struggle for social change. Such organizations are merely appendages to the ruling parties and heads of state (as is the case in most African countries) and are thus of no help in this respect. Indeed, "trade union autonomy is a prime marker for the great divide between democratic and Leninist socialism" (Sklar 1988, 9).

In January 1990, President Joaquim Chissano of Mozambique criticized the traditional dominance of the party and its so-called mass organizations. He demanded that trade unions should be independent and that they be guaranteed the right to strike. In other countries, similar suggestions were made. In South Africa, ANC and COSATU agreed that independent trade union rights should be enshrined in the constitution (ANC/COSATU 1990). South Africa's strong, independent trade union movement, experienced in both fighting and negotiating, could become a guide for Africa for the sound organization of labor relations in a mixed economy. This could have a healthy impact on the role of trade unions in the southern African region in general. If South Africa eventually joins the Southern African Development Coordination Conference (SADCC), trade unions in the region also would be well advised to take a more regional approach in order to counter the regional maneuvering of business in labor relations.

☐ *Debate Guidelines for Transformation of the State*

The mixed-economy concept derives much of its popularity from the fact that it leaves most questions open. Both politicians and experts in and outside Africa will be challenged to define it more precisely. Which mixture will be optimal in the respective sectors? Have there been experiences either inside or outside Africa that could be generalized?

There is a danger in Africa (as well as in Eastern Europe) that after a phase of too much state intervention, the debate will concentrate exclusively on the withdrawal of the state, in the belief that the rest can be left to free market forces. However, as noted, to flourish, market economies (especially social ones) need a state to provide an efficient and predictable legal and administrative framework as well as infrastructure. This is the secret of more or less all successful market economies, not only in Europe but also in Asia.

Africa therefore needs a much more explicit debate about the transformation of the state (and its bureaucracy). South Africa is one of the few countries where such a debate takes place. A neglected part of it (in Eastern Europe as well as in Africa) is what sequence of reforms and timing would be economically and socially the least harmful. Furthermore, the market and planning are not dichotomies, as standard Marxist thinking insinuates. Planning by business and by local, regional, and national state actors is a vital part of successful market economies, although the planning geared to market forces is of course very different from the central planning of command systems. Current developments in Poland and other former socialist countries in the East show how difficult it is for the old bureaucracy to switch from one type to another. It is more than just an institutional and legal problem—it is a difficult and painful process of mental adjustment.

The technocratic role of the state to provide an adequate legal and administrative framework and infrastructure for market forces is very much related to questions about democracy and political organization (one-party or multiparty rule, type of government structure, separation of forces, and so on) that are currently being discussed in Africa. Much has been said recently about the lack of accountability—or to use a broader and more fashionable term, "bad governance"—in most African states (e.g., Carter Center 1989). Accountability in fact is a link between these two issues.

There is little doubt that the era of one-party rule is coming to an end. Encouraged by the events in Eastern Europe, a wave of popular revolt is sweeping the African continent. The first spectacular case, in late fall 1989, was Benin, one of the first African states to adopt Marxism-Leninism as its official ideology (in 1974). Particularly discouraged by the downfall of Eric Honecker (East Germany) and later Nicolae Ceausescu (Romania), African rulers did not dare suppress regional uprisings, as some of them would have done a few years ago. Rather, most of them have tried to accommodate popular discontent by taking up the issue of multiparty rule.

■ No Marshall Plan for Africa

Naturally, the widening gap between the developing countries and the North has led to numerous calls for massive transfers of capital to developing countries—multiple Marshall Plans comparable to the one Europe received from the United States after World War II. In Africa, hopes for such a plan have been particularly voiced in southern Africa but also in other regions, such as the Horn. Several regions outside Africa have made similar demands.

Yet the comparison with the 1948 Marshall Plan for Europe is flawed. First, in recent literature, there is no agreement at all on how important the Marshall Plan really was for rebuilding Europe (e.g., Borchardt and Bucheim 1987).[6] Second, the Marshall Plan, although providing about $13 billion per annum, was not a plan for economic development but a plan to restore the already developed European economies, whose infrastructures were partly destroyed by the war. As one author has written (Garten 1984): "The problem was to restore what had already existed, not to create a more advanced society," the latter being much less amenable to solution by a huge transfer of financial resources. The limitation of absorbing huge amounts of money in a productive way is the most obvious problem. A huge debt burden and the high level of enrichment a small elite in many developing countries enjoys by channeling aid capital into their foreign bank accounts are logical consequences of this limitation. This seems to be the unambiguous lesson of three decades of development aid. As one journalist wrote (*Financial Times*, June 7, 1990): "Despite aid programs that pump more than $10 billion a year (or $83 billion between 1980 and 1988) into sub-Saharan Africa, living standards have declined in the 30-odd years since independence."

The second reason a new Marshall Plan is unlikely is the perceived failure of development aid. For countries to gain a massive transfer of resources, it will not help to appeal either to the guilty conscience of Western nations over their colonial past or to the wealth of the Northern Hemisphere. These appeals are increasingly falling on deaf ears. The results of three decades of development aid are considered to be too meager, apart from the enormous task of economic reconstruction in Europe. As one author from the German left wrote: "The reputation of development aid as an instrument for fighting poverty has been more or less ruined" (Dauderstädt 1990, 5). And for the former "natural allies" of the Third World, the countries of the former socialist bloc, their development aid will come to an end, if this has not already happened.[7] In October 1990, the journal *West Africa* reported that Soviet President Gorbachev, in response to a public outcry, decreed that aid to the developing nations of Africa and Latin America should be slashed immediately.

One could continue quoting alarming statements on the failure of past aid policies in Africa and other parts of the world. One could also enumerate all the well-intentioned programs of the last decade put forward by international organizations—like the Organization of African Unity (OAU), the United Nations, and the Economic Commission for Africa (ECA)—to improve Africa's economic situation. Yet the 1980s were lost as a time for development in Africa (and other parts of the Third World, such as Latin America).

☐ *The Illusion of a Peace Dividend*

On November 25, 1990, the twenty-two member states of the Warsaw Pact and NATO signed a historic agreement in Paris on the reduction of conventional forces in Europe. Yet in parallel to this historic achievement, proponents of "disarmament" are learning about its costs. The systematic destruction of heavy weapons such as tanks, armored cars, and artillery as well as the conversion of the military-industrial complex will prove much more difficult and expensive than realized before. For instance, eight men are required to work one week to disintegrate a Soviet T-55 tank, at a cost of about $25,000.

The "peace dividend" for the Third World that many have been hoping disarmament in Europe would entail will not materialize, at least not in the medium term. "Swords into plowshares" was a nice, romantic slogan. As it turns out, it has little to do with the reality of disarmament. Instead, conventional disarmament in Europe may even have a negative fallout on peace and security in the Third World. The international arms market, the legal as well as the illegal one, will be (and is already) flooded by cheap "disarmed" weapons, either by those that "escape" destruction east of the Urals or those that do not fall directly under the disarmament agreement and its provision for destruction but that will be relinquished as a result of troop reduction. An aggressive sales policy of armament industries in countries of the South (like Brazil, Argentina, South Africa, Israel, Iraq, Pakistan, India, and China) as well as those of the North, facing a reduced market in the Warsaw Pact and NATO countries, will add to this inflationary trend. This is an utterly disturbing perspective in view of the rising potential of socioeconomic and ethnic conflicts in numerous developing countries!

☐ *The Exploding Costs of European Reconstruction*

The aid fatigue just described has to be seen in conjunction with the exploding costs of reconstructing the former socialist countries in the East. The economic, ecological, and social situation in these countries is much worse than was assumed before the iron curtain was lifted. In fall 1990, the euphoric phase of the collapse of unliked, oppressive, and unproductive systems in the East ended. Disenchantment and even despair are rising. Economic descent has begun and will only be halted years from now. Whereas the old systems no longer function, the new market-oriented systems do not yet work. In the cases of the republics of the former Soviet Union and of Bulgaria, Romania, and Poland, even famines (and serious energy shortages during wintertime) cannot be excluded. Convoys with food and medical aid for Poland and the new republics have left West Germany and other West European countries. The European Community ordered a crash emergency program for the republics of the former Soviet Union, above all Russia, to meet hunger and severe energy shortages in the winters of the early 1990s. Only the unification of the former GDR with its economically booming neighbor, the Federal Republic of Germany, is escaping this fate.

It is therefore evident that in the last decade of the century, not only the attention but also the material resources of Western Europe, the United States, and Japan will be concentrated on Eastern Europe and the former Soviet Union. Hundreds of billions of deutsche marks (DM) and dollars must be invested to restart the economies of these countries. The cost of German unification is skyrocketing. Present estimates have already reached the figure of DM 100–150 billion annually for the coming years; another estimate is $1–2 trillion during the next ten to fifteen years.[8] Twelve billion marks will have to be paid for supporting Russian troops on German soil during the next four years. Overall infrastructure (roads and communication systems) is deteriorated and outmoded in all Eastern European countries, even more so in the former Soviet Union. Its modernization is a precondition to foreign investment and economic growth. Ecologically, huge parts of Eastern Europe and the former Soviet Union are in a terrible state. Again, billions of dollars will have to be invested to get it under control. More Chernobyl-like catastrophes or explosions of gas and oil pipelines that would cause devastating effects on the population and ecology are feared in parts of the former Soviet Union and Eastern Europe. The previously mentioned costs of German unification do not include the cost of restoring the ecology of the former GDR, calculated by one economist to be about DM 500 billion (*Herald Tribune,* September 21, 1990).

These figures, which do not include the costs of the 1990–1991 war mounted in the oil Gulf against Saddam Hussein, may suffice to explain why there is no chance for an increase of material resources to Africa. A decrease is more probable, if not certain. This may even be true for food and humanitarian aid, as already mentioned, if one analyzes the grim food and energy situation in several parts of the former Soviet Union and Eastern Europe. Central Europe is getting nervous about a rising flood of immigrants from the East. "The Russians Are Coming" was the title of an article in *The Economist:* this time the reference was not to the danger of a military invasion from the East but to the millions who may start migrating to the West (*Economist,* October 20, 1990).

Africans reasonably may object that the situation in most African countries is much worse than in Eastern Europe, and that therefore, in moral terms, they are more entitled to funds. In principle, this is correct. Millions are starving in different parts of Africa. Unfortunately, apart from the disappointing results of past development aid, Africans have to be aware of the following fact: The massive transfer of capital from Western Europe to Eastern Europe is not merely an investment in the economic future of these countries. It is also an investment in Europe's peace and security, which will be endangered if the present economic decline in the East, on the one hand, and the rise in ethnonationalism, on the other hand, continue. The perspective of an unstable East is of grave concern, particularly in Germany. Ethnic and national conflicts may escalate into violent confrontations (as already has occurred in Yugoslavia and some of the former Soviet republics) and seriously test the European capability of conflict managing and peacekeeping. Europe, as indicated, will have to stop speaking of "tribal conflicts" exclusively when referring to Africa.

As for Europe, this continent would be ill-advised to judge its relations with Africa merely in terms of diminishing strategic and economic interests. Constructive relations with Africa are an important part of an enlightened, nonracist identity and political culture of European countries. Furthermore, the so-called global challenges (poverty, ecology, migration, drug traffic, population growth with the attendant proliferation of diseases, and so on) will affect the countries of Europe more or less directly and force them to take a thorough look at Africa again, rather sooner than later. Europe, therefore, has a deep interest in assisting to make the new realism a success, wherever it occurs.

Besides the improvement of present governmental and nongovernmental development assistance, three topics are salient and must receive increasing attention: First, an even more decisive cancellation of debts is needed with respect to those countries that try a new realistic start. The fact that there is still a net capital flow from the developing countries to the industrialized ones because of debt servicing is a scandal. According to the World Bank, in 1990 developing countries had to repay $27.5 billion more than they received in new credits and grants. The sub-Saharan countries retransferred $500 million more than they received (SADCC 1990, p. 9).The decision of the European Community to cancel almost $6.5 billion of debts of Lomé countries is a small step in the right direction.

Second, trade barriers and unfair subsidies in the three industrialized centers of the world, which make the technoeconomic North-South divide even more insurmountable for developing countries, need to be removed. This is particularly important with respect to agriculture. African farmers do not have the slightest chance of competing with the heavily subsidized farmers in the industrialized countries who receive about $250 billion annually, five times the amount of official development assistance (ODA) (*Süddeutsche Zeitung,* December 12, 1990). For this and other reasons, the price subsidies of the European Common Agricultural Policy (CAP) have to be eliminated. Otherwise, Europe has no legitimacy to ask for market economies in Africa. Although African net food importers benefit from subsidized European agricultural exports, the removal of price subsidies is paramount to giving African agriculture a better chance. Without improvement of the rural sector, there will be no sustained development in Africa.

Third, a more vigorous and better organized human rights policy is necessary to support the process of democratization in African countries. The major aim of such a policy would be not to force upon Africans a democratic model from outside, such as the multiparty system, but instead to create space and assist to keep it open for a relatively free debate on what democratic system is correct for which country. Torture, preventive detention, detention without trial, no due course of law, and pressure and persecution of church leaders, journalists, and lawyers are all part of

The facts and figures mentioned here allow only one conclusion: There will be no significant rise in outside development assistance to Africa in the coming years. A gradual decrease, at least in relative terms, is much more probable. Food and humanitarian aid will become more scarce because of famines, energy shortages, and similar problems in Eastern Europe. African politicians, in their desperate search for more financial aid, are therefore well advised not to listen to Western politicians who promise that the change in Eastern Europe and the former Soviet Union will have no repercussions on development aid available for the South because European countries, especially Germany, can afford both. This is obviously not the case. Africa can no longer hope to be saved from outside.

■ Improving the Future

This is a tough reality. Africans can either react with despair or with a "new realism," dropping past illusions and ideological daydreams and using the dramatic changes of their international environment as a challenge to solve their problems essentially by themselves by mobilizing their own resources and creativity. African politicians and intellectuals have to work hard for a new consensus among themselves and the people on this necessity. It should be at the center of the debate on more democracy, more participation, and more accountability. The result could be what has been lacking so far in many African countries as compared, for instance, with some Asian countries: a profound, realistic, and sustained determination to advance.

This is not an easy demand. Yet an increasing number of Africans are thinking along these lines. The first Annual Progress Report of the 1990s by SADCC (1990, 9) is but one example:

> There is no choice for Africa and SADCC member States, but to effect changes providing for greater economic and political freedoms and to achieve higher levels of efficiency and productivity, better and accountable governance, the development of human resources and the mastery of science and technology.

Although it seems to be a paradox in view of the widening gap between the three world industrial centers and the rest of the world, a determined improvement of the internal and regional conditions is the most realistic and, therefore, most promising way to reduce this gap. The SADCC report obviously has such an approach in mind. A thorough examination of the world market and its sectors where African agriculture and business have a comparative advantage to compete is the other side of this coin.

endeavors by a number of African rulers to suppress this debate. Consistent pressure from outside can help to change these practices. Conditioning development aid in the sense of tying it to the implementation of multiparty rule, as some demand, will achieve very little and is misguided. It underestimates the complexity of the problem of democracy in Africa. There is no unified answer for Africa. Single or multiparty rule is just a small part of the much more comprehensive question of the transformation of the state and civil society in African countries. A stable democracy cannot be imported from outside.

■ Notes

1. An extensive description of Soviet policy on South Africa can be found in Campbell (1986).

2. A view more in accordance with the conventional thinking of the past is taken by Anatoli Gromyko, director of the Africa Institute in Moscow (1989, 52): "New political thinking does not imply renunciation of the class approach, but it develops this approach in a new historical situation."

3. Botswana is an even more remarkable exception to the general failure of development in Africa. Because of sound management of its mineral resources and the economic dependence from South Africa, it has managed an average growth rate of about 8 percent for years. In contrast, the Ivory Coast, for a long time praised as a miracle of economic development along Western ideas, is in a deep economic and social crisis.

4. Some independent Marxists opposed this opinion. As early as the 1960s, S. Amin (1964, 43) presented the thesis that progressive regimes with a socialist orientation had to "break up" the traditional agrarian sector with capitalist development.

5. Even before perestroika, several authors (e.g., Aaby 1978; Kühne 1983) upheld the thesis that Marxism-Leninism would fail in Africa, not least because of its proletarian urban bias against development.

6. Another study, and it is not the only one, points out that "by 1948, when Marshall Plan aid became operative, industrial production in the European countries was already above the 1938 level, including Germany" (Fodor 1984,). To this the same author adds the fact that "the country that received the most American aid [55 percent] was Great Britain, a country that after the war had a much higher level of output than before the war" (Fodor 1984,) He concludes that the Marshall Plan was not decisive for restarting production but for solving a huge foreign exchange crisis of the European economies vis-à-vis the U.S. dollar because of a violent rise in U.S. prices in 1946.

7. Moscow, in its budget for 1990, cut its share of development aid by 30 percent. Soviet aid to Mozambique, which used to be a total of $200 million (U.S.) annually (at the official exchange rate) was cut to $90 million in 1990, with additional cuts likely, as the first secretary in the Soviet embassy in Maputo told the press (*EDICESA*, 1990). For a good account of Soviet assistance to Africa, see Shatalov (1990).

8. Africa's military expenditure has increased and stands now at $250 billion, more than Africa's total debt (*Southern African Economist*, August/September 1990, 10).

3

The Impact of Reduced European Security Roles on African Relations

Edmond Kwam Kouassi
John White

For over two decades, relations between Europe and Africa were marked by the great movement of decolonization, until the independence of Zimbabwe in 1979 completed the independence of Africa from European rule. As a result of their newness and fragility, African states face security issues that go far beyond the usual military matters into political and even economic affairs. Because it was a gradual and largely evolutionary movement, decolonization permitted mutual economic solidarity to be maintained and also a European political and military security policy to emerge in support of the newly independent states.

As Professor Jean-Pierre Cot (1984, 108), former French minister of cooperation, has noted: "Independence was not conceived of as a clean break but rather as the innovation of a complex network of all kinds of connections between the metropole and the new African states. In this kind of arrangement third parties have no place."

Whereas maintenance of economic ties called for a wider project of a multilateral type, such as the association of African countries with the European Common Market, the military security issue was handled on a bilateral basis through mutual assistance agreements. These accords provided for military interventions, always on invitation, on the part of France to defend or restore the security of the state and/or regime. Intervention came in three waves: in the early 1960s to support newly installed regimes, in the 1970s to repel a variety of internal and external challenges, and in the 1990s to manage the democratization process. But increasingly, former metropoles—just as the superpowers—have withdrawn from a security role, leaving a vacuum that African states must find ways to fill. Both internal and interstate security are roles that will require casting for African players.

Since independence, African states have been linked to their former colonial powers by close security agreements. This type of relationship had already existed within the context of "French Union" first, then of

"French Community" as well as that of the Commonwealth for Anglophone African countries. Hence, agreements were already in effect before these African states became independent. British defense agreements did not long survive the changing relations of independence, although military supply and training agreements continue. Nigeria canceled its mutual defense pact with Britain in 1962, but after the Biafran crisis it maintained and renewed cooperative agreements in 1975 and 1976 and beyond (Aluko 1981, chs. 3 and 4). Postcolonial defense agreements also exist between Belgium and Zaire (1978), Portugal and Guinea-Bissau (1978) and Mozambique (1982), and Spain and Equatorial Guinea (1980); these have some security effects. Franco-African relations, however, have exhibited a closer type of security involvement.

■ France's Security Role in Africa

In the relations between France and African states, there are two types of agreements: defense agreements and military assistance agreements, some in the form of secret treaties.

In the first type, thirteen African states have been bound to France by defense agreements. They are the Central African Republic (1960–), Gabon (1960–), Madagascar (1960–1975), Mauritania (1960–1972), Senegal (1960, 1974–), Côte d'Ivoire (1961–), Benin (1961–1974), Niger (1961–1972), the Congo (1960–1972), Chad (1960–1978), and Togo (1963–, 1974–). Cameroon (1960, 1974–) and Djibouti (1977–) have secret defense agreements. There are also multilateral agreements between France and the three original member states of the Conseil de l'Entente (Côte d'Ivoire, Benin, and Niger) (April 24, 1961, with a secret protocol on the quadripartite Defense Council on January 1, 1962), and with the three equatorial African states (Central African Republic, Congo, and Chad) (August 15, 1960, with a secret protocol in the five-party Defense Council on August 25, 1962) that Gabon joined by a protocol (on June 20, 1961) (Decraene 1985; Chipman 1989; McNamara 1989). Burkina Faso has signed only technical military assistance agreements, but it grants France the triple right of overflight, stopover, and transit in order to facilitate the defense of neighboring states linked to France. Among former French colonies, only Mali and Guinea never signed a defense agreement, although the former has had a military cooperation agreement with France since 1977.

Although in principle each state is responsible for its own internal and external security, it still can, in certain circumstances, call upon foreign armed forces to ensure fulfillment of this responsibility on its behalf. Defense agreements between France and African states nominally "give mutual help in assistance to prepare and secure their defense," in the language of article 5 of the French agreement with Madagascar, for example. The purpose of these agreements is to prepare a defense plan to determine the conditions under which military assistance can be used for the necessary material support and troop deployments in time of crisis or threat of crisis. In fact, these Franco-African defense agreements bind their members in much the same manner as the great mutual defense treaties, such as the North Atlantic Treaty, the Southeast Asian Treaty, and the Warsaw Pact. However, there is no provision stating that an attack on one contracting party will be considered an attack on all. The states concerned remain sole judges of the moment when they are attacked or threatened from outside. In the same manner, France can refuse to grant the military assistance requested.

Implementation of the agreements is selective, in accordance with the circumstances and the interests involved. Thus, in the first period of the early 1960s, French troops intervened alongside the government headed by President Ahmadou Ahidjo in Cameroon during the serious political rebellion that shook the western part of the country in the period 1957–1964 and in support of the government of President Leon Mba in Gabon against rioters in 1960 and 1961 and against a coup in 1964. But the French did not intervene on many other occasions: in 1963 in Togo when President Sylvanus Olympio was assassinated; in the Congo when President Fulbert Youlou was overthrown; in later coups throughout the 1960s in Dahomey, the Central African Republic (CAR), Upper Volta, Togo, Congo, or Mali; or in the early 1970s in Upper Volta and Madagascar.

Except for ongoing involvement in the northern rebellions in Chad after 1968, no military interventions were conducted between the mid-1960s and the late 1970s. A second wave of French military activity in Africa can be associated with the tenure of Réné Journiac as adviser on African affairs to President Valéry Giscard d'Estaing. The interventions of the late 1970s were varied in nature. Many were in retaliation: against Polisario attacks on French technicians and government installations in Mauritania in 1977; against the Congolese National Liberation Front (FLNC) invasion of Katanga province with attacks on French personnel in Zaire in 1977 and 1978; and against renewed Frolinat attacks against the government in Chad during 1978 through 1980, but this intervention was also to overthrow the egregious government of "Emperor" Jean-Bedel Bokassa in the Central African Empire in 1979. Some of these interventions protected African security as well as French personnel, but the case of CAR was comparable only to Tanzania's removal of Idi Amin Dada the same year from Uganda, where exceptional measures were needed to handle an egregious situation. In Uganda, the instrument was African; in CAR it was European because France had previously been a close supporter of Bokassa's regime.

During the first period, France did not justify its military intervention other than by reference to the state security agreements. It simply stated (as slightly paraphrased here): "At the invitation of such-and-such state to which it is bound by a defense agreement, France decided to send troops." But after the outbreak of the Chado-Libyan war in 1978, France has given reasons for intervening: a riposte to a foreign military attack on a state that has a defense agreement with France, as in the case of Chad in 1983; the protection of French citizens, as in the case of Zaire in 1977–1978; or the promotion of democracy (plus the protection of French citizens), as in the case of Togo in 1991.

A closer study of these interventions reveals France's desire to assure the security of a regime to which it is attached. Otherwise, how can the deployment of French paratroopers to Lomé (Togo) three days after the terrorist attack on September 23, 1986, be explained, in contrast with nonintervention in the Burkinabe coups of 1980, 1982, and 1983? Whatever their names—for example, "Barracuda" (CAR 1979) or "Epervier" (Chad 1983)—French military interventions are supposed to be backed by a well-established doctrine that is the preservation of Franco-African economic, political, and strategic interests. French calculations have included consideration of how much support the French would have within the African state's army after a coup and of the expected costs of supporting a government against recurring threats from domestic and foreign enemies. Hence, France failed to intervene in 1990 in defense of the Hissène Habré regime in Chad, and it fell to Idris Deby. Rwanda's appeals for assistance against attacks by rebels based in Uganda at the beginning of 1991 apparently were considered more potentially effective and supportive of French interests and objectives, and French troops remained the entire year.

The third wave of French interventions has come at the beginning of the 1990s, following the prodemocratization policy announced by President François Mitterrand at the Franco-African summit at LaBaule in 1990. Despite a clear policy, the French role has not been clear. The intervention in Rwanda protected President Juvenal Habyarimana's Hutu regime against a multiethnic opposition. The briefer intervention in Zaire along with Belgian troops in fall 1991 defied President Mobutu Sese Seko's orders to leave, but it also assured some order and protection for his regime against rioting Zairian troops and a pressing opposition movement. At the end of 1991, French troops were sent to Benin as a threat to intervene in neighboring Togo if the army uprising against the prodemocracy government of Prime Minister Joseph Koffigoh and in favor of President Gnassingbe Eyedema were not brought under control. After the socialist interlude of the 1980s, interrupted only by military interventions in Chad in support of Hissene Habre against the external Libyan attacks, France has shown a continued reluctance to intervene, even to keep order during democratic transition.

On the whole, with a number of African countries, special conventions on maintaining internal order complete the provisions of defense agreements and define the conditions for filling African states' requests for French armed forces, either as indirect intervention through the supply of materials or services or as direct intervention of armed forces. France remains the sole judge of the appropriateness and form of its intervention. It is in the interest of the signatory states that the intervention be limited to their security and to the maintenance of public order and not so much to serve the short-term interests of the policy of the moment.

An indispensable component of the defense agreements is the technical military assistance agreement signed with all Francophone African states except Guinea. Gabon and CAR operate under their original agreements of 1960, and Côte d'Ivoire and Burkina Faso of 1961. Among the other states that signed an original agreement in 1960, Cameroon, Congo, and Senegal renewed in 1974 and Chad in 1976; the rest originally signed in 1961, with Madagascar renewing in 1973, Benin in 1975, Mauritania and Togo in 1976, and Niger in 1977. Mali and Djibouti only signed an assistance agreement in 1977. There are also agreements with the former Belgian territories—Zaire (1974), Burundi (1969), and Rwanda (1975). France is committed to give assistance in personnel (senior officers and junior officers) for the organization, instruction, and training of armed forces of African states, and supplies free of charge all or part of the necessary material and equipment. Senior officers of national armies are thus instructed to call exclusively upon France for the training of their personnel.

Besides defense agreements, special protocols involving strategic raw materials and products have been concluded with certain African states—CAR, Gabon, Madagascar, Mauritania, and Senegal in 1960 and Togo in 1963. These materials and products are: liquid and gaseous hydrocarbons, uranium, thorium, lithium, beryllium, and helium. Signatories of the special protocols and the technical military assistance agreements are committed to follow with France a common and concerted policy about strategic and raw materials. They give it priority in their imports and exports. Moreover, they facilitate the stocking of these products for the benefit of French troops.

■ Evaluation of Franco-African Security Measures

France's role in providing security for selected African states and regimes has produced two different consequences: It has fostered domestic and international stability, but it has also given rise to regional initiatives for collective security.

Though some signatory countries have experienced minor disturbances internally, Francophone Africa in general constitutes an area of relative stability because the threat of external aggression is neutralized. The dissuasive effect of the defense agreements appears to contribute to African security. The regions of endemic insecurity in Africa are those that lack French security agreements—the Horn of Africa, the western Sahara, the frontline states of southern Africa, Liberia and Biafra in West Africa, and Burundi and Uganda in East Africa. States in some of these areas had security agreements with the former USSR—Ethiopia, Somalia, Mozambique, Angola—but these were not effective in providing the same stability. In other cases of recurrent instability, such as Chad and Zaire, French intervention has provided security that local governments and armies were unable to assure.

Neither in theory nor in the constitutional practice of the Organization for African Unity (OAU) is there a definition of a model of collective security. Although the role played by France in the preservation of the security and stability of Francophone African states has been relatively effective, this role is bound increasingly to weaken, for several reasons.

First, for economic reasons, France in the 1970s redeployed its armed forces previously stationed overseas and reduced the number of its military bases in Africa. Thus, under the provisions of the new conventions signed especially with Chad, Senegal, and Gabon, the logistic support that was formerly ensured by French armed forces in Africa was thereafter carried out directly from France (for example, in the interventions in Zaire in 1977–1978 and 1991, in Togo in September 1986, in Gabon and in Rwanda in 1990). Bases remain at Dakar, Senegal (1,200 troops); Bouar, CAR (1,200); N'Djamena, Chad (1,100); Port Bouet, Côte d'Ivoire (500); Libreville, Gabon (500); and Djibouti (3,500).

The French military interventions in Africa have been increasingly criticized by French taxpayers. Thus, during the French intervention in Chad, the French daily *Le Matin* on July 7, 1983, observed: "Today Paris is intervening in Chad in a war of chieftains. Paris is intervening and takes sides for Hissène Habré, master of the capital, N'Djamena."

In the black continent, these interventions are seen as a threat to the independence of African states and thus are bitterly opposed by some heads of state. In April 1979, when Tanzania intervened in Uganda for the overthrow of President Idi Amin Dada, one of its reasons was to prevent calling for foreign forces outside Africa. Nigeria has strongly and consistently opposed the French role in neighboring Chad and elsewhere. On June 25, 1983, President Mengistu Haile Mariam, then OAU chairman, appealed to foreign powers not to intervene in Chad. In the conflict in Rwanda in 1990, President Yoweri Museveni, OAU chairman at that time, criticized the intervention of France and Belgium in support of the Rwandan government, showing that the European security role—as a colonial vestige that compromises the sovereignty of independent African states—

had not yet ended.

With the new orientation of the French cooperative role in Africa, the French government becomes less and less enthusiastic about intervening in favor of African governments that make no effort to promote human rights and democracy in their countries. The refusal of French troops in Chad to prevent the government of Hissene Habre from being overthrown in December 1990 is a case in point.

Finally, France—anxious to help keep its independence in foreign policy—is willing to help African states to lay the foundation of a more autonomous security system at a regional level while maintaining its capacity to intervene for countries in need. These reasons gave rise to regional initiatives for collective security. The only promising historical experience has been that of the Pan-African force set up at the Nairobi summit in 1981 during the Chadian civil war. Unfortunately, this inter-African force failed for many reasons.

First, there was confusion surrounding the definition of its mandate. In the opinion of the Chadian Transitional Government of National Unity (GUNT), the inter-African force should fight alongside the loyalist troops in order to crush the rebellion of FAN (Armed Forces of the North), but the OAU thought this force was in Chad to prevent an external aggression (Libyan) and serve as an interposition force between belligerent factions. The second reason for the failure derives from the absence of prior consent of the belligerents for peace negotiations. Finally, the Pan-African force failed for lack of financial and logistic means. The failure of the first Pan-African force led some states to envisage the establishment of subregional mechanisms for collective security. It was in this perspective that an agreement on nonaggression and defense and a mutual assistance pact were conceived.

At the initiative of the Côte d'Ivoire, Francophone West African states on June 9, 1977, signed in Abidjan an Accord of Nonaggression and Assistance in matters of Defense (ANAD) within a framework of the West African Economic Community (CEAO). This pact aims at achieving an alliance based on the principles of the nonuse of force by member states, their commitment to mutual assistance in case of external aggression, and the pooling of their military potential. The agreement has been in effect since December 1981 through the constitution of an integrated staff of armed forces of the CEAO. Institutionally, only the Secretariat General established in Abidjan is a permanent body, headed by a Senegalese senior officer. ANAD does not provide for permanent forces, but studies have been undertaken to create an allied command. The member states would have to agree on the creation of an intervention force made up of troops from their national armies.

The signatory partners from CEAO are Côte d'Ivoire, Senegal, Burkina Faso, Mauritania, Mali, Niger, and Togo; Benin and Guinea have observer status. From the beginning, Mali and Mauritania adopted a hostile attitude to France as a non-African presence, stating that no agreement could be achieved without the dismantling of foreign bases and the denunciation of defense conventions concluded with foreign powers. Member countries close to France argued that the signatories of ANAD were free as sovereign states to conclude agreements with partners of their choice.

The most important innovation of ANAD lies in its attempt to establish a system enabling member states to be informed of potential violations of their security. However, even in the absence of direct military threats, there may crop up misunderstandings between member states that hold potential for destabilizing political tensions. ANAD's innovation is that it concerns military, political, economic, and even cultural fields in order to lessen potential distrust between neighboring heads of state. Preliminary activities have been undertaken in this privileged field.

An additional protocol on nonaggression was adopted in December 1982 by member states. This agreement provides that border authorities should meet regularly to discuss immigration problems. It also requests member states to organize the exchange of information and mutual help between police and security forces. In addition, the agreement provides for the creation of an arbitrating commission for settling disputes between member states.

Established to defend the economic interests of CEAO by ensuring an indispensable stability of member states, ANAD had to take measures to promote the protection of the natural resources of its members. At the eighth session of the Council of Ministers in Niamey in October 1983, ANAD adopted two protocols that to some extent widened the scope of the treaty. The first protocol deals with the protection of CEAO's economic interests: protection against poaching, devastation of the flora, and the systematic pillage of territorial waters (i.e., obstruction of maritime traffic in areas under members' jurisdiction). The second deals with cooperation in civil defense matters. The civil defense protocol aims at establishing structures adapted to the fight against drought, bushfires, floods, and the threat of maritime pollution. ANAD is still at its beginning stage in search of political will and sufficient funds before taking shape as a subregional reality.

Members' goodwill could not prevent an armed confrontation between Burkina Faso and Mali in December 1985 following a border dispute, and it was only after months of costly conflict that ANAD was able to mediate a settlement. Likewise, the Republic of Togo, shaken by an attempted internal revolt in September 1986, accused Burkina Faso of being one of the countries in which the aggression was initiated. Moreover, Togo appealed to the French government and not to ANAD to send troops. In spite of these incidents, the existence of this type of treaty is clear proof of the perception, by Africa's heads of state, of a real need for security in Africa.

Equally significant is the Pact of Mutual Assistance in Defense Matters (PMA), a larger project concluded by all sixteen member states of the Economic Community of West African States (ECOWAS). The signing of this pact gives birth to the Community Armed Forces (FAC) of ECOWAS. Going beyond the traditional barriers among Francophone, Anglophone, and Lusophone countries, the PMA is a result of the Franco-African summit conference held in Paris in May 1978, which recommended the creation of an operational machinery by Africans themselves. The pact provides a joint action coordinated by a defense council for the defense of an ECOWAS member state against aggression from a nonmember state, mediation in conflicts between member states, and military or political intervention in case of internal conflict encouraged from outside. Community forces do not intervene as long as the conflict remains purely internal. In this regard, the conflict in Liberia has presented a challenge both to action and to definition.

Signed on May 28, 1981, in Freetown, the PMA defense protocol met with abstention from three member states of ECOWAS—Guinea-Bissau, Mali, and Cape Verde—which denounced what they thought to be an instance of excessive French manipulation through ANAD member countries. Other member states, such as Côte d'Ivoire and Niger, saw in the Nigerian army (numerically the second in black Africa after Ethiopia's with a budget of U.S. $1.75 billion) a cause for worry and reservation. On the contrary, Senegal and Togo argued that Nigeria's military capacity could play a stabilizing role in the region, expressing no concern for the alleged intentions of Nigeria to disapprove of defense agreements between Francophone African states and France.

As clear evidence, the stand of Nigeria, headed by General Ibrahim Babangida, on the Liberian civil war destroys the Togolese and Senegalese arguments. The Nigerian forces, which form the greatest contingent of the ECOWAS Monitoring Group (ECOMOG), have behaved like an army of occupation in Liberia. ECOMOG arrived in Monrovia in August 1990, after over half a year of civil war in Liberia. Its mission was not clearly defined, and initially only five ECOWAS members (Guinea, Gambia, Ghana, Nigeria, and Sierra Leone) participated in it; Senegal sent troops in 1992. The involvement has exposed to international public opinion the inconsistencies of the ECOWAS defense policy. Nigeria's partiality and high ambitions caused Mali and Togo to leave ECOMOG and have continued to divide ECOWAS. Support from more conservative Francophone states, including Côte d'Ivoire, Burkina Faso, and Mali, sustained Charles Taylor's rebel forces such that the war spilled over the borders to Guinea and Sierra Leone.

ECOMOG shows the problems inherent in initial attempts of African states to meet their own security problems collectively when the Western tutelary power—in this case the United States—no longer plays its accustomed security role. Moveover, Nigeria, a subregional power, has displayed clear ambition to play a leading role in the subregion of West Africa. If to the mutual distrust is added the fact that the PMA Defense protocol provides for the withdrawal of foreign (i.e., French) forces the moment ECOWAS can ensure the security of member states, there are additional reasons to worry about the future implications of the PMA. Another difficulty, and not the least, is that the protocol does not provide for permanent forces. Although some members in principle express their willingness to place their national troops at the disposal of the allied forces of ECOWAS, such forces can only be organized in a period of crisis at the risk of delaying immediate reaction.

Nevertheless, the ECOWAS and CEAO (ANAD) defense protocols constitute important initiatives in the process of maintaining peace and security in the subregion. These defense and assistance agreements signed by West African states have a double mission. On the one hand, they aim in the long run at replacing agreements existing between France and some African countries by transferring to national armies themselves organized in ECOWAS or CEAO coalitions the stabilizing and dissuasive role previously played by France. On the other hand, they aim at giving to West African forces new functions and missions by expanding the scope of their fields of action at the regional level. When one examines closely the problems created by African experiments in subregional security cooperation, one can only agree with Tshiyembe Mwayila (1988) that contrary to the opinion generally expressed, the regional framework can be a major asset if there is a political will.

■ African States' Arms Imports and Military Expenditures[*]

Africa is almost completely dependent on the outside world for its arms supplies. Implicitly, the military disengagement of the United States, Europe, and the former Soviet Union should lead also to reductions in arms sales and military assistance to African governments and rebel movements. But many of these arms sources may be even more prone to seek African and other Third World arms markets because of the decline in global security concerns. Even if these countries do decrease arms transfers to Africa, would this succeed in forcing the parties in military conflicts to resort to peaceful resolution mechanisms? Alternate sources of arms for Africa also exist, which may be even less subject to restraint.

*This section by John White, The Johns Hopkins School of Advanced International Studies.

Table 3.1 Arms Imports for Sub-Saharan Africa and the African Continent (real value in 1988 $ billion)

Year	Sub-Saharan	North Africa	Total Africa
1978	4.7	6.8	11.5
1979	2.1	7.2	9.3
1980	3.0	6.3	9.3
1981	2.6	7.5	10.1
1982	0.9	8.0	8.9
1983	2.4	5.6	8.0
1984	3.1	5.5	8.6
1985	1.4	4.5	5.9
1986	1.7	3.4	5.1
1987	2.2	3.3	5.5
1988	2.6	2.3	4.9

Source: Arms Control and Development Agency (ACDA), *World Military Expenditures and Arms Transfers 1989.*

of arms for Africa also exist, which may be even less subject to restraint. Thus, in limiting arms as in limiting wars, African states are likely to be obliged to rely on their own will.

Between 1978 and 1988, the latest years for which data are available, Africa's arms imports in real value (measured in 1988 dollars) have generally declined (see Table 3.1). The trend for sub-Saharan Africa has been less evident and smaller in magnitude than that of North Africa: Sub-Saharan Africa's arms imports increased every year from 1985 to 1988, back to levels at the beginning of the decade. In 1988, Africa's arms imports were roughly 42 percent of their 1978 level; sub-Saharan Africa's were 56 percent. Africa's arms imports were at their lowest in 1988; sub-Saharan Africa's apparent half-decade cycles may point to recurrent modernizations, but are probably an aggregate of too many components to be meaningful. This discussion does not take into account the political events of the North and sub-Saharan African regions and those of their constituent states. Hence, only limited insight into the variables contributing to these trends and their relevance can be provided here. Another caveat is the inability to make inferences on the actual quantities of arms imported, based on their real values. The weapons market is not a free, perfectly competitive market in which uniform goods are sold by several sources at published prices and the individual consumer is free to buy from the cheapest source.

The market has increasingly become competitive such that profit margins and price differentials have declined as developing countries and newly industrializing countries (NICs) manufacture and export more weapons. Private middlemen—the most notorious of whom was Adnan

Table 3.2 Arms Exports by Alternate Suppliers to Africa (real value in 1988 $ billion)

Country	1984	1988
Argentina	0.14	0.03
Brazil	0.73	0.38
Chile	0.02	0.28
China	2.25	3.10
Israel	0.52	0.14
N. Korea	0.65	0.47
S. Korea	0.54	0.05
Pakistan	0.34	0.01
Total	5.19	4.46

Source: ACDA, *World Military Expenditures and Arms Transfers 1989.*

Khashoggi—and other intermediaries have recently entered the market and provided client states and militias with more options. Declining real values of arms imports could actually reflect constant or even increasing volumes of arms.

During the 1978–1988 period, the major sources of arms for Africa were the USSR and the Eastern bloc, France, the United States, and Italy. France was the largest Western supplier to Africa; it transferred $4.8 billion, almost as much as the next two major suppliers (Italy and the United States) combined (ACDA 1990).

After these suppliers from the North came eight developing countries or NICs, for which data are provided for 1984 and 1988 (Table 3.2). Their share of world weapons exports increased slightly from 8.8 percent to 9.2 percent over the four-year interval. In 1988, the most recent year for which data are available, the total value of weapons exported by this group of countries was 92 percent and 169 percent of the value of weapons imported by Africa and sub-Saharan Africa, respectively.

In addition to these eight countries, South Africa and a few North African countries are expanding their weapons exports and can serve as convenient sources for clients in black Africa. Perhaps all of the specific items supplied by the developed countries could not now be supplied by alternate suppliers. Nonetheless, the thriving, dynamic weapons market— capable as it is of cloning advanced weapons systems or providing the original weapons through a black market—is not marginal, and the data suggest that Africa is not dependent on the metropoles and superpowers for weapons.

However, other variables affecting African states' arms imports and military expenditures in general have not been considered. Most arms transfers between developed countries and Africa involve large subsidies or donations through military assistance contracts in such a way that these funds are not distinguishable from development assistance. The U.S. government, for example, includes military assistance in the Economic Support Fund, a general category of unrestricted cash transfers to developing countries. Hence, the effect of military assistance on arms imports can only be addressed indirectly by investigating the impact of development assistance. Were military assistance contracts not offered, few African states could afford to purchase weapons from other sources using their own resources.

Development assistance is fungible to the extent that it either is unrestricted in use or provides public goods and services that the government would have provided from local resources. Hence, even if donors suspended all weapons sales to African states, they would nevertheless have to take necessary precautions or they could find themselves sponsoring weapons imports (from third parties) through their aid. Econometric models have been developed to determine which variables influence African government fiscal behavior. Heller's model (1975) documented the tendency to use grants and loans differently: Loans promote long-term investment as opposed to public consumption. White's model (1991) suggests that grants increase military expenditures and arms imports while loans have the opposite effect.

At this preliminary stage, the orders of magnitude of these effects cannot be estimated. However, strong correlations exist between proposed independent variables and military expenditures and arms imports (Table 3.3). To the extent that donors can influence levels of GNP, public expenditures, and debt service—possibly through debt forgiveness, conditions attached to grants and loans, the composition of development assistance, and inducements to citizens to invest in African countries—they can discourage excessive acquisition of arms and thereby encourage peaceful resolution of conflicts in Africa.

■ Conclusion

The lessening of economic affinities between Europe and Africa, the creation of autonomous regional machineries for collective security, and

Table 3.3 Correlations of Military Expenditures and Arms Imports to Variables

	Variable Military Expenditures	Arms Imports
GNP	.90	.74
Public Expenditures	.83	.60
Debt Service	.67	.71
Arms Imports	.73	—

the emergence of alternative sources of arms are indicators of and responses to reduced European security roles in African relations. The evolution of political ideas and the stability of African countries have also been influenced by events in Eastern Europe. The free elections and multiparty systems developing in Eastern Europe have attracted attention in states in West, East, and Central Africa that have single-party systems and have combined with domestic pressures for freedom to produce major effects in South Africa. Africa, it should be stressed, will have to take into account the global progression of freedom and human rights. Even if these are not made preconditions for cooperation, they should be pursued for their own worth. Internal self-help requires the harnessing of latent capacities of African peoples. Another beneficial lesson Africa can draw from the rapprochement between East and West is the merit of peaceful resolution of conflicts as opposed to continued diversions of resources to unnecessary arms acquisitions.

In the new phase, Africa will have to meet its own security needs, because European, U.S., and (former) Soviet commitments in this field have been diminishing. Continental geopolitics have been reshaped in a way that gives rise to subregional hegemons that aspire to play leading roles in maintaining peace and security—Nigeria in West Africa and South Africa in southern Africa. But in the future, if there is a real democracy and a sincere human rights commitment inside the African states, political and social tensions should diminish—and the need for a foreign security role should decrease—because there would be no need for outside intervention in favor of authoritarian regimes.

4

When Weakness Is Strength: The Lomé IV Negotiations

John Ravenhill

The signature of the fourth Lomé Convention in December 1989 failed to attract significant attention from either the media or development experts—in marked contrast to the excitement that accompanied the signing of the first convention in 1975.[1] The reasons are not difficult to discern. The relationship between the European Community (EC) and sixty-nine African, Caribbean, and Pacific (ACP) countries has, over its fifteen years of existence, become routinized, ritualized, and marginalized—routinized in that the energies of the parties are concentrated on the day-to-day implementation of aid and trade procedures that for the most part are now well established; ritualized in that the parties periodically (especially at the time of the Lomé Convention's renegotiation) confront one another with demands that have changed little since the signature of the first convention (particulary true of the ACP group) and that produce equally predictable and ritualized responses; and marginalized in that the ACP countries in general and the institutional relationship with them through Lomé in particular have become less and less important to an EC that not only has undergone significant expansion since 1975 but that looks forward to even greater levels of self-sufficiency with the completion of the single integrated market in 1992.

■ The Context

From a conventional bargaining perspective, the context of the Lomé IV negotiations could scarcely have been less propitious for the ACP group, most of whose members experienced severe economic decline in the 1980s. Thirty-two (thirty-three with Haiti, whose application to accede to the convention was approved during the course of the negotiations) of its members are among the forty-one countries designated as least developed by the UN; the economic weakness of these and other ACP members had been exacerbated by the sustained fall in international commodity prices in the 1980s and by poor government policies. Many members of the group were experiencing severe debt-servicing problems: By the end of 1986, total ACP debt was $130 billion, having almost doubled between 1981 and that year, with $102 billion owed by sub-Saharan Africa. The overall ACP debt-service ratio was estimated to be over 34 percent. Close to half of the group had been forced during the 1980s to reach agreement with the International Monetary Fund and World Bank on structural adjustment programs.

Despite the comparatively favorable access the ACP enjoyed to the European market by virtue of the provisions of the convention, the ACP share in extra-EC imports had declined significantly since the signature of Lomé from 8 percent to 4 percent. In part, given the dependence of two-thirds of the ACP states on nonpetroleum commodities for over 90 percent of their export earnings, this decline reflected the reduced importance of raw materials in total EC imports. In 1975 commodities constituted 26 percent of EC imports; by 1980 their share had fallen to 22 percent and by 1986 to 17 percent. The decline was also a reflection of the fall in oil prices, oil being by far the single most important commodity in ACP exports to the EC. But the decline was also a result of the ACP states' lack of competitiveness despite the tariff preferences provided by the convention and a reflection of domestic production problems; as a consequence, they had even failed to retain their share of the European market for some of their most important exports. The total value of ACP commodity exports to the EC was estimated to have declined from $24 billion in 1980 to under $15 billion in 1987. Meanwhile, although some trade diversification had taken place (McQueen and Stevens 1989), the share of manufactures in ACP exports to the EC had fallen by more than half in the period 1970–1986.

The ACP group on the eve of the negotiations thus was weaker and more distracted by domestic economic problems than at any time in the past. It faced a European Community more self-confident than in any of the previous negotiations, buoyed by the prospects of completing the single integrated market in 1992, and of other European countries lining up to seek admission thereafter. The expansion of the EC that had occurred since the signature of Lomé had already complicated relations with the ACP and made additional concessions in the trade sphere more difficult: Greece and Portugal in particular feared that further liberalization of trade, particularly in agricultural products, would adversely affect their economies. Similarly, Greece opposed an extension of the Lomé scheme for promotion of the ACP minerals sector (SYSMIN) out of fear that it would adversely affect Greece's bauxite production. And although the completion of the single integrated market in 1992 promised some gains for ACP states (particularly with certain member states being required to reduce their consumption taxes on tropical beverages), the new harmonization of regulations, particularly in the health field, posed a potential threat to the access of some ACP agricultural products.

Two other contextual factors were also of significance. The first was the ongoing Uruguay Round of GATT (General Agreement on Tariffs and Trade) negotiations; the anticipated reductions in the EC's common external tariff were expected to cut the preferential margins enjoyed by the ACP. Before the negotiations for the renewal of the convention began, the EC had announced its offer on tropical products for the Uruguay Round, including reduced tariffs on a number of products on which the ACP enjoyed preferential margins. These included coffee, oilseeds, jute and hard fibers, manioc, tobacco, and spices. Because the Uruguay negotiations were not scheduled to end until a year after the fourth convention was due to be signed, there was considerable uncertainty about its final impact on the ACP's position in the EC market. The second factor—unanticipated when the negotiations began but increasingly important as they proceeded—was the dramatic unfolding of events in Eastern Europe. Fear that European assistance to the newly liberalizing economies of the East would come at ACP expense increased the pressure on those states to reach an early agreement on the terms of the new convention.

Yet this conventional perspective on the bargaining strengths of the two groups is incomplete if not misleading for the Lomé relationship. The reason is a paradox—a principal source of ACP states' bargaining strength lies in their weakness. As I have argued elsewhere, the absence of reciprocity in the convention ensures that the only significant allowance the ACP can make toward European interests is actually to sign the convention (Ravenhill 1985b). Negotiations focus not on what the ACP will give in return for concessions from the EC but overwhelmingly on extracting additional concessions from the EC. The one exception in recent talks has been the European attempts to wrest back some of the previous concessions the EC had made on the automaticity (nonconditionality) of the convention's aid provisions. In this context, the further weakening of the ACP group in the 1980s paradoxically may have been to its advantage. Not only did it enable the ACP states to continue to remind the EC that additional concessions in, for example, the trade sphere could not conceivably do major damage to European economies, but it also enabled them to place additional pressure on the EC by demanding that the terms of the convention be improved to compensate for the deterioration in their economic position. And there is evidence that this tactic (reinforced by the EC's own concerns about the deterioration in ACP economies) was successful.

Unlike for the Lomé II negotiations, which occurred when the ACP economies were enjoying relatively high prices for their commodity exports that made the EC Commission unsympathetic toward ACP demands for a major improvement in the terms of the relationship, the deterioration of the ACP economies in the 1980s prompted the Commission to argue that a significant extension of the relationship (through the provision of improved trade access and of structural adjustment financing) was necessary. Compensation was needed, according to Development Commissioner Manuel Marin, for the erosion of ACP trade preferences as a consequence of the Uruguay Round (*Agence Europe,* May 18, 1989). Even the evolution of events in Eastern Europe may have benefited the ACP in the talks: one senior EC negotiator commented that he believed it had been possible to extract an improved offer from the EC member states on financial aid by using the argument that the EC should not, at this time, be seen to be turning its back on its ACP partners (interview, EEC Commission, October 1990).[2] In the context of the Lomé arrangement, the weaker the ACP group, the more successful it may be in extracting further concessions from the Europeans.[3]

■ The Actors and the Structure

As in previous rounds of negotiations, the talks for Lomé IV were multilevel games. On the European side, negotiations took place within the EC itself (with the Development Directorate, DGVIII, having to clear its proposals with other directorates, particularly the External Relations Directorate, DGI, and the Agriculture Directorate, DGVI), between the Commission and the member states, between the member states themselves, between the Commission and the member states on the one hand and various lobby groups (including NGOs) on the other, and between the Commission, the member states, and the European Parliament. The Parliament, although not a new actor in the relationship, had an enhanced role: The Single Europe Act mandated that it be consulted about the negotiations and gave it a veto power over the final package agreed between the EC and the ACP States. And the Parliament did indeed play a role: The insistence of its Development Cooperation Committee that Lomé be significantly improved kept pressure on the member states and the Commission to provide a package acceptable to the ACP; the Parliament was also particularly concerned about ensuring that issues pertaining to the environment and to human rights should figure prominently in the new convention.

On the ACP side, there was a similar multilayered pattern of negotiation, though it was somewhat less complex because of the generally poor communications between ACP member states and with their Brussels-based ambassadors and because of the small size and inadequacy of the ACP Secretariat. The ACP group still had no meaningful existence outside the Lomé relationship: as its secretary-general at the start of the negotiations, Edwin Carrington, noted: "We of the ACP have talked a lot, philosophized a lot, we have studied a lot, we have met a lot. We have not done much else" (Carrington 1990, p. 18).

As was the case in previous conventions, detailed negotiations between the two groups were conducted primarily by the EC Commission (mandated to negotiate on behalf of the Community), and the ACP ambassadors, assisted by the ACP Secretariat. Thematic groups were established that tackled issues in eight areas: agriculture, environment, and fisheries; trade; commodities (including STABEX and SYSMIN); industrial cooperation, mining, and energy; regional cooperation and development of services; financial and technical cooperation, structural adjustment, debt and investment; cultural and social cooperation, population, health, education and training, science and technology, refugees, and the role of women; and the special problems of the least-developed landlocked and island countries. In addition, there was a central negotiating group that dealt with general issues such as the principles and objectives, duration, and geographical coverage of the Lomé Convention, human rights, and the convention's institutions.

Unresolved matters were referred to ministerial sessions that brought together ministers from the various parties to the convention. Five ministerial sessions were held: The first, in Luxembourg in October 1988, was little more than a formal launching of the negotiations; the last, in Brussels in November 1989, saw agreement finally reached (apart from the ritualized last-minute dispute on the size of the financial aid package).

But by far the most important negotiations in terms of outcome took place not between the EC and the ACP but between the EC Commission and the member states. In July 1987, the commission's development director had established a think tank consisting of a half dozen senior members of the Development Directorate to determine the negotiating mandate that the Commission should request from the member states. In the succeeding six months, the proposals were refined within the Commission, with talks taking place not only within the Development Directorate but also with other Commission directorates. In March 1988, the Commission's draft proposals were sent to the European Parliament and to the Council of Ministers.

Difficult negotiations then occurred between the Commission and the member states. In total, the parties spent approximately 150 hours in talks, more than 100 of them taken up just in deciding the Commission's initial negotiating mandate (Nicora 1990; supplemental interviews).[4] A clear North-South division within the EC existed: Germany, the Netherlands, and the UK were willing to grant additional trade concessions but generally opposed significant increases in the convention's aid provisions. On the other hand, the Southern states, most notably Spain, Portugal, Greece, and Italy, were opposed to further trade liberalization. Italy was willing to provide a substantial increase in aid funds; the other Southern countries, the new members of the EC, were far less generously inclined. France took an intermediate position, its stance varying from issue to issue. In general, France, given its traditional interests in ACP states, supported an improvement of the terms of the convention and was willing to provide additional financial assistance;[5] France also was supportive of Commission attempts to improve ACP trade access—with the important exception of those goods that might adversely affect the interests of French producers.

The member states were also divided on the major initiatives that the Commission proposed for the new convention. The most important of these was the Commission's desire to change the emphasis in the aid relationship. Over the course of the 1980s, the Commission increasingly perceived that the traditional emphasis of the European Development Fund (EDF) on infrastructure projects was of decreasing relevance to the immediate needs of the ACP group, especially the African states. Unfavorable external economic circumstances coupled with government maladministration had generated an unprecedented economic decline in many members of the ACP group. The collapse of commodity prices, compounded by the debt crisis, produced a situation of import strangulation: ACP countries were in desperate need of additional foreign exchange to provide the enlargement of import capacity necessary to rehabilitate their economies. This unfavorable economic environment and the ineffectual government policies had placed EC aid projects— whether infrastructure or sectoral assistance—at risk. Moreover, recent attempts at structural adjustment were inconsistent with some dimensions of EC assistance to the ACP: The insistence of the International Monetary Fund (IMF) and World Bank on trade liberalization as part of ACP states' structural adjustment programs threatened the viability of some EC-aided projects that could not survive without tariff protection.

The EC Commission had already moved away from its traditional emphasis on infrastructure projects. In its proposals for Lomé III, it had advocated that greater attention be given to sectoral programs and insisted on the necessity of "policy dialogue" with its ACP partners on their overall development strategies. Lomé III, however, was largely devoid of instruments that could provide the quickly disbursed aid needed to revive import capacity. Perceiving a growing need for support for ACP efforts at structural adjustment, the EC in December 1987 launched a special action program in support of low-income debt-distressed sub-Saharan African countries. The funding, totaling in European currency units (ECUs) approximately ECU 600 million from the Lomé III "reserve fund," was to provide support for essential imports. The new program represented a de facto reinterpretation of the convention. The decision to advocate the inclusion of support for structural adjustment in Lomé IV was a natural extension of this policy initiative. The Commission was concerned, in particular, that under the existing arrangements, it was being looked upon by the international financial institutions as a "social fire brigade," being called in to provide support for victims of a structural adjustment process that it had not participated in designing. Accordingly, the Commission proposed for Lomé IV that there should be a special fund to assist structural adjustment in ACP states; this, it asserted in the draft mandate it proposed to the member states, "would enable the Community and its Member States to play a more active, organized part in consultations and dialogue—with other donors as well as the ACP countries themselves—on general macroeconomic reforms" (CEC 1990, 5).

The United Kingdom and the Netherlands, with Germany generally backing them, were enthusiastic in their support for this initiative and argued that as large a proportion of EC aid as possible should be provided in the form of support for structural adjustment and that it should be linked to the conditionality established by the international financial institutions. They were opposed, however, to the creation of a special fund to support adjustment, arguing instead that this financing should be derived from the regular EDF allocation. France, Italy, Ireland, and Belgium emphasized the need for the EC to continue to emphasize the projects it had traditionally supported and to distance itself from the conditionality imposed by the international financial institutions. The commission itself was split on the matter: Some senior members of the Development Directorate were opposed to the new thrust of EC policy, as were two former commissioners for development—Claude Cheysson and Edgar Pisani. Pisani went so far as to warn that "using the Convention as an instrument for adjustment policies" was an "error," and that "Lomé will not be Lomé if it concerns itself with adjustment. Lomé was made for development" (Pisani 1988).

Arguments over conditionality and the form of aid to be provided also divided the member states on another of the Commission's proposals: that transfers to the ACP from the STABEX scheme should be changed from loans to grants—provided that greater conditionality would be attached to the transfers to ensure their use in support of sectoral adjustment. Again, the Netherlands and the United Kingdom opposed the proposal, whereas France supported it.

Divisions within the EC over the central issues of trade and financial aid delayed agreement by the Council of Ministers on a negotiating mandate for the Commission. Even though last-minute negotiations provided an outline for the Commission on the eve of the formal opening of the talks in October 1988, several key issues, especially in the trade field, remained unresolved. The inability of the EC to reach a position on key issues inevitably delayed the negotiations and complicated the task of the ACP states.

For its part, the ACP group entered the negotiations even less well prepared than on previous occasions. Although a number of preparatory studies were commissioned by the ACP Secretariat, these were not as extensive as those prepared for previous negotiations. Nor did the Secretariat receive the same support as in the past from the UN Conference on Trade and Development (UNCTAD) or the British Commonwealth Secretariat. Despite the efforts of its very able secretary-general, Edwin Carrington,[6] the underfunded Secretariat was unable for the most part to provide the technical backup needed to justify the ACP case. Rather than attempting to establish priorities in the demands that came from the various states, the ACP in practice—as in other rounds of Lomé negotiations and, indeed, as in so many other North-South talks—tended to aggregate all demands into a long shopping list.

The divisions within the ACP group, evident in previous negotiations, were even more to the fore. These were primarily geographic: The African states, most of which were interested above all in the size of the aid offer, were suspicious of Caribbean countries that they perceived as having the luxury of being able to take a harder line in the talks because the items of particular interest to them (bananas, rum, sugar) were covered by special arrangements in the convention. The Anglophone-Francophone divide was of continuing significance; again, it was the Francophone countries that were most concerned with a quick settlement of the negotiations in order to ensure continued aid flows. A further line of cleavage was according to level of development. Some of the more developed states resisted special treatment for their less-favored colleagues for fear that it would adversely affect their own gains from the convention. Kenyan President Arap Moi, for instance, on a visit to the EC Commission in March 1989, was quoted as opposing differential treatment for the least-developed ACP states on the grounds that it penalized "good Kenyan management." "We cannot," he asserted, "wait for the poorest to rejoin us" (*Agence Europe,* March 10, 1989).

The very structure of the negotiations tended to place the ACP group at a disadvantage. The day-to-day negotiations pitted the EC Commission with its considerable resources against ACP ambassadors whose abilities and expertise varied considerably and who had little technical backup from the ACP Secretariat. As in previous negotiations, the Commission claimed that some ambassadors were adopting positions their home governments did not support, and threatened to go over their heads to deal directly with governments in their national capitals. Given the disunity of the group and its lack of support staff, it was not surprising that the ACP was unable to respond quickly to EC proposals. And as Myriam Vander Stichele (1990) points out, the ACP states complicated their task by insisting on renegotiating every part of the third convention—all 294 articles, 8 protocols, and 54 annexes.

■ The Course and Content of the Negotiations

☐ Opening Positions

As in previous negotiations, the ACP opening position emphasized that an incremental improvement of the terms of cooperation was insufficient. Three other themes were prominent. First, the group viewed Lomé as a contractual relationship between equal parties, and the initial convention as a trade-off of nonreciprocal access to the European market for ACP exports in exchange for security of supply of raw materials for European consumers. Trade, therefore, was the centerpiece of the convention—despite the prominence given to the financial assistance provisions under Lomé III. Second, the Group stressed the acknowledgment that the convention had made of the important principle of differential treatment according to levels of development. According to the memorandum on guidelines for the negotiations prepared by the ACP Secretariat, the convention implemented the UNCTAD II resolution that there should be special and differential treatment for groups of developing countries. For the ACP states, this principle justified the last of the major planks in their position: that the rights they had acquired ("acquis") under the provisions of the previous conventions must be maintained. According to the group, the "acquis" included

1. Equality of status of the partners under the convention;
2. The full recognition of and mutual respect for the sovereignty of each partner—for its political, social, cultural, and economic choices;
3. The interdependent nature and mutual-interest character of the relationship;
4. The security of the relationship based on a system of law and on the existence of joint institutions;
5. A global approach incorporating a diversity of instruments to cover the various fields of cooperation and enabling a balanced response to the various and differential needs according to economic structures, levels of development, and priorities as defined by the ACP states in their sovereignty; and
6. The right to progress and innovation without prejudice to earlier acquired rights.

Furthermore, according to the ACP Secretariat in its background memorandum for the negotiations, the "preservation of their preferences in the Community [was] a vital part of the 'acquis'." One of the ACP states' initial demands, therefore, was that their levels of preference in the European market must be maintained and that any loss of such preferences must be offset by clear quantifiable compensation. As in previous rounds of negotiations (Ravenhill 1987), the ACP opening position included a number of broad demands of principle (a useful tactical device when the group was unable to agree on priorities). In the trade field, these demands included the removal of all tariff and nontariff barriers to ACP exports, including those covered by the EC's Common Agricultural Policy; the abolition of the convention's safeguard clause; and significant relaxation of the rules of origin that determine the extent of domestic transformation that must occur within an ACP state for a product to be classed as an export of that state. The group also demanded that a special fund be established to promote the processing, marketing, distribution, and transport of their commodities. Virtually all of these demands had been raised in previous rounds of negotiations; they had been rejected repeatedly by the Europeans as an unacceptable basis for discussion.

On STABEX, the ACP demanded that the transfers be made in grant form rather than loans. The dependence and fluctuation thresholds that had to be satisfied in order for countries to be eligible for transfers should be reduced from 6 percent to 3 percent (from 1.5 percent to 0.5 percent for the least-developed countries). The long-standing demand that STABEX transfers should be indexed to take account of inflation in the prices of imported manufactured goods was repeated. The system should automatically include exports to other ACP states; it should be extended to cover all of a country's exports if more than 50 percent are directed to non-EC markets. On SYSMIN, the convention's scheme to promote production of ACP minerals for the EC market, the group called for an extension of the coverage of the system—both in terms of the minerals included and the ability to provide funding to develop new mines instead of primarily intervening to maintain the production of existing facilities.

Anticipating the EC's initiative on structural adjustment, the ACP gave cautious support to the idea—providing that it was clearly established that funding for structural adjustment would be in addition to the conventional EDF programs, and that funding would not be subject to the conditions imposed by the IMF and the World Bank. The ACP seized the opportunity provided by the EC's concern with structural adjustment to argue that it should include as part of the arrangements for the convention debt relief to the ACP states. Originally, the ACP states argued that both bilateral as well as multilateral (EC) debt should be included; they later retreated to the demand that all outstanding loans in the Lomé framework (with the exception of European Investment Bank investments) be transformed into grants.

On another EC initiative—the proposal that the convention last for more than the customary five years—the ACP states were in favor provided that the convention was not to be of indefinite duration (as the Commission had proposed for Lomé III) and that the financial aid package would be renegotiated after five years. On proposals to extend the convention to include Haiti, the Dominican Republic, and Namibia, the ACP failed to adopt a united position. There was support for the accession of Namibia but suspicion toward both Haiti and the Dominican Republic—especially from Caribbean states that saw the Dominican Republic as a potential competitor in exporting sugar and bananas and as a country with a poor record in regional cooperation and in its treatment of migrants from Caribbean islands. There was general concern that the admission of the Dominican Republic, which Spain was strongly advocating against British and Dutch resistance, would open the way for the extension of the convention to Central America—and thus to a diminution of existing ACP states' preferences in the EC market.

The EC's opening position and tactics were also familiar from previous rounds of negotiation. The ACP demands for the contractual elements of the convention to be respected and, in particular, for the implementation of the principle of completely free access of their products to the European market were brushed aside with the familiar argument that Lomé was a practical arrangement rather than one based on abstractions. The ACP states already enjoyed free access to the European market for the overwhelming majority of their products; their poor trade performance therefore was largely of their own making. As the Council of Ministers noted in its response to the Commission's proposal for a negotiating mandate: "The improvement of the ACP's commercial performance depends above all on the competitiveness of their export production, and thus on their own efforts at restructuring and diversification, which the Community is willing to support." Similarly, the director of DGVIII, Dieter Frisch, argued in a speech to the Royal Commonwealth Society in November 1988 that "the real problem lies not with the access regime but with the structural weakness, the lack of competitiveness, of many of our ACP partners' products. . . . [T]inkering with the access regime . . . is not tackling the roots of the problem." The emphasis therefore had to be on setting the correct macroeconomic climate to support efforts at rehabilitation and growth.

There could be no guarantee of the margin of preference enjoyed by the ACP in a changing world economy. Although the ACP states might lose some of their preferential margins in Europe as a result of the Uruguay Round, they would be compensated by gains in other markets. Development Commissioner Joseph Natali, at the start of the negotiations, argued that "Lomé will have no claim to remaining a model if the negotiators are out only to defend acquired advantages or outdated ideas." The Commission's starting point, as outlined in its draft negotiating mandate, was that "there is no reason to seek a wholesale renegotiation of the Convention. The new Lomé III approach and methods should be consolidated and built upon." Consolidation was also the catchword in discussing the trade regime. The "already generous provisions," the Commission argued, "leave very little scope for further liberalization. The main objective of the forthcoming negotiations should therefore be to consolidate the existing arrangements by extending them for a longer period" (CEC 1990).

The main thrust of the Commission's argument was that the deterioration in ACP economies necessitated a new approach to cooperation under Lomé: "The main problems facing the ACP countries," the Commission asserted, "are structural and persistent, whether we are talking about the insecurity of food supplies, threats to the environment or dependence on commodities; cooperation in all these essential areas must be long-term." A convention of longer duration would bring "stability, predictability and security" and provide a stable framework for the activities of the private sector. The Commission was also obviously weary of the seemingly interminable negotiations not only with the ACP but also with the member states. A convention of longer duration, the Commission asserted, would avoid the problem of having to renegotiate provisions when they had scarcely been implemented and certainly had not had time to bear fruit. "Every five years the negotiation takes up time and energy which could be better spent elsewhere. Since the negotiations tend to go over everything, even the best-established parts of the agreement, they are often protracted and difficult" (CEC 1990).

Besides a convention of longer duration, the deterioration in the ACP countries' economic circumstances, the Commission argued, required EC involvement in financing structural adjustment programs. The EC, the Commission continued, would play an independent role in structural adjustment and be able to act as a go-between in negotiations between ACP states and the international financial institutions. In his speech at the opening of the negotiations, Development Commissioner Natali declared that although there would be a need for coordination between the EC and the international financial institutions over conditionality, "it is clear that the Community cannot agree to its aid being governed by conditions drawn up only by others nor by negotiations in which it has played no active part." One of the fears was that EC assistance could be used by ACP states to repay their obligations to the IMF and the World Bank. Another, as previously mentioned, was that these institutions' insistence on trade liberalization could undermine the viability of EC projects in some countries (as had happened with palm oil in Ghana). Furthermore, the Commission envisaged that it could provide financing to ameliorate the social costs of adjustment—a dimension of adjustment lending particularly favored by the European Parliament.

The new emphasis on structural adjustment financing was one facet of a more general EC push to increase conditionality in the relationship, seen also in its proposals for a stricter linking of STABEX transfers to sectoral restructuring (again, a long-standing EC aspiration in the relationship), and for human rights to be given a more central position in the new convention. The EC clearly felt that the "new international economic order" (NIEO) rhetoric of equality of partnership and noninterference—with which the first convention had been endowed—was no longer relevant to the circumstances of the 1990s. Not only was the EC intent on increasing its input into ACP states' macroeconomic management, but it wished to be active in the promotion of democratization. The major initiative on this subject that emerged from the deliberations of the Commission's think tank was a proposal to support "decentralized cooperation." The idea was that decentralized public authorities, cooperatives, trade unions, and voluntary organizations in ACP countries would be able to approach the EC Commission delegate in their country directly to seek support for their activities. This, the Commission hoped, would promote democratization and empowerment at the grassroots level.

☐ *The Process*

The ritualistic ACP demands for the incorporation into the new convention of general principles—such as completely free access for their exports, abolition of the safeguard clause, or provisions for debt relief—were soon abandoned; the ACP knew from past experience the EC would not agree to them. The negotiations thus moved quickly toward the discussion of specifics, but progress was often slow because of the inability of the EC member states to reach agreement on proposals. In the trade regime, the focus was on improved access for a number of ACP agricultural products that competed with production within Europe. Here, the EC Commission acted as an advocate for the ACP in talks with EC member states. Indeed, the Commission was so frustrated by the slow and grudging response of its members that it took the unusual step in April 1989 of publicly advocating a change in the basis of treatment for ACP agricultural products: Instead of access being determined under the existing list that detailed those products permitted entry to the EC market, Development Commissioner Manuel Marin proposed that free access would be the rule except for commodities on a "negative" list.

Although the proposal was eventually rejected by the member states (which did not reach agreement on their trade offer to the ACP until the end of July 1989), it does underline the role played by the Commission in the negotiations as an advocate at times of ACP interests. Also of interest here is the part played by the new commissioner for development and vice-president of the Commission, Manuel Marin. On trade and aid issues alike, he was more outspoken in the course of the negotiations than were his predecessors in criticizing the unwillingness of member states to make what he regarded as necessary concessions. The extent to which his interventions actually changed the outcome is impossible to say; they did, however, embarrass member states (Marin was regarded as a neophyte in EC negotiations by some) and maintain pressure for additional concessions.

Agreement was reached surprisingly easily on many of the areas of the convention, including structural adjustment, decentralized cooperation, the environment, promotion of ACP service industries, the terms of financial assistance, and industrial cooperation. As in previous negotiations, the main sticking points were trade and the size of the financial aid package. The ACP states succeeded in extracting some marginal improvements in access to the EC market for forty agricultural products. Here they were aided by the Spanish desire to ensure that the Dominican Republic be included in the convention; this enabled the Commission and some member states to pressure Madrid for additional concessions in the trade sphere. On some issues, such as ACP debt to the EC and the arrangements to allow ACP bananas into the EC market post-1992, the ACP had to settle for a promise that the EC would "sympathetically" review these issues in the future.

The financial aid package for Lomé IV was the last issue to be resolved. The EC had always left the announcement of the size of the package to the last ministerial session in each of the previous renewals of the convention to ensure that the package be "non-negotiable." For their part, the ACP states had ritually denounced the package in the Lomé II and III negotiations and succeeded in extracting a minor improvement in the EC aid offer. In this round of talks, the ACP states tried a new tactic: They threatened to refuse to agree to the other elements in the convention, particularly the trade package, until after the EC had made its financial aid offer. Britain and Germany countered by asserting that no offer would be made until the ACP agreed to the trade package; the ACP states backed down. They did, however, reject the initial aid offer, which amounted to less than they had been told, informally, they would receive.

Again, disputes between the EC member states played a significant role: Britain and the Netherlands had initially insisted Lomé IV should be funded only at the same level in nominal terms as the previous convention. The ACP had requested a total of ECU 15.5 billion (compared with ECU 8.5 billion for Lomé III) to allow for inflation, the accession of additional countries to the convention, and new areas of cooperation. Commission Marin, again in a negotiating ploy, had publicly advocated a package of ECU 12.8 billion (not including funds from the EIB). At the last moment, the Spanish government insisted that its contribution to the new package should not be in excess of that for Lomé III (Spain gains very little return from EEC aid through winning EDF contracts). An initial offer of a total of ECU 11.9 billion—including ECU 1.2 billion in European Investment Bank (EIB) loans—was rejected by the ACP.

The role of the French presidency of the Council of Ministers was decisive in determining final agreement on the size of the aid package. The French government had indicated informally to the Commission and to the ACP that it would be willing to provide an additional ECU 100 million so long as the convention was signed during its presidency (which was to expire at the end of 1989). In two previous rounds of negotiations, the French government had played an active role, only to have the convention concluded during the Irish presidency, which was able to claim the credit for the successful outcome of the negotiations; Paris was determined that this would not happen for Lomé IV. With all parties aware of the French offer, there was considerable pressure to reach a quick agreement. The ACP accepted a revised package of ECU 12 billion, the additional funds being provided by France, Germany, and Italy (with Britain refusing to make a supplementary contribution).

■ Lomé IV: Something Old, Something New

That the negotiations for a fourth Lomé Convention would reach a successful conclusion was inevitable. Both parties had too much at stake in the relationship to allow it to lapse. For the ACP states, the concerns were predominantly material. Despite their complaints at the erosion of their trade preferences and the fact that the vast majority of their exports even without the convention would enter the EC market duty-free—either because they attract zero tariffs or because they would enter under the EC's General System of Preferences (GSP)—the trade preferences do make a difference at the margin, particularly the access for some agricultural products that compete with EC production and for certain processed tropical products. The convention also provides somewhat more security of trade access (despite the existence of a safeguard clause) than is available to other countries under the GSP. Most important, at a time when aid flows from other sources are at best stagnating, the convention provides a substantial flow of funds—on very favorable terms—to ACP states. The ECU 12 billion of Lomé IV, however inadequate for meeting the needs of the ACP group, make the EDF one of the most significant aid agencies.

The ACP Secretariat's own assessment of the convention at the beginning of the negotiations had been substantially more positive than on previous occasions. The Secretariat had noted that the contractual basis of the convention allowed planning, that its consultative provisions facilitated a "genuine search for solutions of mutual interest and benefit," and that EDF resources facilitated planning and budgeting because of their predictability and availability. The convention was "an instrument of economic security" that helped to insulate to some degree a large number of ACP states "from the worst hazards of economic life." "The ACP," the memorandum concluded, "can hardly call for a more firmly stated commitment to partnership."

On the EC side, there would have been considerable embarrassment if the convention had not been successfully renegotiated. As the commission noted in its proposal to the Council of Ministers for a negotiating mandate, the convention was "the main pillar of the Community's development policy." In addition to this centrality, continuation of Lomé enabled member states to claim in other forums that they were making special efforts for the least-developed states. There were also, of course, direct bureaucratic interests in the continuation of the relationship—Lomé is the primary raison d'etre of the Commission's Development Directorate. Beyond the Commission, however, there were other groups, including some in the European Parliament, and nongovernmental organizations (NGOs) that had their own interests in seeing the relationship renewed.

For the member states, the material gains from Lomé are limited: It is difficult to see what the convention provides that they would not otherwise be able to obtain through bilateral relations with the ACP states or with other countries. But there is no doubt that Lomé IV does assist in sustaining some bilateral relations with the more significant ACP economies such as Côte d'Ivoire, Nigeria, and Zimbabwe—relations that member states probably value more highly than the convention itself. And there are still some sectors of European industry for which the ACP economies remain significant trading partners.

Outside the trade sphere, where European concessions on access were modest (although more substantial than many expected on the rules of origin and safeguards issues), the new convention did bring some significant gains, most noticeably in the terms of the financial assistance package. Why, given the ACP states' weakness, were they able to extract additional concessions from the EC? Part of the answer lies in their very weakness: The paradox of the relationship is that this weakness is their principal negotiating strength. The decline in ACP economies in the 1980s prompted a reconsideration of the relationship by the EC: There was obvious concern that the viability of existing aid projects would be thrown into doubt unless significant improvement occurred in the macroeconomic environment.

The ACP group's weakness was at the root of its most viable bargaining tactic: its ability to embarrass the EC by publicizing its lack of generosity. This was particularly true of negotiations in the trade regime. Here, however, the ACP states also proved to be dogged negotiators—much tougher, Commission officials acknowledged, than they had anticipated before the negotiations began.

The ACP cause also benefited from European allies. Here the Commission was most important. There is little doubt that the ACP would not have achieved as much in the trade and aid spheres had it not been for the Commission's continuous attempts to force the Council of Ministers to improve its offers. By publicly putting forward positions on aid and trade that went beyond the initial offers made by the council, Development Commissioner Marin placed the council on the defensive. It may have been only a bargaining ploy, as for instance in the commission's advocacy of an aid package of over ECU 12 billion excluding EIB resources, but it had some effect. Commission officials asserted that the final aid package was funded at a higher level than they had anticipated at the beginning of the negotiations (interviews, Brussels, October 1990). Finally, individual ACP states and the group as a whole benefited from having champions among the member states. Former colonial ties continued to exert an influence as ex-metropoles championed the interests of some of their former colonies. And of considerable significance for the group as a whole was that the final negotiations took place under the French presidency of the Council of Ministers. Ever eager to benefit from the grand symbolic gesture in favor of less-developed countries, the French were willing to exert pressure on other members of the council, and to put additional financial resources of their own into the relationship, in order to ensure that the negotiation of the convention was successfully concluded during their presidency.

I have argued before (Ravenhill 1985b) that the advantage to the ACP in renegotiating the convention is that there is a "foot in the door" effect: Each time the convention is renegotiated, the ACP states can use the existing benefits they enjoy as a lever with which to pry open the door a little further. The EC's position is less comfortable: In each renegotiation, it has to improve the terms of the convention or face embarrassment. Why, then, did the ACP agree to a convention of ten years' duration instead of the previous five-year period? Perhaps the two most important factors here are (1) a cost-benefit calculation on the part of the ACP that suggested that the extent of gains from renegotiating the convention did not significantly outweigh the costs of investing so many resources in lengthy negotiations; and (2) that for many states, the most important part of the convention is its financial aid provisions and these will be renegotiated after five years.

Ironically, it is now the EC that is unhappy with the ten-year duration of the convention. The dramatic developments in Eastern Europe in 1989 have convinced the EC that it should place far more emphasis in its external relations on the need for democratization and for a move to market-based economies. For some members, therefore, Lomé IV—with its rhetorical emphasis on equality of partnership, respect for the sovereignty of the ACP states, and avoidance of political interference—is a legacy of the 1970s that is increasingly irrelevant to the 1990s. Already, in the EDF committee, member states have been increasingly insistent about taking into account human rights and democratization issues in decisionmaking on funding aid projects.

The new chapter on structural adjustment opens the way for the EC to impose far greater conditionality in the relationship than previously. Even though the actual provisions for structural adjustment financing for Lomé IV amount to only ECU 1,150 million, or about 14 percent of EDF grants, the EC has given clear signals that it intends to link part of the other EDF funding through national indicative programs to structural adjustment objectives. The ACP may well discover that the financial assistance provisions of the convention that they have negotiated are implemented in a way very different from what they anticipated.

This fluidity exists because the Lomé Convention has always been an essentially declaratory document rather than a contract. Over the years, as successive rounds of negotiations have specified additional objectives and new instruments of cooperation, it has become even more so. The advantage for the partners is that it gives them considerable flexibility and enables the convention to be redefined to meet changing needs (as seen in the provision of structural adjustment assistance in Lomé III). For the ACP, the danger is that the convention gives significant discretionary power to the EC Commission (as the implementing agency) to reinterpret the arrangements as it sees fit.

■ Conclusion

The renewal of the Lomé Convention in 1989 maintained a pattern of negotiations that was characteristic not only of previous Lomé talks but was also observed in its Yaoundé predecessors (Zartman 1971). The most important negotiations continued to occur within the European Community, in particular between the member states at the Council of Ministers level. As it had done on previous occasions, the EC Commission, although a considerable source of frustration for the ACP in its role as negotiating partner for detailed talks, was an ally to the ACP in helping to prise concessions from the member states. Once the EC had agreed on its position, it was very difficult for the ACP to budge it. Certainly, as the EC expected (hence its enthusiasm for a convention of longer duration), the ACP states were able to move the EC marginally toward its demands, but inevitably the outcome was far short of the demands of principle that constituted the ACP opening position.

An emphasis on the centrality of the bargaining between the Europeans is not to suggest that the ACP states were completely lacking in influence over the outcome of the negotiations. They did play an important role in shaping the agenda. This was particularly the case, for instance, in defining the conditions for and permissible usage of structural adjustment assistance and in ensuring that debt relief figured prominently in the talks.[7] Similarly, in the trade sphere, ACP pressure for modification of the rules of origin and safeguard clauses brought significant improvements over the Lomé III terms. As had always been the case, the principal weapons in the negotiating armory of ACP states were their ability to embarrass the EC by pointing to their own weakness and to the Europeans' miserly approach and an ACP persistence that eventually wore down exasperated European negotiators and extracted concessions at the margin (which seldom imposed a significant cost on the EC).

As in the past, the weakness of the ACP Secretariat hampered the group; the lack of detailed technical information made it difficult for negotiators to argue other than along the lines of general principles. The deterioration of the Secretariat as a consequence of the failure of member states to pay their budgetary contributions reflected not only the desperate financial situation of many group members but also divisions within the membership and a lack of faith in the efficacy of the group. The ACP continued to exist only for the purposes of the convention, and even then the day-to-day implementation of the relationship lay between the EC Commission (with its own delegates in all ACP countries) and ACP national governments. The ACP Secretariat and the Brussels-based ambassadors were simply bypassed. There was also a lack of communication between the Brussels ambassadors and their Geneva counterparts on issues before UNCTAD.

To some extent, the ACP states thus have themselves to blame for the demise of Lomé as a model for North-South relations: ACP countries did not take the relationship seriously enough to invest the modest resources required to finance a secretariat that could provide them with the necessary detailed technical support. To be sure, such a secretariat would not have changed the outcome of the negotiations in any fundamental way. It should, however, have enabled the ACP to make additional gains that although marginal, would nevertheless have been valuable to individual members of the group. European negotiators expressed surprise that the ACP had not pursued some issues on which the Europeans believed it would have been possible for the ACP to extract concessions (interviews, Brussels, October 1990).

With little prospect of significant reversal of Africa's economic decline in the coming decade (Ravenhill 1990), and new opportunities for the EC opening up in Eastern Europe, the ACP states are likely to continue to decline in significance as economic partners for Western Europe. Africa's raw materials will continue to be of interest, but with commodity prices likely to remain low and African supply uncertain, Europe is unlikely to be motivated by fears of raw-materials shortages to provide significantly more assistance to the ACP. The EC has already signaled that it regards the convention's trade preferences as being of little importance to the ACP and susceptible to reduction in accord with European objectives in the Uruguay Round. The enlargement of the community to include Spain and Portugal has admitted countries that not only compete directly with some ACP states in agricultural production but that are keen to improve EC links with non-ACP Southern countries with which they have traditional ties. Thus, although the provisions of Lomé IV will be in force for ten years, the ACP can expect to see the actual value of the trade provisions continue to be whittled away as preferential margins are reduced.

The third decade of the Lomé relationship will almost certainly be focused on the aid relationship. The actual aid figures will be renegotiated midway through the convention, though there is little reason to expect that the procedures will be different from before: The Europeans will argue at length before making an offer that the ACP will ritually reject before returning to the table shortly afterward to accept a marginally improved offer. The most contentious issue in the 1990s is likely to be more aggressive efforts by the EC to move away from the NIEO rhetoric and notions of equality of partnership with which the convention was originally imbued and to impose increased conditionality on ACP recipients. In the 1980s the ACP could rely on allies within the EC Commission and some member states to help resist such tendencies; in the 1990s they are unlikely to be so fortunate.

■ Notes

1. The signature of the convention was originally scheduled for December 28, 1989; it was brought forward to December 15 for fear that the later date would ensure that it received no media coverage and would interfere with ministers' Christmas vacations. In any case, the dramatic developments in Eastern Europe completely overshadowed the renewal of the treaty.

2. The Commission had made a similar argument in its draft negotiating mandate regarding the completion of the single market: "The Community should show that regardless of its own internal problems and priorities, it has no intention of turning in on itself, but plans to reaffirm its solidarity with its partners by increasing its financial support and adapting its operating methods to meet the new problems emerging."

3. Other things being equal, of course. As a reviewer of this manuscript pointed out, the ACP states were disadvantaged by the general decline in interest on the part of Europe in development issues and by the apparent "aid fatigue" that had afflicted most member states by the mid-1980s. This overall context plus the Community's unwillingness to make any significant extensions to the relationship severely constrained the range of possible outcomes in the negotiations.

4. The supplemental interviews were with negotiators. Nicora was the head of the Commission task force set up for the Lomé IV negotiations.

5. France had earlier advocated additional funding to make up the deficit

on STABEX transfers caused by the inability of the system to cope with the decline in commodity prices during Lomé III.

6. Carrington, never popular with many African states, was essentially a lame duck because he was due to step down as secretary-general at the end of 1989.

7. The EC frequently argued during the talks that the total amount of ACP debt to the EC as a multilateral organization as opposed to that owed to the member states was minimal, and that the latter could not be discussed within the framework of the convention. In early 1991 the member states rejected a Commission proposal to cancel outstanding ACP debt to the EC qua EC, asserting that the subject must be addressed on a case-by-case basis.

5

The Impact of 1992 on EC-ACP Trade and Investment

Carol Cosgrove

Lomé IV, concluded between the European Community (EC) and sixty-nine African, Caribbean, and Pacific (ACP) states in 1989, provides a ten-year framework for their cooperation. It coincides with the intensive EC program for creating the single European market (SEM) on December 31, 1992. At the same time, the wider European economic and trading environment has increasingly liberalized with the collapse of communism in Eastern Europe and the approaches by the Scandinavian and other members of the European Free Trade Association (EFTA) for full membership in the EC. Indeed, within Europe there is a growing agreement on the desirability and eventual feasibility of creating a European economic space, or, to quote former Soviet President Mikhail Gorbachev, a "common European homeland."

ACP states believe that their interests are directly affected by the revolutionary changes taking place in Europe. The result has been deep uncertainty, doubt, and fear that their trade and financial relations with Europe will be disrupted. Many ACP spokespersons have expressed their suspicions that ACP interests will not be protected in the momentous events reshaping the European continent. The ACP states are indeed confronted with a bewildering and often intimidating range of challenges in the European marketplace. Nevertheless, EC Commission officials have repeatedly proclaimed that there will be exciting opportunities for the ACP states deriving from dynamic growth and expansion of the newly uniting European economies in the 1990s.

How real are these opportunities? Even if they exist, are the ACP states sufficiently robust to take advantage of them? What is likely to be the impact on their fragile economies, at least in the short term, of incipient diversion of aid, finance, and trade opportunities to other priority regions, not least Eastern Europe? Will Europe's resurrection advance or diminish ACP prospects for economic development?

■ The Single European Market and Plans for Economic and Monetary Union

The goal of the single European market is to establish a truly common market on the basis of full economic integration that will involve greater social cohesion among the European people and enable them to enjoy higher living standards. The SEM program was launched with the Single European Act in 1985, followed by the White Paper by Lord Cockfield, a vice-president of the EC Commission (CEC 1985). The Cockfield White Paper set out almost 300 specific measures that were essential if the EC were to achieve a single market by December 1992. By February 1991, agreement was reached on more than 200 of these measures; the remainder constituted a priority agenda for the European Community in 1991 and 1992.

The creation of the European Monetary System (EMS) is an integral part of this goal. First established in 1979, it includes all twelve EC member states. Two of them, Greece and Portugal, have not yet joined the Exchange Rate Mechanism (ERM), preferring to permit their currencies to float freely in view of the vulnerability of their economies. The ERM commits the participating member states to maintain strict parities between their values, in the context of a basket of currencies defined in European currency units (ECUs). The Spanish peseta and the United Kingdom pound sterling fluctuate within a wider band than the strict parities that apply to the currency values of the other member states.

At the heart of the present plan, a European system of central banks would constitute a vehicle for creating a monetary union and eventually a single currency. The idea could develop into a "Eurofed," along similar lines to the United States Federal Reserve Bank, although events were some way from this goal at the beginning of the 1990s.

The critical issue is the extent to which power should be exercised at the EC level over macroeconomic policies in the member states. This fundamental political issue preoccupied the EC states throughout 1991 and beyond, along with the allied question of how much independence European central banks should maintain in the future. Whatever the outcome of this debate, there seems little doubt that these essentially domestic issues in Europe will continue to inhibit the capacity of the EC to participate in international diplomacy into the 1990s. ACP states are concerned that the stresses and strains of achieving the EMS will constitute too great a distraction.

■ Implications of Lomé IV

□ Trade and Aid Provisions

Lomé IV maintained the principal provisions of the previous Lomé regimes: free access to EC markets for the ACP states on a basis of nonreciprocity, and a wide range of financial and technical assistance provided on mainly nonreimbursable terms. The trade arrangements were marginally adjusted with the intention of providing even better access conditions for some ACP products than those previously upheld, and the opportunity to protect ACP interests if adversely affected by such mechanisms as a "safeguard clause" were adjusted in favor of the ACP states.

In terms of financial and technical assistance, the existing mechanisms for the economic development of the ACP states were broadly maintained and enhanced. The European Development Fund (EDF) was replenished to a total of ECU 12 billion (approximately $13 billion), to be disbursed between 1991 and 1995. The principal instruments for disbursement remained direct grants for economic projects and programs, support for the stabilization of ACP exports (via STABEX and SYSMIN), special loans and rebates, contributions toward risk capital, and a new mechanism with reserved funding of ECU 1,150 million for debt release and rapid economic assistance to the ACP states. These measures are designed to ensure that the EC can help preserve social stability and encourage ACP states to adopt structural adjustment policies. Overall, Lomé IV funding for the ACP states represents a nominal increase of 40 percent over Lomé III, although when demographic growth and inflation are taken into account, it is frankly doubtful whether Lomé IV funding constitutes any increase in real terms (Cosgrove and Laurent 1991).

☐ *The Single European Market*

Some of the trade provisions of Lomé IV were specially adjusted to take account of the pending single European market. For example, ACP exports (with certain crucial derogations regarding agricultural products) enjoy duty-free entry under the common external tariff of the EC. The latter is in the process of being replaced by a new harmonized system (HS), where each tariff will bear a new nomenclature. ACP exporters, especially customs regarding ACP products seeking to take advantage of Lomé duty-free access (OJEC, 1989).

Specific limits on ACP duty-free entry to the Single Market were spelled out in protocols attached to Lomé IV, which in large part perpetuated the previously established provisions of Lomé III. These special protocols to Lomé IV govern trade in beef and veal, sugar, rum, and bananas. All of these products, for one reason or another, are regarded as sensitive in the EC.

In the case of beef and veal (of particular concern to Botswana, Kenya, Swaziland, and Zimbabwe), European production is in surplus. Within the terms of the Common Agricultural Policy, beef and beef products from third countries are permitted to enter the EC only by detailed arrangement. ACP states benefit from a special protocol attached to the Lomé Convention permiting an overall annual quantity of imports from ACP states that ranges from 30,00 to 39,000 tons. The establishment of the SEM will not have any direct impact on this provision, beyond the fact that the SEM should encourage greater freedom of circulation for ACP meat and processed meat products within the EC in the 1990s. As such, there is no reason to believe that the 1992 agenda will have any adverse effect on the ACP states.

Sugar has traditionally been a highly political product in the context of EC-ACP cooperation. Among the ACP members most directly affected are Mauritius, Fiji, and the Caribbean states. From the beginning of the Lomé regime in 1975, the EC has had surplus sugar production. When the United Kingdom joined the EC, the British government negotiated special conditions of access for cane sugar from certain British Commonwealth ACP countries whose economies had come to depend on cane sugar exports to Britain and could not easily be diversified.

In 1973, the first sugar protocol was negotiated with the EC and then attached to Lomé I. It remained unchanged in Lomé IV, with the guaranteed purchase by the EC of up to 1.3 million tons of ACP sugar at guaranteed prices. Within the framework of the SEM, ACP sugar, which traditionally had been exported to the United Kingdom, will be able to circulate throughout the EC. In the longer term, there is no doubt that attention will be paid to the paradox of EC surplus production of beet sugar alongside its commitment to import ACP cane sugar.

The present EC sugar regime has a destabilizing effect on international sugar markets, but it is likely to remain in its present form at least through the early 1990s. The operation of the SEM and the spending priorities of the European structural adjustment funds to modernize Spanish and Portuguese agricultural processing could well have the combined effect of reducing market opportunities for cane sugar in the EC. There is little doubt that any diminution of cane sugar imports from ACP states would have a deleterious impact on many fragile ACP economies. Much of ACP sugar is exported from small island economies that have extremely limited options in terms of agricultural diversification. Countries such as Mauritius in the Indian Ocean, Fiji in the Pacific, and Saint Lucia and Barbados in the Caribbean have few alternative crops given the hurricanes, cyclones, and soil conditions prevalent in these territories. Without guaranteed markets for cane sugar, their economic prospects could be bleak. The future of these island economies depends directly on the political goodwill of the EC member states, especially the United Kingdom, and their willingness to perpetuate the sugar protocol as a special arrangement to support them.

Rum is of the most direct interest to the Caribbean states. Essentially a processed sugar product, it received special attention in the protocol attached to Lomé IV. The new arrangements constitute a distinct and positive advantage for the ACP states and herald benefits stemming directly from the push toward the 1992 benchmark. Hitherto, ACP rum exports have been subject to national tariff quotas in each EC market. In anticipation of the SEM, the Lomé IV rum protocol provides for a rapid increase in rum quotas after 1993 and the eventual abolition of quotas after 1995. There is likely to be considerable expansion of ACP rum exports throughout the EC, especially to the German market, which represents a bonanza for rum-producing ACP states, principally in the Caribbean.

Bananas, also a highly political product, fall under a protocol that represents one of the most vexed and difficult aspects of EC-ACP trade. The EC, ever since its origins in 1958, has sought to protect traditional European banana markets for suppliers from former colonial territories in Africa and the Caribbean. Lomé IV provides for the renewal of the banana protocol as it existed under Lomé III. This maintained protection for bananas in the French, Italian, and British markets from ACP states; it also included special protective measures regarding Greece, Spain, and Portugal, all of whom had traditional domestic suppliers.

At present, bananas are not permitted to circulate freely within the EC. Indeed, bananas are ranked alongside armaments, drugs, and valuable antiques as excluded products within the terms of the SEM—clearly a rather bizarre grouping. It must be inconceivable that frontier controls would remain in place throughout the EC to secure ACP banana interests.

ACP bananas cannot compete with the so-called dollar bananas coming from Latin America, which are generally of higher quality and are produced more cheaply than ACP bananas. It is reasonable to assume that in a free market, ACP bananas would be unlikely to maintain their market share. Lomé IV commits EC member states to protect ACP banana interests, but it is difficult to imagine under what conditions ACP bananas could compete effectively in the SEM. This issue is likely to cause considerable problems in the context of ACP-EC relations later in the 1990s.

For its part, the EC has committed substantial structural adjustment finance to support the weaker, less competitive ACP economies in the SEM. It is difficult, however, to see how relatively limited short-term finance can compensate for the long-term displacement of export earnings—hence economic development potential—that ACP banana producers are likely to suffer as the SEM regime for bananas comes into effect during the early 1990s.

☐ *Impact on Nontraditional Exports*

Under the Lomé regime, ACP exports of nontraditional products have enjoyed a relative degree of protection in individual EC markets by virtue of the operation of the General System of Preferences (GSP), the Multi-

Fibre Agreement (MFA), and various controls concerning bilateral trade agreements and voluntary export restraints. These quantitative restrictions have served to ensure not only that the European market has been highly regulated, but also that the ACP states have not been exposed to full-fledged competition from Asian and Latin American exporters. The creation of the SEM, however, means a harmonized and eventually uniform trade regime throughout the EC. Among other things, it will mean common rules regarding trademarks and counterfeiting, export credits, reciprocity from trade in services, and the replacement of national quota restrictions by those of the EC. The net effect of all these measures is likely to be that the European market will become increasingly competitive and that ACP producers will be the least likely to succeed.

The precise impact on ACP exports will depend to a great extent on the way in which EC national quotas are gradually eliminated and what replaces them. At the present time, it is not clear how EC member states will manage this transition to the SEM. It should be remembered that this transition from national- to EC-level quantitative restrictions is taking place simultaneously with the Uruguay Round of GATT negotiations. The uncertainty regarding the outcome of the global trade talks adds to the unsettling environment in which the ACP states find themselves as they enter the 1992 arrangements.

Because the goal of the SEM legislation is to ensure that all products and services circulate freely within the EC, national quantitative restrictions will become irrelevant. Currently, the EC member states are negotiating the replacement of national quotas with EC-wide ones and other measures with equivalent effect. This new arrangement will have a direct impact on the EC market for textiles, process engineering products, industrial items, and processed agricultural goods.

The ACP states are wary of the possible implications for them of what they see as liberalization under the SEM regime regarding other developing countries' trade access within the framework of GSP, MFA, and other arrangements. Because ACP states currently benefit from general duty-free treatment in the EC market, any tariff reduction by the EC on a most-favored nation basis or under the GSP automatically reduces the preferences enjoyed by ACP exporters.

In 1989, the firm of CTA Economic and Export Analysts Ltd. of Reading, United Kingdom, undertook an extensive analysis for the EC Commission of the extent to which ACP trade preferences in the EC market had been eroded by concessions already made under the GSP and other arrangements with Asian and Latin American developing countries between 1976 and 1988 (CTA 1989). The study, though not definitive, indicated that although preference erosion had taken place, ACP interests were only marginally affected. Indeed, the CTA study showed that ACP exports are less responsive to changes in world demand than are exports of other developing-country ACP competitors. The implication is that ACP exports are supply-inelastic. They were price-competitive without the benefit of preferences for only very few of the products studied. For the remaining products, ACP preference-adjusted prices were often considerably higher than those from other developing countries. This suggests that preferences enjoyed by the ACP states in the EC market establish an essential floor to ACP export performance.

Overall, the findings of the CTA study indicated that the existence (or absence) of preferences had a random impact on ACP export performance for the products examined, both on a product-specific and group basis. In general, the results seemed to show that Lomé trade and tariff regimes themselves do not ensure ACP competitiveness in EC markets against competition from other developing countries or EC suppliers. Other factors play a much more important role, including climatic variations, political upheavals, financial constraints, overvaluation of currencies, raw-materials shortages, production and quality-control problems, inadequate marketing, and unreliable transportation and distribution systems. Two other factors that affect the ACP states and other developing countries as well are instability of world commodity prices and increasing competition from Eastern Europe within the EC itself.

It would seem that the ACP economies have not benefited as much as the states had hoped from successive Lomé aid and trade regimes. Relatively limited trade diversification has occurred in the ACP economies, and ACP exporters of value-added products find themselves under increasingly competitive pressures. To some extent, more realistic currency valuations would improve their competitiveness. ACP economies, heavily dependent on raw-materials exports, will need significant structural adjustment assistance and debt relief if they are to adapt to the dynamic international environment of the 1990s in general and the liberalized SEM market in particular.

☐ *Taxation*

The European Community, the United States, and Japan are discussing the abolition of revenue taxes on tropical products within the context of the Uruguay Round. These negotiations are proceeding in parallel with the proposed harmonization of revenue taxes within EC countries in the context of the 1992 agenda. Some EC member states maintain high internal taxes on coffee, tea, cocoa, and bananas, products traditionally regarded as "luxuries" that could be taxed legitimately. These taxes apply to imports from ACP states as well as other developing countries. ACP states would benefit from the proposals in the Uruguay Round negotiations for eliminating those taxes not covered by the preferential provisions of the Lomé Convention. The harmonization and eventual elimination of revenue duties on tropical products could stimulate demand for ACP commodity exports in the EC market, but only if ACP supplies are competitive in terms of price and quality.

☐ *Franc Zone and European Monetary Union*

In the context of 1992 and EC-ACP trade and investment, there is little doubt that the future of the franc zone is of critical importance. The franc zone economies in West and Central Africa, in which currencies are dominated in terms of the CFA franc, maintain direct links with the Bank of France. In 1990 the CFA franc was effectively pegged to the ECU as realignment between the French franc and other EC currencies became more infrequent and inflexible. If the Delors Plan for a European monetary union proceeds in the mid-1990s, the future of the relationship between the franc zone and the Bank of France must be called into question.

The West and Equatorial African Francophone ACP states have long enjoyed the benefits of the franc zone and their continued special relationship with their former metropole, France. Shantayanan Deverajan and Jaime de Melo examine the relative performances of members and nonmembers of CFA franc Africa in recent years in Chapter 8.

The French government currently advocates the substitution of this special relationship with a new one, possibly based within a subset of Lomé IV, involving direct links between the CFA franc and a proposed European federal reserve bank. Other EC member states are much less sympathetic to the maintenance of direct financial relations with what they perceive as unstable economies in Africa. Any diminution or weakening of franc zone links could well result in a diversion of investment and financial flows in general from France to the Francophone franc zone countries (ODI 1990).

African franc zone countries fear a greater loss of control over their exchange rate determination as the 1992 program unfolds. Although the precise structure of European monetary union has not been decided, the majority of EC currencies are already very tightly aligned to one other. Inflation in a European monetary union seems likely to follow the previous German experience, based on tight monetary policy and an increasingly fixed exchange rate. In this scenario, the African CFA zone countries will find it difficult to maintain their competitiveness because their currency will in effect be overvalued. A further source of concern is their inability to influence collective EC actions at a time when France is increasingly distracted by European policy imperatives.

To some extent, the move toward economic and monetary union in Europe has prompted African states to look again at their priorities. In the view of the executive secretary of the Economic Commission for Africa (ECA), Adebayo Adedeji, Africa should promote monetary and other forms of financial integration vigorously in order to resolve the monetary and other problems associated with the inconvertibility of its currencies. The ECA would like to see the franc zone dissolved within a broader African financial grouping, with greatly increased financial cooperation between participating African countries. To some extent, the Lomé Convention could contribute toward this goal (Adedeji 1991).

☐ *Aid and Investment*

Throughout the Lomé IV negotiations, ACP spokespersons persistently voiced their fears of substantial diversion of EC aid and investment away from their economies to the fledgling democracies of Eastern Europe and the less-developed regions of the EC. They pointed to the massive expansion of European structural funds targeted to less-developed regions in Greece, Spain, Portugal, and southern Italy and the significant built-in incentives in this aid to promote commercial and state-funded projects in those regions. The integration of these lagging regions into the mainstream European economy was perceived as a direct threat to the prospects that ACP states had of attracting aid and investment. The liberalization of Eastern Europe and the opening up of the Eastern European economies to EC aid and investment represents, from an ACP perspective, further significant pressures. ACP states allege that the EC is no longer interested in its ACP partners and that it currently permits Eastern Europe to dominate its horizons.

The EC Commission response, predictably sharp, insists that "our partners must understand that the Community in Western Europe cannot ignore what happens with their immediate neighbors, and must be available to support the process of liberalization of the economies and political systems in these countries. This priority is very normal and nobody can criticize us for intending to make every economic and financial effort to help in that process" (Dieter Frisch, quoted in *West Africa,* February 20, 1990). EC officials insist that there is no evidence of any aid or investment diversion away from the ACP states and that allocations of aid for Eastern European countries is definitely not at ACP expense. Nevertheless, it would be foolish to deny that aid budgets are finite, and if we view the total aid budget as a cake (or as the French call it, a Camembert), the size of the wedge allocated to the ACP is likely, directly or indirectly, to affect the slice available for the Eastern European countries and vice versa.

There is no mechanism within the EC for directing private investment.

Eastern Europe, with relatively well-developed industrial infrastructures, a well-trained industrial labor force, and close proximity to the principal European markets, is likely to be an attractive magnet for private investment. In any evaluation of locations for private investment projects, there seems little doubt that Eastern European countries could well win out over less-developed ACP economies. Even EC member states, such as Spain and Portugal, allege significant potential diversion of investment away from their economies to those of Czechoslovakia and Hungary— witness the switch to several major Japanese projects from southern to Eastern Europe in 1990. The results of any diminution of aid to and investment in the ACP states are likely to have a severe impact (Cosgrove 1981).

■ Conclusions

ACP states are confronted by a bewildering number of challenges regarding their relations with Europe in the 1990s (OJEC). To some extent, Lomé IV offers new opportunities, not least in terms of the expansion of STABEX and more generous rules of origin. Moreover, the creation of the single European market and a wider European economic space could generate more dynamic economic growth throughout the European continent. This in turn could conceivably stimulate import demand for ACP tropical products. Similarly, opportunities opened up by Uruguay Round trade liberalization could encourage ACP exports. But it is unclear when these measures will be implemented. For many of the poorest ACP states, the trade provision of Lomé IV and the implications of the SEM are unlikely to make a significant difference to their economic prospects in the 1990s.

The effects of the Gulf War could well distort ACP economic development. ACP oil-rich countries such as Nigeria, Cameroon, Gabon, Angola, the Congo, and Trinidad and Tobago all experienced a welcome upsurge in their foreign exchange receipts. For the most part, however, the ACP states will be seriously affected by any rise in oil prices, which are likely to trigger adverse economic conditions in the majority of the ACP states. The diminution of the so-called peace dividend, which was formerly predicted by the U.S. government at around $189 billion a year between 1991 and 1994, now seems less likely to materialize.

Finally, the debate on the SEM and the liberalization of Eastern Europe already has political repercussions on EC-ACP relations. The emergence of multiparty systems and democracies in Eastern Europe has prompted many Western politicians to look for the same metamorphosis from their partners in Africa. Thus, an additional impact on the SEM and the opening up toward Eastern Europe is a greater focus on participation and dialogue, with EC governments stressing the need for African democracy as a counterpart to economic development. The EC increasingly insists on participatory development on the part of the ACP states. This means involving the people at the grassroots level in economic development priorities and ensuring popular validation of what is done in their name. This would be an uncomfortable process for most ACP states, which still regard the Lomé Convention as an economic rather than a political framework for development.

6

The Common Agricultural Policy and African Countries

Ousmane Badiane

A number of factors explain the interest of developing countries, particularly African, in the Common Agricultural Policy (CAP) of the European Community (EC). The most important of these factors are (1) the overriding role agriculture plays in a typical developing country; (2) the relatively high degree of openness of these economies that renders them particularly vulnerable to changes in international markets; (3) the increasing reliance on international trade in securing food consumption in these countries; (4) the dominant presence of the EC on major international agricultural markets; and (5) the essentially inward-looking orientation of the Common Agricultural Policy.

One hitherto neglected feature of the CAP, which by no means is less important than these five factors, has been brought to light recently by the ongoing Uruguay Round of negotiations. That is the strong connection between the CAP and global protectionism in agriculture. Moreover, as the GATT (General Agreement on Tariffs and Trade) negotiations have revealed, the implications of the Common Agricultural Policy extend far beyond the narrow sphere of agricultural policies. Also, its link to the structure and reforms of economic policies in developing countries has gained more visibility.

The objective of this chapter is to analyze the impact of the CAP on African economies, taking into consideration the linkages just mentioned between the CAP, worldwide agricultural protectionism, and economic policies in developing countries. Thus, the approach here consists of a brief review of the conception and evolution of the CAP, a discussion of why African countries are especially vulnerable to it, and finally an analysis of its effects. The trade effects from the point of view of African countries are discussed in terms of the broader implications of CAP for international markets. In the discussion of the welfare effects, the conventional comparative static analysis is extended to include the linkages already mentioned and to give a more comprehensive and dynamic view of the interactions between African economies and the CAP.

Finally, another characteristic of African countries is added to this analysis: the preferential arrangements linking them to the CAP. Because Chapters 4 and 10 contain interesting political economic analyses of these arrangements, this chapter is restricted to the analysis of the effects of a specific part of these arrangements, the export earnings stabilization facility (STABEX). Also included is a concise evaluation of the CAP-related arrangements between the EC and African countries.

It should be noted that the focus here is not on the myriad of domestic impediments to efficiency and growth in the agricultural sectors of African countries. I argue, however, that these impediments, to the extent that they are policy-related, have a much closer relationship to policies in developed countries than normally recognized, just in the same way recent events in Eastern Europe are linked to the ongoing democratization process in Africa.

■ Conception and Evolution of the Common Agricultural Policy

Article 39 of the EC treaty lays down the following main objectives of the CAP:

1. To raise productivity in the agricultural sector by promoting technical progress, rational development of production, and optimum utilization of factors of production (growth objective);
2. To guarantee a fair standard of living to the farming population by raising their earnings (income objective);
3. To stabilize domestic agricultural markets (stability objective);
4. To assure the availability of food supplies on domestic markets (supply objective);
5. To meet domestic agricultural demand at reasonable prices (distribution objective);
6. To contribute to the harmonization of developments in world trade by abolishing barriers to trade (trade objective).

The EC Commission opted early on for the use of inward-directed and protectionist policies to achieve these goals. It insisted, from the inception of the CAP, on the necessity to shelter the domestic agricultural market from fluctuations on world markets and to support farm prices above their international levels. The EC's argument was that conditions in the EC were different from those in competing export countries and that observed international prices were distorted by state intervention (Rosenblatt et al. 1988).

In accordance with this mandate, the CAP operates through a combination of border regulations, internal market intervention, and direct production support. Border regulations are based on threshold prices set above world levels and at which export supplies are allowed to enter the EC market. Variable levies are applied in the case of imports, or restitutions paid in the case of exports, to bridge the difference between the threshold and international prices for the different commodities. Fluctuations in world prices are absorbed through adjustments in the levies and restitutions, and domestic import and export supply prices remain unaffected. In order to support internal prices above their international levels, the EC also intervenes directly in the domestic market by buying surplus quantities if domestic prices fall below a given level, the so-called intervention price.

The noticeable inwardness of the EC market regulations is to a large extent the consequence of the institutional scaffolding of CAP. The principal actors within the CAP decisionmaking system, the EC Commission and the Council of Ministers of Agriculture, primarily set the orientation of the agricultural policy. Accordingly, agricultural market regulations have been guided more by budgetary restrictions and the income and stabilization objectives than by welfare and allocative considerations.

Through the tremendous changes in its productive capacity, the EC progressively moved from an import situation into one of permanent exports. The CAP, primarily designed to deal with import markets, became increasingly inefficient in coping with the new situation. The system of variable import levies, for example, is effective in protecting domestic markets against competing imports and fluctuations on international markets. When domestic surpluses became the normal situation in EC agricultural markets, intervention buying and the payment of export restitutions substantially raised the costs of operating the CAP. By the mid-1980s, coresponsibility levies, equivalent to producer taxes, and production quotas were introduced into the CAP to contain output expansion and reduce its cost.

Although the EC's role in international markets has markedly increased over the last few decades, the CAP still remains essentially an inward-directed system. The reluctance to adjust the CAP has been shown to have serious effects on world markets, effects that are contrary to its trade objective mentioned previously. Through its impact on international agricultural markets, the CAP is very likely to affect the primarily agrarian African economies.

■ Why African Countries Are Especially Vulnerable to CAP

One reason African economies are vulnerable to CAP effects on international agricultural markets is the dominant role agriculture plays in the domestic economies and in foreign trade in these countries. Primary agriculture and processing industries are by far the largest sectors, both in terms of employment and foreign exchange earnings.

African countries are also vulnerable to the CAP because of the high degree of openness of their economies. For the large majority of African countries, the share of exports in gross domestic product (GDP) fluctuates around 30 percent. And a large share of these exports is generally composed of raw and processed agricultural commodities.

Because of their increasing dependence on trade to secure domestic food consumption, African economies have become increasingly exposed to the effects of changes on international agricultural markets. The ratio of food imports to domestic food production, with cereals used as an indicator, has increased from 10 percent in the early 1960s to 30 to 40 percent at the end of the 1980s (see Figure 6.1). African countries not only resort increasingly to food imports to satisfy domestic consumption but also rely heavily on agricultural exports to finance their food import bill. The average ratio of food imports to agricultural export earnings has been as high as 30 percent throughout the last three decades (Badiane 1990).

Perhaps the most important factor explaining the vulnerability of African countries to the CAP is the high degree of trade intensity between these countries and the EC. As shown by Figure 6.2, African countries display a significantly higher intensity of trade with EC countries than do the developing countries in Asia and Latin America. Therefore, CAP-induced price and quantity changes in EC domestic markets are likely to affect these countries more than most other developing economies.

■ Effects of CAP and Agricultural Protectionism on African Economies

The standard approach in investigating the impact of the CAP is to ask what the effects of its elimination would be. Treated this way, the impact that the CAP may have on developing countries goes far beyond what can be considered as its direct impact on domestic EC and international agricultural markets. In order to have a full appreciation of the potential implications of liberalizing the CAP, it is useful to take into consideration its links to (1) global protectionism in world agriculture; (2) agricultural trade pessimism among developing countries; and (3) exchange regimes and the attitude toward foreign trade generally in these countries.

The GATT negotiations have recently brought to light the close relationship between EC policies and global protectionism in agriculture (Valdes and Zietz 1990). Reluctance on the part of EC countries to reform the CAP has been a major obstacle to the integration of agriculture into

COMMON AGRICULTURAL POLICY AND AFRICA

Figure 6.1 Ratio of Cereal Imports to Domestic Cereal Production in Africa

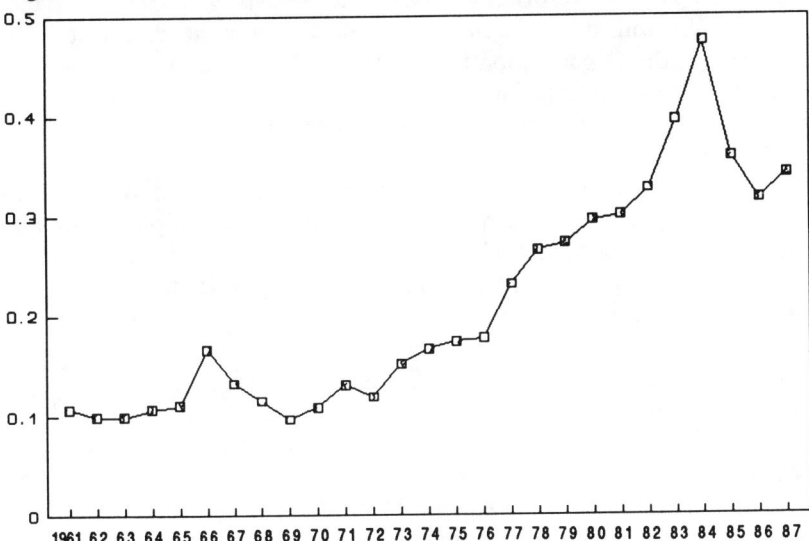

Source: International Food Policy Research Institute (IFPRI) database.

Figure 6.2 Degree of Trade Intensity with the EC

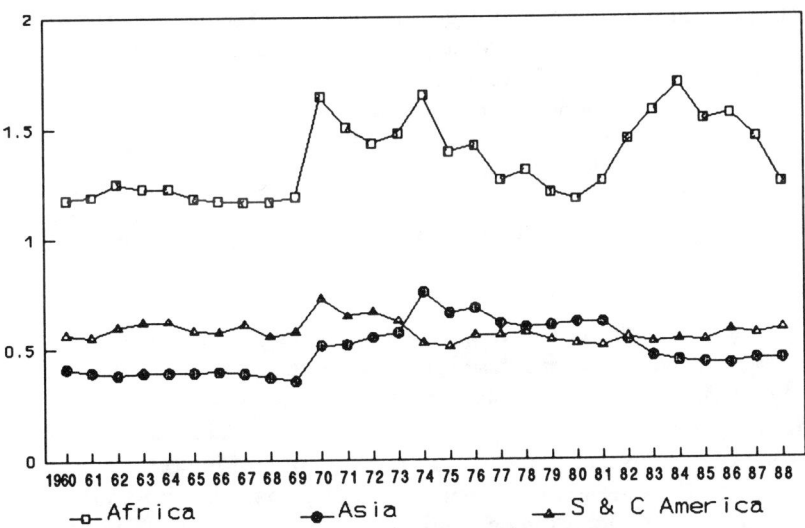

Sources: United Nations Conference on Trade and Development (UNCTAD), *Handbook of International Trade and Development*, various issues.

the GATT. Because reforming the CAP can be expected to speed up the process of liberalization in agriculture in the world—or at least in member countries of the Organization for Economic Cooperation and Development (OECD)—the importance of such a move for any developing region can be seen from the changes that global agricultural reforms may have on developing countries.

The link between CAP and OECD policies is a crucial one for two main reasons. First, their respective architects may be tempted to find in each other's actions a rationale for the measures they adopt. Second, and perhaps more important, is the fact that the two policies tend to amplify each other's effect on international agriculture. Koester and Bale, for instance (1984, p. 13), show how effects on world dairy, grain, and sugar markets are accentuated when CAP measures are combined with sugar protection in the United States.

As the evidence presented in the next section shows, the impact of CAP on the international trading environment probably has been negative. To the extent that a more favorable trading environment will reduce trade pessimism among developing countries, CAP-led policy reforms may be expected to contribute to the reduction of distorting policy intervention in these countries. In such a case, extra gain from CAP liberalization will accrue to developing economies because of the induced improvement in the domestic policy environment.

Developing countries seem to be too willing to point to protectionism in OECD countries to legitimize their interventionist policies. As a Dominican minister participating in an EC-organized seminar on the Lomé arrangements puts it: "How could [developing countries] compete if their markets were not protected, when developed countries had a very efficient protectionist policy even if they did not call it that?" (*Courier*, 1990 no. 123, 7–8.) Furthermore, reforming the CAP and reducing OECD protection to ease the integration of agriculture into GATT, as advocated by developing countries, would raise the pressure on the same countries to adjust their policies in sectors outside agriculture. To the extent that changes in international agricultural policies induce adjustments in the economies of developing countries, they will gain additionally.

The remainder of this chapter discusses the potential impact of the CAP on African countries, based on these broader interrelationships. The effects of the CAP and agricultural policies in other OECD countries result from (1) the active support of domestic production; (2) the subsidizing of surplus exports; and (3) the restriction of imports from third countries. The CAP affects agricultural trading countries directly through the reduction of domestic demand for third country exports and/or the increase in EC supply on export markets. It affects them indirectly through its impact on the level, structure, and stability of world agricultural prices.

Table 6.1 Sources of EC Imports of Selected Agricultural Commodities

Commodity	Percent Share of Intra-EC Imports		Absolute Changes in 1976–1978 to 1986–1988 (in mill. tons)	
	1976/78	1986/88	Total Import	Intra-EC Imports
Cereals	36.9	77.2	− 7.7	+ 10.0
Oilseeds	4.3	18.3	+ 5.9	+ 2.9
Vegetable oils	34.8	47.2	+ 1.7	+ 1.2
Sugar	29.0	37.3	+ 0.1	+ 0.4
Oilseed cake	18.0	20.1	+ 10.7	+ 2.3
Bovine meat	85.4	85.5	+ 0.3	+ 1.2

Source: EC Commission, Eurostatistics, "Analytical Tables of Foreign Trade," Nimexe (various issues).

☐ Effects on Agricultural Trade

The net impact of the CAP on individual African and developing countries' trade depends, on the one hand, on how it affects both demand for and entry of their exports in the EC markets. On the other hand, it depends on how demand in non-EC markets is affected and to what extent individual countries succeed in adjusting to induced changes.

Another important feature of CAP protection is the inability of exporting countries to improve their competitiveness on internal EC markets through price-reducing productivity increases. The substantial discrimination against outside imports arising from these measures has led to the progressive displacement of third-country exports by intra-EC imports. Thus, aggregate imports into the EC stagnated throughout the second half of the 1970s. The share of intra-EC imports rose, however, by more than 5 percent, with a concomitant decrease of 10 percent in the share of third countries (OECD 1987).

The changes for the different commodities from the period 1976–1978 to the period 1986–1988 are recorded in Table 6.1. Whereas combined intra- and extra-EC imports of commodities such as sugar and bovine meat remained almost constant throughout the ten-year period, imports of oilseeds and cake rose by approximately 17 million tons, and imports of cereals fell by nearly 8 million tons. A comparison of the last two columns of Table 6.1 reveals that with the exception of oils and cake, extra-EC imports have declined for all major agricultural commodities. This displacement is the strongest for cereals; the 8-million-ton decrease in combined imports is accompanied by an increase of 10 million tons in intra-EC imports. In the remaining markets where combined imports have risen, intra-EC sources account for by far the largest part of the changes in supply. For oilseeds and vegetable oils, the share of import expansion between 1976–1978 and 1986–1988 that originated within the EC was 50 and 70 percent, respectively. For sugar and bovine meat, products for which combined import growth has been the smallest, changes in intra-EC imports are as much as four times higher than the change in total imports.

The figures in the first two columns of Table 6.1 give an idea of the ultimate impact of the CAP on demand for third-country exports on major agricultural EC markets. They show a significant expansion of the shares of intra-EC sources in domestic consumption. The strongest expansion has been observed for oilseeds and cereals. For the former, the domestic market share has risen from below 5 percent to nearly 20 percent, whereas for the latter, it has almost doubled. On the other hand, the change in intra-EC share has been negligible for oilseed cake, mainly from tropical origin, and for bovine meat, for which intra-EC shares have already reached a very high level.

As the CAP has reduced the potential outlets for third-country exports, it has also boosted export production in the EC and thereby increased competition on remaining export markets. For instance, Schmidt et al. (1987) found production in EC dairy and grain sectors to be 3 and 16–18 percent higher, respectively, than without the CAP. In addition, results obtained by Koester (1982) indicate that the effect of CAP measures on EC grain production could be as high as 40 percent. During the last one-and-a-half decades, the average annual growth rate of cereals production in the EC has exceeded 2 percent. Wheat production has increased by 3 to 4 percent annually, against 3 to 5 percent for milk products, poultry, and sugar. Oilseeds production has achieved annual growth rates above 9 percent. Pork production has expanded at the same rate as cereals, whereas growth rates for milk and beef production have ranged between 1 and 2 percent (Koester and Terwitte 1988).

The strong expansion of production and the stagnating domestic consumption have led to substantial surpluses on major agricultural markets (Koester and Bale 1984, table 4). To export the surpluses resulting from the various forms of production support, the CAP-policy mix was completed by subsidy schemes for exports, which enabled the EC to expand substantially its exports to third markets. For instance, Koester and Bale (1984) show that from the mid-1970s to the mid-1980s, the EC share in world exports rose by two-thirds to reach 11 percent for cereals. It nearly tripled for sugar and bovine meat, reaching 14 and 30 percent, respectively. For butter, the share of EC exports jumped from around 20 to about 45 percent. The increasing role of the EC as a major exporter and competitor on world agricultural markets is displayed by the fact that it alone accounted for between half and more than three quarters of world export growth for major commodities (Koester and Bale 1984, table 1).

Table 6.2 Estimates of CAP Effects on International Price Changes (percent change following complete price liberalization)

Source (Base year)	Wheat	Course Grains	Rice	Ruminant Meat	Non-ruminant Meat	Sugar	Milk
Koester/Schmitz (1982) (1979)[a]						12.0	
Koester (1982) (1975-77)[a]	9.6	14.3[1]					
Koester/Valdes (1984) (1980)[a]	4.6			10.5[2]	5.9[2]	9.7	28.3[3]
Sarris/Freebairn (1983) (1978-80)[a]	9.2						
Anderson/Tyers (1984)[5] (1980)[a]	13.0	16.0	5.0	17.0	1.0		
Tyers/Anderson (1986) (1985)[b]	0.7	2.5	0.7	9.5	1.7	2.6	11.8
Matthews (1985) (1978-82)[b]	0.7	2.9[1]	0.1	4.5[6]	3.6[3]	6.0	10.5[4]
Tyers/Anderson (1986) (1980-82)[c]	6.0	5.0	3.0	18.0	4.0	7.0	25.0

Source: Rosenblatt et al. 1988, p. 42.
[a] EC-9; [b] EC-10; [c] EC-12
[1] Figure refers to barley only.
[2] Figure refers to beef only.
[3] Average value of the estimated effect on the prices of pork and poultry.
[4] Figure refers to butter only.
[5] Same results reported in Tyers (1985).
[6] Average value of the estimate effects on the prices of beef and mutton.

Besides the displacement of extra-EC imports and the accentuation of competition on world export markets, CAP policy measures also affect African and other developing countries through their impact on the level and stability of world agricultural prices. A number of studies have estimated the incidence of eliminating the CAP measures on international prices. Table 6.2 summarizes some of the results that consistently indicate that CAP measures have depressed world prices. Furthermore, results obtained by Burniaux and Waelbroek (1985) indicate that world market prices would be, on average, 15 percent lower than without the CAP. Anderson and Tyers (1984) found that world cereals and beef prices would rise by 13 to 17 percent after elimination of the CAP. Estimates by Swampson and Snape (1980) and Koester and Schmitz (1982) also indicate price-depressing effects on dairy, beef, and sugar markets.

In addition to the impact on the level of international prices, CAP measures have also been shown to exacerbate price volatility on international markets. It is known that not all trade barriers have an impact on world price stability but that some are particularly suited to transfer instability from one geographical area to others and to destabilize world markets (Bale and Lutz 1978). Whether and how far individual policies increase instability on international markets is a function of the extent to which they affect the transmission and absorption of fluctuations between domestic and foreign markets. In other words, a given policy stimulates world price volatility if it reinforces the transmission of short-run variability in domestic markets to international markets through changes in traded quantities. It increases instability also if it reduces the capacity of the economy to adjust domestic production and consumption to short-run external changes. One can, therefore, expect the various CAP measures previously described to have a significant impact on the instability of world agricultural markets.

First, the inward orientation of the levy and restitution policies already mentioned have the particular effect of insulating producers and consumers in the EC from fluctuations on foreign agricultural markets. Second, direct purchase and public storage serve to shelter the same producers and consumers from domestic supply variations. Third, world market price expectations are made irrelevant to EC private stockholders in that annual and seasonal changes in EC prices are politically determined and normally sufficient to compensate for storage costs. If one considers also the practice of export restitutions, it can only be by chance if EC exports follow the patterns necessary to stabilize international agricultural markets (Koester 1982).

Given the relative importance of the EC as a source of supply and destination of exports, the consequences of these measures are twofold. On the one hand, they reduce the stabilizing potential on international markets by preventing a large share of trade quantities to adjust to changes in market conditions. On the other hand, they place the adjustment load to market disturbances on non-EC markets and trading partners.

Available empirical estimates indicate that CAP measures have accentuated instability on world agricultural markets. For instance, estimates in Tyers (1990) show that liberalizing the CAP would reduce the weighted average coefficient of variation of prices for major agricultural commodities from 34 to 26 percent. Similarly, Anderson and Tyers (1984) found that abolishing the CAP would decrease instability on world cereals markets by between 50 and 30 percent. Sarris and Freebairn (1983) point out that liberalizing the CAP would reduce the standard deviation of the world market price for wheat by 35 percent.

The interdependence between agricultural policies in the EC, the OECD, and developing countries and the need to consider their combined effects are particularly important for the analysis of induced world market instability. Johnson (1991) pointed out that world cereals markets were stable during the 1960s despite significant production variability. Com-

Table 6.3 Impact of National Food Policies on the Stability of World Agricultural Prices (percent decrease in coefficient of variation around price trend levels following liberalization)

	Wheat	Coarse Grain	Rice	Ruminant Meat	Dairy	Sugar	Average
EC	32	15	16	37	50	22	24
All Industrial Market Economies	43	11	26	71	58	30	32
Industrial Market Economies plus Developing Countries	74	57	76	83	77	80	71

Source: Based on Tyers 1990, table 7.2, p. 43.

pared with the period between 1971 and 1975, production shortfalls in the first half of the 1960s were two times higher. World prices, however, were far more stable during the 1960s than during the beginning of the 1970s. Johnson found the explanation in the shift from open national agricultural domestic and trade policies to increasingly inward-oriented policies, essentially designed to stabilize internal markets. In the attempt to stabilize internal markets, domestic policies increasingly insulate them from international markets.

As shown in the previous sections, the more a policy insulates domestic markets from international ones, the more it contributes to world price volatility (Tyers 1990). The likely aggregate effect of agricultural policies in the EC, the OECD, and developing countries can be inferred from the figures in Table 6.3. Liberalizing food markets in the EC reduces instability in major world agricultural markets by 24 percent. If liberalizing the CAP is combined with agricultural liberalization in other industrial and developing countries, international price instability decreases by 32 and 71 percent, respectively.

A direct evaluation of trade effects for African countries has not been undertaken in this section. However, it should be clear from the foregoing analysis of the repercussions of CAP measures on the EC and international agricultural markets, and from the previous discussion of their vulnerability, that African countries are very likely to be affected—and negatively. For instance, Figure 6.3 shows how the change in the pattern of instability on international agricultural markets depicted by Johnson (1991) has been transmitted to African economies. The observed increased instability of agricultural export earnings from the beginning of the 1970s must have severely affected the process of sustained development in these countries. And as suggested by the figures in Table 6.3, about 30 percent of policy-induced instability on international agricultural markets is directly linked to CAP measures.

Figure 6.3 Index of Real Agricultural Unit Export in Africa

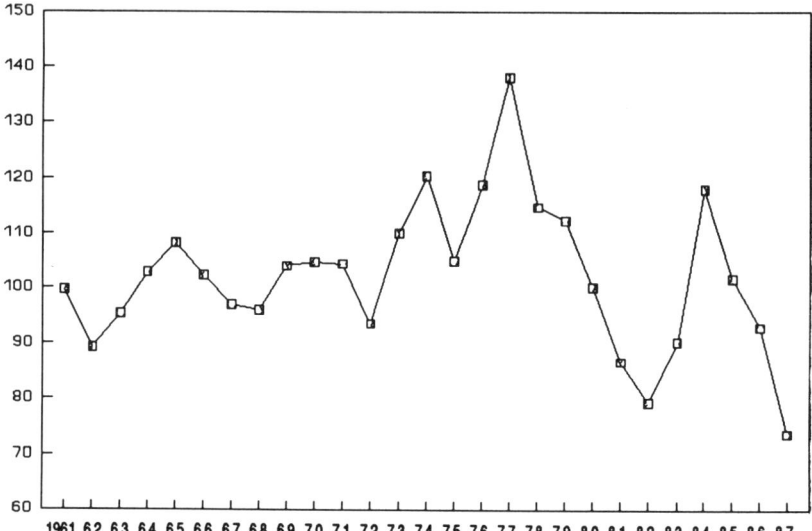

Sources: IFPRI database; World Bank, International Economics Department, International Commodity Markets Division, and International Economic Analysis and Prospects Division.

Note: Agricultural Unit Export is deflated by the manufacturing unit value (MUV) index.

☐ *Effects on Welfare*

The impact of the CAP on welfare in agricultural trading countries arises from its effects on producer and consumer benefits and on the terms of trade for these countries. The conventional approach to estimating the welfare implications of the CAP is to look at the changes that its removal would induce at these different levels. The standard comparative static analysis of this issue often concludes that the elimination of the CAP and other OECD agricultural policies would raise world prices and that the resulting loss to consumers in most developing countries would exceed the gain accruing to producers. Net food importers, in particular, are found to lose from agricultural trade liberalization in the EC (Matthews 1985). These results, however, may underestimate the benefits to developing countries of liberalizing the CAP; various reasons exist for this premise.

First, the often dramatic price increases upon which the findings are based are not likely to hold in the short run. This is true because not only do the elasticity parameters underlying many estimates reflect rather long-term changes but also, as Koester and Bale (1984) have pointed out, high levels of protection for almost three decades have had a lasting impact on the rate and direction of technological change and on the structure of agricultural production. Consequently, liberalizing the CAP would not automatically translate into a downward shift of the aggregate agricultural supply curve. It may rather have a stronger impact on the structure of production in the agricultural sector as efficient farmers expand at the cost of less-efficient farmers. The induced increase in efficiency may well in the short run offset the effect of reduced protection levels. The stronger structural effect would sustain high production levels in the EC for some time, and world market prices would most likely fall in the longer run, after agricultural production growth slowed in the EC.

Second, if price increases are more likely to occur in the longer run, then ignoring the possible efficiency gains through technical innovations in developing countries clearly underestimates the benefits of liberalizing EC agricultural policies for these countries. In this case, it would be useful to adopt a more dynamic approach that incorporates the progressive adjustment and the induced technical changes in the production sectors of developing countries. Such an approach, as adopted in Anderson and Tyers (1984), is very likely to change the outcome usually predicted by the findings derived through conventional analysis.

Third, as already stressed in the previous sections, a reform of agricultural policies in the EC will most probably induce similar changes in other OECD countries and encourage policy reforms in developing countries beyond the agricultural sector. The induced changes in world market prices following further adjustment in national policies will certainly differ from the changes resulting directly from the CAP reforms. Accordingly, welfare effects can be expected to differ from what is usually predicted by conventional analyses.

In the following paragraphs, I attempt to build into the analysis of the CAP effects on African countries the possible dynamic efficiency effects and the changes in policies in OECD and developing countries that are likely to accompany the CAP reforms in the long term. The previous section stressed the depressing and destabilizing impact of the CAP on international agricultural prices. Consequently, and if we assume for the moment the full transmission of world price changes, the abolition of the CAP would have the double effect of raising the mean level of profitability and reducing the expected variability of profits in the agricultural sector of African countries. To the extent that higher and stabilized levels of profits translate into higher rates of induced technical innovation in agriculture, reforming the CAP would accelerate the rate of agricultural growth in African countries and shift the supply curve to the right in the longer term (Anderson and Tyers 1984). Therefore, the level of agricultural production in African countries associated with the liberalization of the CAP most probably will exceed the level predicted by conventional findings.

Furthermore, the rate of technical change is also a function of the structure of domestic incentives facing the agricultural sector. This explains the need to include in the analysis the link between the CAP and general agricultural policy reforms in OECD countries, on the one hand, and sectoral and economywide policies in developing countries, on the other. As the ongoing GATT negotiations have demonstrated, these two factors are closely linked: A change in agricultural policies in industrial countries will induce changes in the policy environment surrounding the agricultural sector in developing countries. This is true because the improved environment on international agricultural markets would raise the willingness of developing countries to integrate into world agricultural markets by adjusting their trade policies. It is also true because developing countries would have to change their policies in the nonagricultural sector as well, in reciprocity to agricultural liberalization in the EC and other OECD countries (Valdes and Zietz 1990).

It follows from the foregoing discussion that the gains resulting from higher efficiency in production through induced innovation and improved domestic policies have been left out of the traditional analysis of CAP effects. However, these gains can be substantial and are likely to outweigh the loss suffered by consumers. Graphical analysis of the efficiency effects (see Figure 6.4) is a means of depicting typical treatment of agriculture and the nonagricultural sector (for convenience, labeled "industry") in most African and other developing countries. National-sector and economywide policies tend to discriminate against agriculture and favor nonagricultural production. This generally induces a wage gap (Wi - Wa) between industry and agriculture. Labor is assumed to be mobile between sectors and used with sector-specific factors. The curves kd and ec represent the marginal product and demand curves for labor in the industrial and agricultural sectors. At the prevailing wage ratio, the distribution of labor between industry and agriculture is given by point L on the abciss. The distortion of relative wages induces a loss in efficiency equal to the triangle formed by the curves kd and ec and the labor ratio line at L.

Let us suppose that the long-run world price increases resulting from liberalization of the CAP and agricultural policies in other OECD countries are transmitted to domestic sectors. This would induce innovations in the agricultural sector and shift the marginal value curve of labor from ec to fh. The resulting welfare gains to producers in the agricultural sectors in African countries are given by the area enclosed by cefh.

Furthermore, let us suppose that the domestic policies in African countries have raised the private marginal value product curve for labor in industry, PMVPi, above the social product curve SMVPi. Eliminating domestic policy distortions in response to agricultural liberalization in the EC and other OECD countries would shift the private marginal value curve of labor in industry down to SMVPi. This raises the welfare gains

COMMON AGRICULTURAL POLICY AND AFRICA

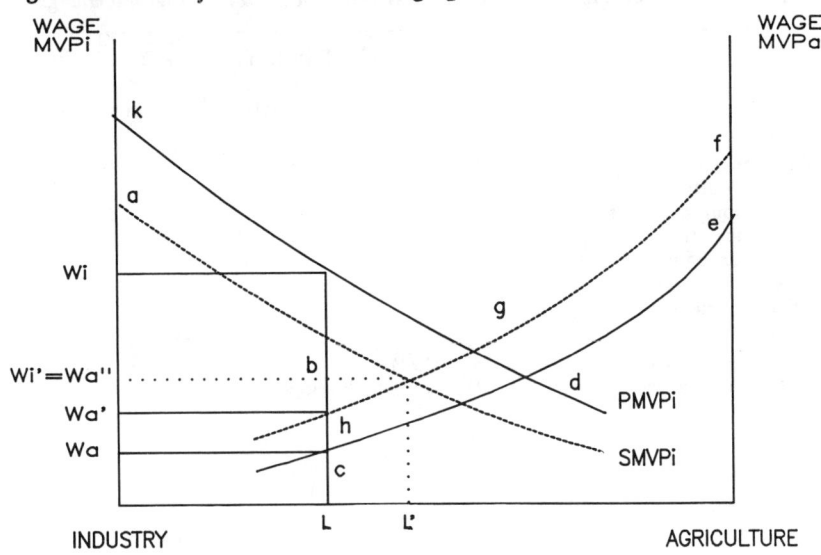

Figure 6.4 Efficiency Effects of Liberalizing Agricultural Trade

Sources: Based on Badiane (1990) and Anderson and Tyers (1984).

by the area enclosed by abhgk. The total welfare effects on the production side of abolishing the CAP and the probable policy changes in national policies accompanying it are equal to the area delineated by the points abcefgk. These effects are much larger than what is captured by the limited traditional approach and are very likely to exceed the loss incurred on the consumption side.

Estimates based on a similar approach are presented in Table 6.4. It shows that if international agricultural policy reforms are accompanied by broader reforms in developing countries, world market price changes would be far less detrimental to food-importing countries, as findings in Table 6.2 suggest. The general improvement in domestic policies can be expected to have a much greater impact on agricultural production, particularly in African countries, as reflected by the changes in self-sufficiency ratios. The last row of Table 6.3 supports the argument that if the gains in efficiency are fully accounted for and the links between international agricultural and domestic policies are considered, African countries are presently suffering from the CAP measures. However, any analysis of the effects of the CAP on African countries must necessarily include the specific trade arrangements that exist between the EC and African coun-

Table 6.4 Long-Term Effects of Agricultural Trade Liberalization (percent change)

	OECD Liberalization	+ Developing Countries Liberalization	+ Trade Policy Reforms in Developing Countries
World prices	12	1	-3
Food self-sufficiency[a]			
Developing countries	21	21	28
Sub-Saharan Africa[b]	27		1
Welfare expenditure			
Developing countries	12	64	56
Sub-Saharan Africa[b]	0.6		6.6

Source: Based on Anderson and Tyers (1984).
[a] Self-sufficiency in base period is 92 percent for developing countries and 45 percent for Sub-Saharan Africa.
[b] Nigeria excluded.

tries and that can be considered as a by-product of the CAP. This issue is dealt with in the next section.

☐ *The Effects of Africa-EC Trade Arrangements*

Trade arrangements between the EC and African countries are embedded in the wider framework of the former Yaoundé and now Lomé conventions. Besides the trade arrangements, the conventions define the guidelines for industrial and financial cooperation between the EC and selected African, Caribbean, and Pacific countries (ACP). Frequently, trade preferences through the Lomé conventions are cited as evidence that African countries are not affected negatively by the CAP measures. This would hold if the trade provisions would shelter African exports from the effects of import restrictions through the CAP and from induced effects in international markets. The first point is investigated by looking at the degree of preferential treatment African countries really enjoy. Furthermore, Figure 6.3 and Table 6.3 suggest that international price instability has been a major problem for African exporters and is closely linked to the CAP. Accordingly, the STABEX scheme of the convention is used to evaluate the degree to which induced CAP effects are compensated for by the Lomé arrangements.

In accordance with Article 168 of Lomé IV, agricultural products originating in ACP states are imported into the EC free of customs duties and equivalent charges. Subparagraph (2)(i) of the same article, however, introduces an important modification from the point of view of CAP protectionism: Only "those products shall be imported free of customs duties for which Community provisions in force at the time of importation do not provide, apart from customs duties, for the application of any other measure relating to their importation." Preferential treatment is, accordingly, granted in the first place to non-CAP commodities, although specific preferences apply to commodities covered by the CAP regime. However, preferential margins received over competing exporters are generally low and cannot be expected to raise competitiveness of African exporters significantly (Koester and Herrmann 1987, 11–13).

It is often stated that African countries do not perform well on EC markets, not because of CAP restrictions but rather because of weak performance of their domestic sectors. The previous discussion of the efficiency effects of the CAP pointed out that performance in African countries is closely related to conditions of international markets—price distortions, trade uncertainty, greater instability—and, therefore, affected by the CAP and agricultural policies in general. Furthermore, effective preferential treatment by the EC would mean higher incentives for African countries to export to EC markets. Independent of the overall performance level of African export sectors, EC shares in African exports should, consequently, increase over time. Figure 6.5 and Table 6.1 demonstrate that EC shares in African exports have, at best, stagnated, even though imports into the EC have been expanding.

This trend is not particularly surprising. Although it is known that the major obstacle to expanding exports to the EC stems from heavy protection of commodities under the CAP regime, trade preferences under Lomé basically exclude such commodities (articles 168, 177). Furthermore, the Lomé trade arrangements guarantee only limited preferences in relation to third countries because generally low tariffs are applied to commodities not under the CAP regime (Koester and Herrmann 1987, table 4.1).

The other important component of the Lomé trade arrangements is the system of stabilization of agricultural export earnings (STABEX). The objective of STABEX is to help remedy the effects on African and other ACP countries of fluctuating export earnings. Payments are made to countries to offset the fall in export earnings from a basket of forty-nine commodities (articles 186, 187). Given that a link has been established between the CAP and increased instability on international markets (Table 6.3), and the potential impact of that instability on African export earnings (Figure 6.3), the need to evaluate the stabilization effect of the STABEX scheme is obvious.

For that purpose, twenty-three African ACP countries that received more than five STABEX payments between 1975 and 1988 have been selected for analysis. For each of these countries, the instability of export earnings with and without STABEX payments has been computed using as an indicator the coefficient of variation around trend levels (Table 6.5). It can be observed that although total transfers to some countries have

Figure 6.5 EC Shares in African Exports of Selected Agricultural Commodities

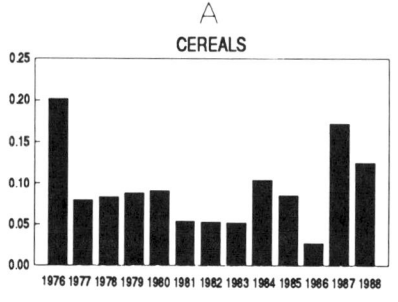
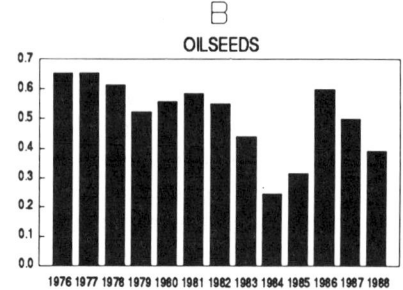
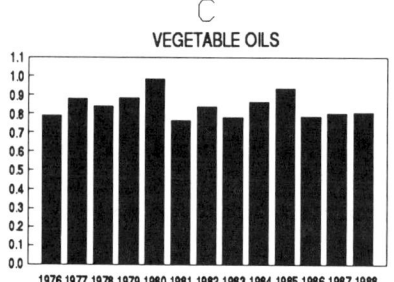
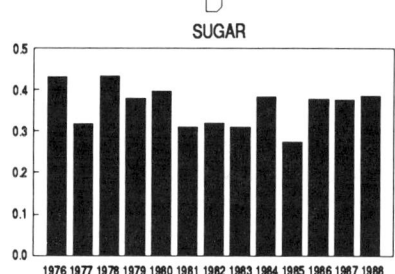
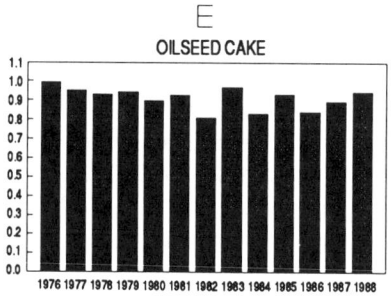
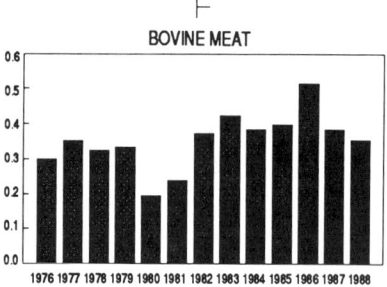

Table 6.5 Stabilization Effect of STABEX on African Export Earnings (1975–1988)

Countries	Total STABEX Payments 1975–1988 in 1,000 ECU	Instability[a] of Earnings Without STABEX Payments (%) (A)	Instability[a] of Export Earnings with STABEX Payments (%) (B)	Changes in Instability of Export Earnings (%) 100(A-B)/A
Benin	40,584.15	79.83	75.84	4.99
Burkina Faso	15,626.18	25.88	25.39	1.89
Burundi	40,537.78	31.66	26.81	15.32
Cameroon	133,751.58	32.70	31.29	4.31
Central African Republic	40,296.02	22.85	19.48	14.75
Chad	51,364.71	42.39	38.04	10.26
Comores	17,001.91	39.31	36.18	7.96
Côte d'Ivoire	374,584.04	21.05	20.01	4.94
Ethiopia	123,907.15	19.33	17.60	8.95
Gambia	38,241.76	27.27	22.41	17.82
Guinea-Bissau	17,819.18	29.57	23.36	21.00
Lesotho	5,655.27	30.18	29.19	3.28
Madagascar	20,242.50	17.08	16.98	0.59
Mali	40,755.11	22.96	22.30	2.87
Niger	29,264.39	43.65	42.06	3.64
Rwanda	52,989.82	30.19	26.00	13.88
Senegal	262,242.81	22.37	20.85	6.79
Sierra Leone	18,328.40	22.43	22.42	0.04
Sudan	146,401.01	25.62	24.51	4.33
Swaziland	21,414.19	25.13	25.05	0.32
Tanzania	50,473.95	21.05	21.26	-0.99
Togo	53,564.06	18.33	18.16	0.93
Uganda	20,595.45	29.40	29.19	0.71

Sources: For export data: UNCTAD, "Handbook of International Trade and Development," various issues. For STABEX payments: EEC Commission, "Commission Report on the Operation During 1988 of the Export Earnings Stabilization System Set up by the Third Lomé Convention," May 1989. For exchange rates: EC Commission, Eurostatistics, "Data for Short-term Economic Analysis," various issues.

[a] Trend-corrected coefficient of variation is used as indicator.

been considerable, the overall stabilization effect has been limited. The last column of the table reveals that for two-thirds of the countries, the change in export instability resulting from STABEX payments does not exceed 5 percent. It is greater than 10 percent for only six out of twenty-three countries. Thus, while the CAP destabilizes international export markets, the special arrangements hardly contribute to stabilizing the export earnings of African countries (Table 6.5, column B), which remain highly vulnerable to increased export price instability (Figure 6.3).

■ Conclusions

My purpose in this chapter was to analyze the impact of the CAP on African economies. This evaluation shows that African countries are particularly vulnerable to CAP measures and that the trade arrangements under the Lomé conventions have not generated benefits large enough to offset the likely CAP effects. It also shows that the typical approach to analyzing the implications of the CAP, which tends to be static and too narrowly focused, clearly underestimates the effects of the policy. The proposed dynamic approach, which takes into consideration the linkages between the CAP, worldwide agricultural protectionism, and economic policies in developing countries, suggests that net importing African countries would most probably gain from CAP liberalization. This is explained by the fact that reforming the CAP would induce worldwide reform of agricultural policies and of nonagricultural policies in African countries. The resulting long-term efficiency gains through induced innovation in African countries are expected to outweigh the loss stemming from higher world market prices.

7

Europe 1992 and Foreign Direct Investment in Africa

Persephone Economou
Michelle Gittelman
Mulatu Wubneh

■ **Introduction***

Europe 1992 confronts Africa not only with challenges and opportunities, but also possibilities of serious market and foreign investment losses. An integrated Europe would provide a large regional market for Africa's products, a strong entrepreneurial group with the resources to enhance the flow of investment, and a traditional ally with the potential to accelerate the transfer of skill, management, and technology.

A united Europe could also force African countries to make hard decisions about their dependence on Europe. Yet it is fear of commercial and investment exclusion that has dominated Africa's reaction to Europe 1992. There is a concern that Europe would be a "fortress" that would put up protectionist ramparts. With the incorporation of Spain and Portugal into the European Community (EC) and the opening up of Eastern Europe to trade and investment, Europe could become an inward-looking giant that would divert its attention and resources to its own continent. The Iberian countries as well as Eastern Europe have the advantage of proximity, market, infrastructure, and skilled labor that can make investment in these regions more attractive than in Africa.

Whether the fears and anxieties of African governments will turn out to be justified remains to be seen. But if the challenges and opportunities of Europe 1992 are to be met, Africa must organize itself to be on a competitive ground. Africa has the strategic resources and the potential market to entice investors. At the same time, it needs to build on the recent positive changes in policy and attitude toward foreign direct investment (FDI) and the restructuring of its society to improve the economic and

*This section is by Mulatu Wubneh.

political environment.

In contrast to the 1970s and 1980s, when foreign investment was viewed as a form of neocolonialism, today it is widely welcomed by many African governments. It is recognized as a means to meet the gap in domestic capital and to gain access to foreign technology, expertise, and markets. Many African governments have either promulgated new foreign investment laws or have made adjustments to their investment codes or guidelines in order to attract foreign capital and technology. Since 1988, a number of African governments have become members of the UN-sponsored Multilateral Investment Guarantee Agency (MIGA). MIGA, a World Bank-affiliated agency, guarantees foreign investment against losses resulting from noncommercial risks such as expropriation, civil unrest, and restrictions in currency transfers. Many countries have also adopted far-reaching economic reforms, including devaluing currencies, trimming bureaucracies, tightening fiscal controls, and liberalizing trade and investment regimes.

Despite these changes in policy and attitude, FDI inflow to Africa has remained erratic in the last decade. The long-term trend shows a persistent decline in investment, particularly from France and Britain, the traditional large investors in Africa.

Although there are limitations on reliable statistics, data published by the Organization for Economic Cooperation and Development (OECD) and the United Nations (based on IMF data) appear to indicate some firm trends of foreign investment in Africa. Total world inflow of FDI reached a record high of $152 million in 1988 (Table 7.1). Some four-fifths of this inflow went to developed countries. FDI in developing countries has continued to decline in the last two decades. Developing countries' share dropped from 32 percent in 1975 to 18 percent in 1988. Developing countries' share of FDI may further decline in the 1990s if the efforts of the former Soviet Union and Eastern European countries to attract foreign investment prove successful (UNCTC 1990b). Many of the East European countries have introduced and/or improved legislation and incentives to attract foreign investment. Furthermore, countries such as the United States that traditionally had been the leading investors abroad are now major host countries. The decline of the dollar since 1985 has induced a significant inflow of foreign investment into the United States to purchase land and other assets and to create new capacity; this flow increased from 13 percent of all FDI in 1970 to 41 percent in 1988 (UNCTC 1990a, 29).

Among the developing countries, Latin America has lost its lead as a major recipient of FDI to South and Southeast Asia. In Africa, both in absolute values and in percentage shares, FDI stagnated. Three important factors are worth noting in analyzing FDI in Africa. First, although FDI has shown an increasing trend during the period 1980–1985 compared with

Table 7.1 Inflow of Foreign Direct Investment, 1970–1988 (in $ millions)

Region	1970 $	1970 %	1975 $	1975 %	1980 $	1980 %	1985 $	1985 %	1988 $	1988 %
Developed Countries	9,122.4	81.3	14,910.0	68.4	41,280.3	79.2	35,604.7	72.8	123,891.3	81.5
Developing Countries	2,102.5	18.7	6,877.9	31.6	10,867.3	20.8	13,286.5	27.2	28,025.0	18.4
Africa	320.4	2.9	477.0	2.2	365.0	0.6	2,587.3	5.3	2,118.8	1.4
Latin America and the Caribbean	1,167.2	10.4	4,041.3	18.5	7,196.4	13.8	5,567.9	11.4	11,305.3	7.4
South and East Asia	596.4	5.3	1,648.9	7.6	3,233.2	6.2	4,584.5	9.4	13,864.4	9.1
Other	-0.7	0.0	661.3	3.0	47.6	0.0	402.5	0.8	329.7	0.2
World	11,224.9	100.0	21,787.9	100.0	52,147.6	100.0	48,906.2	100.0	151,916.3	100.0

Source: UNCTC. Based on IMF, Balance of Payments data tape as of November 20, 1990.

Table 7.2 FDI Inflow to Selected African Countries (in $ millions)

Region	1980	1985	1987	Average 1975-80	Average 1981-87
Africa	311.9	2570.6	2227.2	816.8	1727.9
Oil-Exporters					
Algeria	348.8	0.0	3.9	165.8	-4.3
Cameroon	129.8	316.3	12.0	47.4	117.9
Egypt	547.9	1177.8	947.8	376.1	801.1
Nigeria	-1089.4	469.1	600.0	163.3	397.5
Tunisia	234.3	107.6	91.8	103.8	170.9
Middle Income					
Botswana	111.5	53.6	113.5	44.3	61.9
Côte d'Ivoire	94.6	29.1	68.3	63.5	41.3
Ghana	15.6	5.6	4.7	15.7	7.4
Kenya	79.0	18.1	67.9	52.9	25.8
Morocco	89.8	20.3	59.5	45.2	44.5
Zaire	109.6	69.2	-55.0	73.4	-19.7
Zambia	61.2	51.8	31.6	36.9	22.5
Low Income					
Benin	4.3	0.0	0.0	2.7	0.4
Burkina Faso	0.0	-1.4	0.0	1.7	1.0
Ethiopia	1.0	0.0	-3.0	0.2	0.0
Malawi	9.5	0.5	0.0	6.9	0.6
Mali	2.3	2.8	-5.9	1.6	0.1
Sudan	0.0	-2.8	0.0	0.0	0.9
Uganda	4.0	-4.0	0.0	1.8	-0.3

Source: UN, Economic and Social Council, 1990. Based on IMF and information from OECD.

1975–1980, about 83 percent of the FDI during the period 1981–1988 went only to the major oil-exporting countries. Egypt, Nigeria, and Tunisia alone accounted for about 79 percent of the FDI inflow to Africa. Second, much of the FDI inflow to Africa includes reinvestment of unremitted profits rather than new investment. For instance, unremitted profits accounted for nearly all of "new" FDI in Nigeria for 1970–1974 and for about 83 percent for 1982–1984, further illustrating that foreign investment in Africa has been much lower than the figures would suggest (Cockcroft and Riddell 1990, 8). Third, among the non-oil-exporting countries, the inflow of FDI has declined significantly in the last decade. With the exception of Botswana, most of the middle-income, non-oil-exporting African countries, including Côte d'Ivoire, Kenya, Zambia, and Zaire, experienced significant loss in FDI during the period 1981–1987 compared with 1975–1980. For a majority of the low-income African countries, FDI inflow ranged from a negative balance to a few million dollars per year in most cases (Table 7.2). In comparative terms, in 1987 the whole of Africa received substantially less FDI inflows than Singapore (UNIDO 1990, 11).

Unfortunately, the upturn for Africa, particularly Sub-Saharan Africa, was far less marked than trends for the developing world.

Africa's share of the stock of FDI declined from about 6.6 percent in 1960 to 2.8 percent in 1980 with a slight increase to 3.5 percent in 1985 (Wubneh 1990, table 2). In terms of the various economic sectors, investment in Africa is dominated by the primary sector, particularly petroleum and mining. Investment in manufacturing, services, and the primary sector have remained around 30, 20, and 50 percent, respectively, since the mid-1960s (UN 1988, 5; Green 1981, 338–339). In comparison, investment in developing countries in primary, secondary, and tertiary sectors in 1982 was 19, 44, and 38 percent, respectively.

■ Foreign Direct Investment in Africa, 1970–1988

Historically, FDI in Africa is closely linked to colonial ties. It is estimated that in the early 1980s, British and French transnational corporations (TNCs) accounted for 40 and 18 percent, respectively, of all foreign-owned corporations operating in Africa, as opposed to 22 and 8 percent, respectively, for all developing countries (Tiewul 1986, 43; UNCTC 1985, 27; Green 1981, 343). By contrast, only 16 percent of foreign-owned enterprises in Africa were affiliates of U.S.-based TNCs compared to 31 percent for all developing countries (UNCTC 1985, 29).

These trends have significantly changed in the last decade. Table 7.3 presents FDI flow from Development Assistance Committee (DAC) members of the OECD to sub-Saharan Africa. Although the overall pattern is somewhat erratic, there was a large disinvestment in the mid-1980s, a positive trend in 1986–1987, and then a decline in 1988. According

Table 7.3 Distribution of Foreign Affiliates in Sub-Saharan Africa (SSA) by OECD Country of Origin, 1986–1987

Home Country	Total Number of Affiliates		Share of SSA	
	In SSA	In All Countries	In Developing Countries (percent)	In All Countries (percent)
United Kingdom	1,571	24,534	23.0	6.4
France	357	4,462	29.6	8.0
Germany	138	8,337	9.4	1.7
Netherlands	123	4,647	12.7	2.7
Belgium	76	1,162	35.9	6.5
Italy	47	1,513	13.5	3.1

Source: United Nations Center on Transnational Corporations (UNCTC), Billion Dollar Club database.

to the OECD, FDI accounted for 8.8 percent of the 1981 total net resources flow to Africa, but dropped to 2.3 percent in 1985 before it showed a slight increase to 5.1 percent in 1988 (OECD 1990a, table III.5). Unfortunately, the upturn for Africa, particularly sub-Saharan Africa, was far less marked than trends for the developing world. These trends are confirmed by other studies on British and French TNCs in Africa.

In a recent analysis of British investment in fifteen English-speaking African countries, Bennell (1990, 56) discovered that British industrial FDI inflow to Africa had declined from around 4 percent of the total overseas industrial investment in the mid-1970s to 0.5 percent in 1986. In terms of absolute values, the figures declined from 67 million in 1978 to 27 million in 1986. Bennell's study further noted that nearly one-third of the British companies that had industrial investment in Africa in the late 1970s had already disposed of their investments by mid-1989, and most of the disengagement occurred in the last decade. The largest number of companies that have exited withdrew from Zimbabwe (37), Nigeria (23), and Zambia (17).

Two reasons may explain why British corporations are moving out of Africa in such large numbers. First, the rate of return on investments in Africa has declined significantly over the years and more precipitously in the last decade. According to the World Bank, rates of return in sub-Saharan Africa have dropped from around 30.7 percent in 1961–1973 to around 2.5 percent in 1980–1987 (World Bank 1989a, 26). However, one needs to exercise caution in interpreting these figures because the World Bank data are based on aggregate values. Although returns have declined over time, particularly returns for industrial investment, nonindustrial returns are above the global rate. According to Bennell (1990, table 10), the rates of return on British nonindustrial investments in Africa were at least 4 percent above the global rate—in 1981 and 1984, the rates of returns for nonindustrial investment in Africa were 17.2 and 22.1, respectively, as opposed to global rates of 12.4 and 9.8, respectively.[1]

The major reason for the large withdrawal of British firms is related to the second factor—the chronic and persistent shortage of foreign exchange. Bennell (1990) found that nearly 75 percent of the respondents to his questionnaire ranked foreign exchange availability as the most serious constraint facing their companies. Chronic shortage of foreign exchange would impinge on the ability to purchase inputs and remit profits. Other problems that have often been cited by other researchers include currency depreciation, price controls, government bureaucracy and corruption, and generally depressed economic conditions as factors affecting foreign investment in Africa (Baker 1983; World Bank 1989a; Cockcroft and Riddell 1990; Group of Thirty 1984; Wubneh 1990).

Although probably not on a similar scale as that of British firms, French TNCs in Africa are also undergoing a disengagement process.

There has been substantial disinvestment from Burkina Faso and the Congo. For Côte d'Ivoire, average annual inflow of FDI declined from $63.5 million in 1975-1980 to $41.3 million in 1981-1987; and for Senegal, the average annual inflow dropped from $17.5 million in 1975-1980 to $8.4 million in 1981-1987 (UNESCO 1990, 5; Cockcroft and Riddell 1990, 9).

U.S. companies are also believed to be pulling out of many African countries. According to the U.S. Department of Commerce (1988, 103), U.S. investment in Africa has declined from an average annual rate of 22.2 percent in 1977-1980 to an average annual rate of 2.0 percent in 1980-1986.

In both Lomé I and Lomé II, private investment received little attention. While negotiating for Lome III, EC member countries wanted to introduce contractual arrangements to promote European private investment in ACP economies, particularly in the mining sector. Subsequently, title IV of Lomé III tried to outline some basic principles governing private investment. The principles were related to ensuring fair and equitable treatment, maintaining a secure investment climate, and protecting private investments. But the specific investment relations were left up to individual members to be covered through agreements with individual ACP governments rather than through Lomé III.

Chapter 3 of Lomé IV addresses investment relations between EC and ACP countries. It defines the basic investment principles and measures member states can take to promote private investment: establishing cooperative arrangements, sharing investment information, providing technical assistance, and encouraging private investment. Lomé IV also sets aside risk capital of up to ECU 825 million to promote investment in the private sector. Chapter 3, section 2, of the agreement recommends talks about investment protection through insurance and guarantee schemes. Provisions are included for the development of a model protection agreement that would cover such issues as legal guarantees, equal treatment, protection against expropriation and nationalization, and the free transfer of capital and profits (CEC 1990, 5; *Courier* 1990).

■ A Typology of Foreign Direct Investment*

It is useful to distinguish among the three broad types of foreign direct investment, each of which responds to different determining variables and serves different corporate objectives. It thus follows that each will be differently impacted by the European unified market. The three types of foreign direct investment are resource based (supply seeking), import substituting (market seeking), and rationalized (efficiency seeking) (Dunning 1988).

The first type, resource-based investment, is made to secure access to resources found in the host country, usually exported for further process-

---

*This section is by Persephone Economou and Michelle Gittelman.

ing in the home country. Such investments characterized the early overseas activities of TNCs in developing countries; these ventures were concentrated in the mineral and commodity agricultural sectors (notably in copper, iron ore, bauxite, oil, bananas, and sugar). Key locational determinants, besides the availability of the resource, are worldwide supply and demand conditions; transport and processing costs; and government policies regarding foreign ownership of the host country's resources. During the colonial period, the European powers made the first resource-based investments, thus laying the foundation for the pattern described, in which investment by EC members (the UK and France in particular) is highly concentrated in their former colonies.

The second type of investment, import-substituting investment, is geared toward production to serve the local market and thus to replace imports from abroad (although frequently imports of consumption goods merely give way to intermediate and capital-goods imports to supply local production). Key locational determinants of this type of investment are the attractiveness of the local market ("pull" factors), coupled with restrictions, particularly tariff barriers, that render imports uncompetitive with locally produced goods ("push" factors). In Africa, as will be shown later, a good deal of foreign direct investment in the manufacturing sector is of this type, concentrated in low value-added sectors such as basic chemicals, tobacco, and processed foods and beverages.

The last type is rationalized, or efficiency-seeking, investment. It is a more recent form of TNC activity and is geared toward capturing the benefits of integrating a group of geographically dispersed but specialized operations. The firm establishes a division of labor among the parent and its subsidiaries and locates production according to the comparative advantages of host countries. Such investment is thus complementary with trade, as affiliates based in different countries trade among themselves; a key determinant of rationalized investment patterns will be the absence of trade barriers among the host countries involved, coupled with a comparative advantage in a segment of the investing firm's value-adding activities. Indeed, the early years of European integration attracted a good deal of this type of investment by U.S. TNCs, which integrated their European affiliates into regionally based, vertically integrated supply networks (UNCTC 1991a), and the current phase of European integration is causing a good deal of new investment of this type by Japanese firms in the early 1990s.

■ Sectoral Distribution of Foreign Direct Investment in Sub-Saharan Africa

Traditionally, foreign investment in Africa has been concentrated in extractive activities, such as petroleum exploration and mining, and in agriculture, forestry, and fisheries. In 1982, the primary sector accounted for about one-half of the foreign investment stock in Africa, a proportion that had remained unchanged since 1975. Manufacturing accounted for approximately 30 percent of the total stock in Africa and services for the remaining 20 percent (Dunning and Cantwell 1987). Mining and petroleum industries are still attracting a substantial proportion of foreign investment in Africa and are particularly important for Nigeria, Gabon, Botswana, Zambia, and Zimbabwe.

The sectoral distribution of foreign affiliates in Africa (Table 7.4) indicates that the majority of them are now involved in manufacturing activities. Because the data on foreign affiliates do not provide an indication of the level of foreign investment, it is useful to note that for at least one country (United Kingdom), the share of foreign investment stock in manufacturing in all Africa exceeds that of the primary and services

Table 7.4 Industrial Distribution of Sub-Saharan (SSA) Affiliates of EC Transnational Corporations

Industry	Number of Affiliates in SSA	Share of Affiliates in Total for SSA (percent)
Primary	316	12.9
Agriculture	19	0.8
Mining/quarrying	297	12.1
Manufacturing	1,093	44.6
Chemicals	220	9.0
Food, beverages, tobacco	293	11.9
Petroleum refining	138	5.6
Electrical machinery	135	5.5
Industrial machinery	83	3.4
Metal industries	55	2.2
Transport equipment	43	1.8
Wood and paper	23	0.9
Textiles	18	0.7
Other	85	3.5
Services	696	28.4
Utilities	19	0.8
Construction	99	4.0
Trade	41	1.7
Tourism	7	0.3
Transport/commerce	80	3.3
Finance/insurance	422	17.2
Other	28	1.1
Unallocated[a]	347	14.2
Total	2,452	100.0

Source: UNCTC, Billion Dollar Club database.
[a] Reflects affiliates whose industry has not been specified.

Table 7.5 Industrial Distribution of FDI Stock to Africa from Selected EC Members (in millions of national currency; percentages in parentheses)

	United Kingdom			The Netherlands	
	1981[a]	1987	1987[b]	1980	1988
Africa					
Primary	390	535	310	443	637
	(20.4)	(31.1)	(21.9)	(52.6)	(55.3)
Manufacturing	836	669	669	277	270
	(43.8)	(38.8)	(47.4)	(32.9)	(23.4)
Services	686	519	519	123	245
	(35.9)	(30.1)	(36.7)	(14.6)	(21.3)
Total	1,911	1,723	1,413	843	1,152
	(100.0)	(100.0)	(100.0)	(100.0)	(100.0)
Developing countries					
Primary	864	4,107	441	5,661	5,491
	(13.9)	(29.5)	(4.3)	(37.8)	(29.4)
Manufacturing	2,648	3,694	3,694	4,852	7,047
	(42.5)	(26.6)	(36.1)	(32.4)	(37.8)
Services	2,714	6,113	6,113	4,466	6,115
	(43.6)	(43.9)	(59.7)	(29.8)	(32.8)
Total	6,226	13,913	10,247	14,979	18,653
	(100.0)	(100.0)	(100.0)	(100.0)	(100.0)

Sources: Central Statistical Office, Business Monitor, Census of Overseas Assets, various issues; Marius van Nieuwkerk and Robert P. Sparling, *The Netherlands International Direct Investment Position,* The Netherlands Bank, Monetary Monographs No. 4, and unpublished data.

[a] Excludes oil companies, banks, and insurance companies.
[b] Excludes the energy sector (oil companies).

sectors (Table 7.5). Chemicals, food, tobacco, and other manufacturing activities, which include textiles, have been the prominent recipients of foreign investment flows in manufacturing in the period 1986–1988.

The high share of manufacturing foreign direct investment indicates that import-substituting industries have attracted a large share of foreign affiliates in Africa; because Africa's exports of manufactured goods to the EC are extremely low, it can be assumed that the investment in this sector is not export oriented. However, in the food and beverages sector, Africa accounted for 20 percent of the EC's total imports, consisting mainly of coffee, tea, cocoa, and fruits and vegetables (in 1987). TNCs play an important role in the processing and shipping of these commodities (Cantwell 1989). Thus, investment in those sectors is likely to be a mix of both import-substituting and resource-seeking types of investment.

Foreign investment in resource-based activities in mining and quarrying, including petroleum and natural gas, appears significant both in terms of the share of foreign affiliates and of the stock of foreign investment. The share of the primary sector in total British stock in Africa has increased in importance between 1980 and 1987, a pattern exhibited in outward investment from the United Kingdom to all developing countries. Similar data for the Netherlands provide further evidence as to the increased importance of foreign investment stock in the primary sector of Africa in the 1980s.

Services account for 28 percent of all foreign affiliates from the European Community in Africa. Banking and finance account for 60 percent of all foreign affiliates in services and 17 percent of all foreign affiliates in Africa from the EC. Commercial banks headquartered in the EC are extensively involved in retail banking in Africa. The nontradable nature of these activities is among the factors that account for the large concentration of foreign affiliates in finance and insurance.

EC investment in Africa is undertaken by relatively few companies. About 30 percent of all EC TNCs in Africa are in the manufacturing sector, primarily in food, beverages, and tobacco. EC TNCs in services are concentrated in finance and insurance and in construction.

Several sectors have been hit hard by recent trends of investment withdrawal from Africa. Netherlands' share of manufacturing investment in Africa declined from 45.3 percent in 1975 to 6.1 percent in 1987. For the United States and Japan, respectively, the shares declined from 9.5 percent to 6.1 percent, and from 12 percent to 5 percent during the same period (UNESCO 1990 6). Mining has also been affected by declining trends. Africa's share of new investment in mining during the period 1975–1990 stagnated for Germany, at around 14 percent, and declined for Japan, from 7 percent in 1975 to 5 percent in 1988 (two countries for which regional data are available). Furthermore, except in Botswana, there has not been any significant project in mining taking place in Africa in the last fifteen years (UNESCO 1990). Oil exploration in Africa has also suffered a decline. Capital expenditure in Africa by U.S. oil companies declined by more than 60 percent during the period 1982–1986 (UNESCO 1990, 9). Low oil prices and uncertainty about the global financial outlook are believed to be the major reasons for the major decline in oil investment.

■ Sectoral Implications of 1992 for EC Investment in Africa

The possible effects of 1992 on investment from the EC, and the mechanisms by which those effects will be channeled, will differ according to the type and sector of investment concerned. For the framework previously presented, it should be stressed that both resource-seeking and rationalized types of foreign investment are trade-related—they are investments geared toward exporting the output of the foreign affiliate (whether in raw or processed form) to foreign markets. Such investment is thus complementary to increased trade flows, and changes in the latter—whether up or down—could have a corresponding impact on the former. In contrast, import-substituting investment is geared toward selling the output of foreign affiliates locally and thus is sensitive to market conditions in the host country, particularly in regard to market size and growth rates, access to intermediate inputs, and protection from competing imports. The locational distribution of import-substituting investment, then, is primarily sensitive to changes in domestic market conditions in the host (recipient) country, and relatively insensitive (except in a very indirect sense) to changes in domestic conditions in the home (investing) country.

Because the Europe 1992 plan represents a fundamental change in market conditions in the EC rather than in foreign markets, it will not have a direct, immediate effect on the level of outward market-seeking investment by European TNCs, whether in developing countries or elsewhere. As already shown, a large proportion of manufacturing investment in Africa is of the import-substituting type, and European unification carries no direct implications for much of this investment. Indirectly, however, it is likely that market integration in the EC will cause the aggregate level of market-seeking investment from Europe to rise and its sectoral composition to change in the long term as European TNCs reap the gains of increased specialization and accelerated technological progress, increasing their competitive position in world markets (particularly in relation to U.S. and Japanese TNCs, relative to which European TNCs currently place third in most high-growth sectors).

Although 1992 will almost certainly lead to an increased internationalization of TNCs from the EC—indeed this is one of the primary objectives of the 1992 program—the geographical distribution of this increased outward investment will turn on domestic conditions in the array of foreign markets facing investors. With the formation of a regional trade bloc in North America, the loose economic integration of fast-growing Asian countries, and the rise of potential growth markets in the East, the prospects for most sub-Saharan African countries to attract significant new market-seeking investment from the EC are likely to be rather slim.

As for the other two types of FDI, both resource-seeking and rationalized investments are trade-related and supply-oriented and will be more directly influenced by the 1992 program. Africa is currently not a significant location for rationalized investment. However, this is one area where Europe 1992 is likely to have an effect on investment in developing countries. Increasing competition within the integrated market will put pressure on European firms to raise efficiency and lower costs. Many are likely to deploy rationalized investment strategies in pursuit of this objective by involving a greater specialization of affiliates and switching to new supply locations, particularly for multistage, assembly-intensive manufacturing processes. Such a scenario presents both opportunities as well as threats for developing countries.

In order to lower production costs, companies may increase their foreign investment in developing countries, particularly in those that have a comparative advantage in labor-intensive, low- to medium-technology goods. The output from those investments would then be exported back to the EC for further processing or final assembly. However, if external barriers are erected against such imports from low-cost locations, there is a threat that investment otherwise intended for developing countries will be diverted instead to an EC location. Indeed, it is likely that some portion of Japanese investment currently being directed into the EC is a response to fears of possible protectionism, and would otherwise have been invested in Asian locations for export to EC affiliates. However, this type of investment diversion is triggered by the static effects of protectionism; in the long run, investment in developing countries could rise as the dynamic economic effects of EC integration (i.e., economies of scale and an overall rise in economic efficiency) enable EC countries—particularly in the South—to shift out of sectors that compete directly with developing-country imports.

Currently, as described, the amount of rationalized investment from the EC in Africa is marginal. Attracting more such efficiency-seeking investment in the future will require fundamental changes in the supply conditions that currently prevail in most sub-Saharan African countries; such changes include improving process and product technology; upgrading human and infrastructural resources; and developing a comparative advantage in sectors that most lend themselves to rationalized production. Thus, although 1992 carries important implications for the level and distribution of rationalized investments in developing countries, the impacts on Africa are likely to be slight in the short to medium term.

It is in the area of resource-based investment that most of the impact of EC 1992 is likely to occur. As mentioned earlier, European TNCs play a major role in African resource-based industries. Here, a distinction needs to be made between resource-based investments in the minerals and energy sector and those in the agricultural (raw or processed) sector. In the former, particularly in petroleum, trade and investment levels tend to be determined by long-term supply and demand conditions that are likely to be independent of the direct effects of removing nontariff barriers in the EC. However, the magnitude of 1992's impact on the structure and performance of EC industry might be sufficiently great to cause a fundamental shift in the pattern of demand for those commodities, resulting in changes in the level and composition of foreign investment. In contrast, the removal of barriers to intra-EC trade could have an immediate impact on the level and composition of EC consumption of certain agricultural goods, and thus affect FDI more directly in those sectors. For both types of investment, however, the primary channel for changes in the level of FDI in Africa will be through changes in the level and/or composition of its exports to the EC.

It is beyond the scope of this chapter to explore all the possible trade implications of EC 1992 for Africa's resources and how these might be translated into corresponding changes in foreign investment in those sectors. In aggregate, estimates from a recent study (which used an assumed 5 percent growth in EC GDP induced by the 1992 program—probably a conservative estimate) indicate that exports of primary products to the EC from developing countries would increase by $5.1 billion, of which $1.4 billion would be composed of nonfuel primary products, and that these countries would see a positive trade effect of some $400 million. In terms of the increase in fuel exports, Africa (including oil exporters) and the Middle East would be the primary beneficiaries (Matthews and McAleese 1990). An increase of exports of this magnitude could translate into higher FDI in African resource-based industries if current capacity levels are insufficient to meet the projected growth in demand. The projected increase in demand, however, could be more than offset by the development of new technologies that will render European industry cleaner and less energy- and materials-intensive. Importing primary products from nearby Eastern European countries could also cut into African gains from growing European demand for resources.

In the area of food and agricultural products, a few examples stand out as being directly influenced by the 1992 harmonization of rules. It has been estimated that the elimination of excise taxes on coffee as part of fiscal harmonization will increase ACP exports (because of increased demand for coffee) to the EC by an estimated ECU 189 million (Davenport 1988). In another important sector, imports of cocoa could fall after EC-wide standards for chocolate confectionary are established; the UK currently requires a lower cocoa content in its confectionary than other EC countries, and this may lower EC demand for cocoa once mutual recognition of standards is introduced. Other agricultural products that are likely to involve changed demand levels are palm oil, cotton, tobacco, and sugar. Foreign investment plays an important role in the extraction and processing of all of these commodities. In the case of sugar, one company, the British firm of Tate and Lyle, processes cane sugar from Africa for consumption in the UK; the raw product is regulated by the Lomé sugar protocol, which guarantees a given quota to several sub-Saharan states. After market unification, cane sugar from Africa could be replaced with beet sugar grown and processed in the rest of the EC (Stevens 1990). The result could be a reduction of foreign investment by Tate and Lyle, which in the mid-1980s had fourteen affiliates located in seven sub-Saharan African countries.

■ Restructuring of EC Industry: A New Role for Sub-Saharan Africa?

Besides the sectoral implications of 1992 for European investment in Africa, the high levels of concentration in a few countries and the distribution of that investment leave African host countries vulnerable to change in the post-1992 period. This is compounded by the fact that a small number of TNCs dominate foreign participation in many important sectors, such as Lonrho in mining and Unilever in food processing. A change in the foreign investment strategy of a single firm from the EC might have a relatively minor impact on the structure of the home industry but could have important repercussions for host countries in Africa.

The pattern presented in Table 7.6, in which a large proportion of investment is concentrated in the former colonies of the investing country, suggests that these colonial affiliations (and perhaps more important, the bilateral preferences that later evolved from them) are a major determinant of European TNCs' investment choices in Africa. The question may be asked whether the 1992 program will dissolve those relationships, not only by shifting preferential agreements with ACP countries to a Pan-European dimension but by changing the very character of EC firms, such that they too will evolve into truly Pan-European entities. If this occurs, the concern for African countries is how such a change in the nationality of European TNCs would affect these firms' investment stakes in Africa, which today reflect very national interests. This question is of particular importance with respect to TNCs from the United Kingdom, France, and Belgium; their overseas investments have a strong bilateral flavor.

Current evidence suggests that EC firms are indeed moving from a position of "national champions" to one of Pan-European operations. In the pre-1992 industrial structure of Europe, large firms, supported by preferential policies from their governments, dominated their home markets but had very narrow market shares in other EC countries. Now TNCs from EC countries are moving swiftly beyond their borders to build up substantial market shares in the rest of the EC. Data on intra-EC FDI reveal that average annual flows among member states increased from $4 billion in the early 1980s (1980–1984) to $20 billion by the end of the decade (1984–1989), and throughout the decade, intra-EC FDI flows grew twice as fast as did EC FDI to the rest of the world. In 1980, intra-EC FDI stock was only one-fourth of total foreign investments by EC countries; by 1988, this ratio had risen to one-third (UNCTC 1991b). As a result of the more regional orientation of EC foreign investment, the structure and performance of EC industry are likely to change considerably as EC TNCs become truly European in character.

Data on mergers and acquisitions confirm this. Between December 1988 and December 1989, the total value of foreign acquisitions by EC firms rose

Table 7.6 Number of Affiliates and Share in Sub-Saharan Africa (SSA)

	Number of Affiliates	Share in SSA (percent)
United Kingdom		
Zimbabwe	404	25.7
Nigeria	167	10.6
Kenya	243	15.4
Zambia	147	9.3
Malawi	86	5.5
Total	1,047	66.5
France		
Côte d'Ivoire	69	19.3
Cameroon	52	14.6
Gabon	40	11.2
Senegal	35	9.8
Nigeria	27	7.6
Total	223	62.5
Germany		
Nigeria	44	31.7
Zimbabwe	10	7.2
Kenya	9	6.5
Liberia	6	4.3
Côte d'Ivoire	6	4.3
Total	75	54.0
Netherlands		
Nigeria	24	19.5
Zimbabwe	15	12.2
Zaire	13	10.6
Liberia	11	8.9
Kenya	10	8.1
Total	73	59.3
Belgium		
Zaire	12	15.8
Kenya	9	11.8
Nigeria	9	11.8
Burundi	7	9.2
Congo	6	7.9
Total	43	56.5

Source: UNCTC, Billion Dollar Club database.

by 7 percent, but purchases of other EC firms grew by 116 percent, raising the proportion of intra-EC to total acquisitions from 17 percent to 40 percent. France, Germany, and the United Kingdom were the largest purchasers of other EC firms, accounting for 33 percent, 26 percent, and 19 percent of total intra-EC purchases (KPMG 1990). Such figures give ample evidence to support predictions that 1992 would cause a major restructuring of EC industry and would drive firms aggressively to seek out new markets and production locations in neighboring EC countries.

An analysis of the sectoral composition of this cross-border activity reveals that with the exception of food, beverages, and banking, the most active intra-EC restructuring is taking place in industries with weak FDI linkages to Africa: Wholesale distribution, engineered products, chemicals, paper, banking, and electrical and electronics products top the list. A relatively low proportion of corporate assets were traded in the extractive and oil and gas industries (KPMG, *Dealwatch*, various issues). This does not mean, however, that similar restructuring in those industries will not occur in the future, only that firms in other sectors were among the first to feel the direct effects of the 1992 program. The chairman of British Petroleum, pointing to overcapacity in the EC petrochemicals industry, predicted a serious profit squeeze that would lead to a restructuring of national firms to a regional orientation, as had already happened in other EC industries (*Financial Times* 1990).

The restructuring of EC industry from a national to a Pan-European orientation leads to questions about the level and composition of European investment in Africa. If French companies acquire significant Italian interests, for instance, and if their relationship with the French government is distanced in the process, will this weaken the role of French West Africa in the investment strategies? If, as is likely, German investment capital plays a more important role in the EC region as a whole, to what extent will this dilute the strongly bilateral investment relationships between other EC countries and their ex-colonies? As the commercial interests of individual EC countries merge via a large-scale restructuring of capital, will this lead to a similar restructuring of investments by European TNCs in Africa because the latter reflect historical, bilateral relationships in which one of the parties will soon be unrecognizable? Although the answers lie in the future, trends are clear.

■ African National Policies and Foreign Investment*

Historically, the policies of African countries toward TNCs were quite diverse and depended on a number of factors such as political and eco-

---

*This section is by Mulatu Wubneh.

nomic ideology, history, and size of the respective country. Foreign investors were often viewed as extensions of colonialism in the early years following independence. Nationalization of foreign-owned companies were extensive, and where there was no outright expropriation, foreign investors were required to accept minority state participation (UNESCO 1990, 12).

Between 1982 and 1987, more than one-third of the African countries have either introduced new codes or have made adjustments to their investment codes or guidelines (UN 1988). The major elements of the legislation are often related to the country's development objectives, which are then followed by specific provisions governing establishment, ownership, and operating environment of FDI. Some of the specific provisions concern authorization and registration, taxes, remittances of profits and capital, and employment and training of local personnel. Recent legislative developments include the establishment of special agencies with overall responsibility in investment matters (e.g., Ghana's Investment Center), the development of export zones (e.g., Ghana, Togo, Kenya), and the privatization of state and parastatal enterprises (e.g., Nigeria, Guinea, Togo). Although it is difficult to develop a typology of FDI legislation in African countries because of their diversity and complexity, Islam and Majmudar (1990) maintain that three clusters of countries can be identified based on the direction of change of their codes:

1. Countries that pursued restrictive policies toward FDI in the 1960s and 1970s, but have adopted major liberalization measures since the 1980s. In this group could be included Ghana, Senegal, and Somalia.
2. Countries that pursued liberal policies in the 1960s and 1970s and generally continued to do the same in the 1980s. However, they have introduced certain changes to liberalize some aspects of FDI policies and have tightened the restrictions in others. A majority of the African countries probably fall in this category, including Burkina Faso, Central African Republic, and Niger.
3. Countries that have maintained a restrictive stance even though they have amended some sections of their FDI laws during the 1980s. Benin, Ethiopia, Guinea, and Tanzania could fall in this group. Most of these countries followed or, at some time in their history, adopted socialist ideology to guide their economic policy. The major problem facing many of these countries is that the policy changes they have introduced have not been perceived as credible and permanent, factors that are important in winning the confidence of investors.

Table 7.7 presents a summary review of the characteristics of FDI legislation of twenty-four developing countries analyzed by Islam and

Table 7.7 Major Features of FDI Laws in Less Developed Countries

Regulatory Issue	Major Features
Authorization and registration	With a few exceptions, enterprises require authorization from the government prior to commencing business.
Domestic tax concessions	Exemption from or reduction of income tax, turnover tax, real estate tax, tax on dividends and remuneration of expatriates is available for a period ranging from 2 to 15 years.
Import duty concessions	Exemption from import duty on raw materials, machinery, and spare parts not available locally is available from 2 to 15 years.
Remittances	Remittance of profits and repatriation of capital allowed freely by most countries.
Ownership and control	Foreign investments with 100 percent ownership are permitted, but joint venture undertakings with partly local ownership are preferred by many countries.
Employment of local personnel	Foreign enterprises are generally required to employ and train local personnel. Only a few countries specify specific targets.
Other concessions	Exemption from or reduced rates on registration and mortgage fees, export duty and real estate levies, discount on lease of land, accelerated rate of depreciation and investment allowance.
Minimum capital requirements	Minimum capital requirements are usually stipulated in local currency.
Exclusions	Industries engaged in purely commercial activities; armament or public utility are generally excluded from foreign investment.
Local content	The use of local materials and resources is encouraged, but very few countries specify particular proportions.
Foreign exchange balance	The transfer of profits and dividends is made subject to being covered by foreign-exchange balance of the enterprise.

Source: Islam and Majmudar 1990, p. 8.

Majmudar. Many of the African countries have incorporated new measures beyond the traditional incentives such as liberalization of tax regimes, elimination of provisions on exclusion of certain sectors and requirement of local participation in ownership of foreign-controlled enterprises, simplification of administrative procedures, and the streamlining of regulatory frameworks. Unfortunately, because many of these liberal measures were introduced in the last decade, their impact has not been adequately assessed.

The liberalization codes introduced by African governments are welcome, but it is important to note that these new investment laws provide necessary but not sufficient conditions for attracting new investment in Africa. As a UNIDO report (1991, 34) put it: "No amount of policy reform directed at foreign investors (better investment codes, faster procedures, liberal treatment, tax holdings) or at macroeconomic variables (inflation, wage, exchange rates) is likely to offset structural economic weaknesses." What Africa needs is to (1) capitalize on the unique opportunities the region possesses, (2) restructure its political and economic environment to create a conducive climate for development, and (3) develop new strategies that can lure investors into the region. Each of these concepts is examined in detail next.

■ **Capitalizing on Unique Opportunities**

Africa's unique opportunities lie largely in its rich mineral resources, believed to be among the largest in the world. There is already evidence that many African countries have potential for high-value as well as strategic and industrial minerals (World Bank 1989a, 122). Legislation that permits liberal mineral regimes can attract investment in the mining sector. Ghana's Minerals and Mining Law of 1986 is believed to have had a major impact in increasing mining production and in attracting substantial amounts of foreign investment into the country. Between 1986 and 1989, seventy prospecting licenses were issued, a third of which went to predominantly foreign-owned companies, and four mining leases were granted (UNIDO 1991, 86).

Oil is another important resource that could attract investors because Africa's important oil deposits, such as the Rift Valley and much of the Gulf of Guinea, are yet to be prospected. Although oil exploration in Africa has declined in the last decade, largely because of the crash in oil prices, the success rate for oil exploration is very high. According to a recent UN report, there has been one discovery for every two to five exploration wells in the Gulf area of Africa compared with a world average of one for every five to six wells (UNESCO 1990, 21).

Privatization, which many African countries are increasingly implementing, is another area that could create new opportunities for potential investors to assume full ownership or to participate in joint ventures. Several African countries, including Nigeria, Ghana, and Togo, have announced their intention to sell their state and parastatal enterprises. Although investors are cautiously watching developments, it is believed that with proper packaging of incentives and guarantees, the privatization move would eventually entice many foreign investors.

■ **Restructuring the Economic and Political Environment**

Improving Africa's economy is going to require that African governments change their approach—in particular, putting greater stress on the primary sector while at the same time trimming their military expenditures. Africa today not only is facing an economic crisis dramatized by famine, malnutrition, high unemployment, refugees, and abject poverty, but also is burdened by serious political problems, including one-person rule, violation of human rights, interethnic and interregional conflict, and the lack of tolerance for minority groups. These problems have projected an image that Africa is a region riddled by crisis and not conducive to investment.

In the economic sector, the performance of the African economy has slipped backward over the years. According to the World Bank (1989a, 122), the average annual growth of GDP among sub-Saharan African countries for the periods 1973–1980 and 1980–1987 were 2.5 and 0.5 percent, respectively, compared to 5.9 percent for the period 1965–1973. In comparison, the GDP growth for all low-income economies (those with GNP of $400 or less) for 1973–1980 and 1980–1987 were 4.6 and 6.0 percent, respectively. These poor performances can be partially explained by the fact that African economies are based on the export of one or two primary commodities whose terms of trade have deteriorated significantly in the last decade. The values of African exports have declined at an annual rate of 7 percent during the period 1980–1987, whereas those for Western Europe have increased at an annual rate of 5 percent, those for the United States at 3 percent, and those for Asia at 8.5 percent (GATT 1988, 19). A whole range of institutional, financial, and infrastructural constraints have negatively affected Africa's economy in the last two decades (see World Bank 1989a, 16–33, for details). The deterioration of the economic conditions was exacerbated by the drought that has claimed the lives of millions in the Sahel and northeast Africa and has put millions of others in a precarious situation. The drought as well as interethnic and interregional conflicts have forced more than 1.4 million people to become refugees; they account for the second-largest (after Asia) refugee population in the world.

Another major economic problem affecting investment in Africa is the lack of a large market. In a survey of major corporations conducted by the Group of Thirty (an independent international organization headquartered in New York), over 80 percent of the respondents ranked access to the host country's market among the top three factors influencing investment decisions. The market shares in Africa are small and fragmented, and the purchasing power of African economies is limited. For instance, with a combined population of 7 million, Burkina Faso, Malawi, and Mali have a GNP of about $1 billion, or one-tenth of the GNP of Guatemala, a middle-income country with a comparable population (UN 1988, 14).

Many African governments have adopted structural adjustment measures based on advice from the World Bank and the International Monetary Fund. These measures are aimed at "getting prices right" by adopting austerity measures to reduce government costs, devaluing currencies, and undertaking privatization of public enterprises. Structural adjustment programs are highly criticized as being harsh and inhuman because of their effect on the poorest of the society—indeed, a number of countries experienced food riots and violent demonstrations. Despite the criticisms, many Western governments are using structural adjustment as a condition for providing aid and other types of assistance, and some maintain that structural adjustment programs are essential if African countries are to create a conducive environment for investment. Under Lomé IV, over ECU 1,150 million is set aside for projects designed to help ACP members weather the difficult times brought about by structural adjustment programs. Lomé IV also includes a new chapter about enterprise development, which states that the "private sector needs to be made more dynamic and play a greater role, in particular through small and medium-sized enterprises, which are better suited to conditions prevailing in the ACP economies" (*Courier* 1990).

A regional integration process similar to the EC arrangement is another important concept that African governments should consider to enhance the flow of FDI. At present, less than 5 percent of Africa's products are exported to African countries. This is largely because the economies of African countries are similar to one another; what African countries produce and export are mainly primary products, whereas they import manufactured goods. As a result, they have relatively little to exchange with one another. Because of the low level of economic development and the relatively small population—factors that restrict the purchasing power—investment opportunities in Africa are limited. Through market and product integration (e.g., removal of nontariff barriers), African countries can increase trade among each other and thereby investment opportunities. At present there are several regional cooperative arrangements—for example, the Economic Community of West African States, Inter-Governmental Agency on Drought (in the Horn of Africa), and the Communauté Economique d'Etats de l'Afrique Centrale—but their effectiveness has been limited largely because of the lack of political will on the part of member countries. These regional cooperatives have to be restructured in a similar manner as the EC arrangement by developing secure and lasting cooperation based on a freely negotiated and legally binding contract.

In the realm of political climate, as a result of the political crisis that engulfed Africa in the 1970s and 1980s, many investors have developed a perception that investing in Africa is "unsafe." Various studies (e.g., Baker 1983; Group of Thirty 1984; Helmboldt et al. 1986; Wallace 1990) have documented that the hostile attitude of host governments toward private investment and the prospect of political instability were among the factors that influenced investors not to invest in Africa. Other political factors are related to slow response of host governments, complicated requirements, and inefficiency and corruption of bureaucratic processes and government decisionmaking.

African governments need to change the overall political climate so that they can create a conducive atmosphere for development. One of the important tasks in restructuring the political environment is resolving the issue of the role of foreign investment in national development. The debates on the merits and demerits of this issue tend to be murky because many African governments continue to send conflicting signals on whether they welcome or resist foreign investment. Although many countries recognize the importance of FDI, TNCs are often viewed as being exploiters rather than partners that can help in the development process. It is therefore essential to (1) define the national objectives and the role TNCs can play in realizing the objectives, (2) spell out the requirements and circumstances for investment, and (3) with commitment and clear purpose, seek out foreign investors in sectors where foreign investment is considered beneficial.

A second important factor in improving the investment climate would be to develop legislation that is consistent, credible, and permanent. Investors often complain that government policies in Africa tend to be transitory and, in some cases, capricious. Many African countries have a history of altering investment legislation frequently. Because predictability is an important factor in the investment decisions of TNCs, government policies should be clear and consistent; when legislative changes are made, retroactive application of the new change on already-established firms should be avoided.

A third important factor affecting the politico-economic environment is related to the slowness and corruption of the African bureaucratic structure. Delay often occurs because of technicalities in requirements, indecisiveness in decisionmaking, and in some cases corruption. African governments must restructure their bureaucracies to provide prompt response to investors; they also must establish "one-stop" offices with the responsibility of facilitating investment procedures and requirements. An investment promotion center (IPC) that can assist in facilitating investment decisions by providing information, technical assistance, and administrative linkage, and that also can serve as a clearinghouse to help identify projects in host countries as well as TNCs that are seeking investment opportunities, can expedite the investment process.

■ **Developing New Strategies to Lure Investors into the Region**

The process of developing enticement strategies include some of the following measures:

1. Countries should pursue a policy of "targeting" investors and aggressively following up to recruit potential investors. Experiences in many Asian and Latin American countries have demonstrated that the passive approach of developing a package of incentives and identifying a "shopping list" of projects for investment is not likely to have a major impact on investment. African governments must actively pursue and specifically target TNCs to entice them to invest in a particular project or in a particular sector.

2. Local entrepreneurs should be encouraged to undertake joint-venture investment with TNCs. They could enter these arrangements as equity shareholders and providers of finance, technology, and managerial skills.

3. Governments should institute the strategic planning process. This concept, widely used in the private sector, is a systematic method for identifying and accomplishing the most important actions in view of strengths, weaknesses, threats, and opportunities (Bryson 1988). It is a focused approach that concentrates on issues that are critical to an organization. African governments can use the process to identify the internal and external environments affecting FDI, to set specific goals and strategies by which they can enhance the flow of FDI, to formulate action plans, and to evaluate the results periodically. Such a focused approach can help establish priorities and deal effectively with the ever rapidly changing circumstances affecting the global flow of investment.

4. Countries should undertake an information campaign to gild Africa's image. An information campaign that explains the attitude of host governments is critical in improving Africa's image in the international world. Africa, more than any other region of the developing world, suffers from adverse media exposure. Many firms make decisions based on the information they receive through the mass media. The negative view of Africa that is now prevalent can only be eliminated by developing an information campaign that explains that African society is undergoing a serious economic and political change and opportunities for investment are brighter than ever. Further, this strategy can be strengthened by seeking home countries' assistance to encourage their TNCs to invest in Africa as well as the assistance of TNCs that have had investment success

in Africa.

5. Government programs should give priority to the development of an infrastructure base, such as roads and railway lines that have become bottlenecks in exploiting resources. A partnership can be worked out in which the government would be willing to eliminate long-term structural obstacles to FDI by using public funds or official development assistance to provide infrastructure, train labor, and help in developing resources in return for the expanding or undertaking of new investment by TNCs.

■ Note

1. Similarly, the average annual rate of return of U.S. investment in Africa for the period 1980–1986 was 20.6 percent. The corresponding figures for Europe, Latin America, and Asia (including the Middle East) were 13.3, 12.2, and 28.5 percent, respectively (U.S. Department of Commerce 1988, 111–112).

8
Relative Performance of CFA Franc Zone Members and Other Countries

Shantayanan Devarajan
Jaime de Melo

Among the many facets of Europe's relations with Africa, the link between France and the thirteen members of the CFA franc zone stands out as a unique institution. Before African independence, CFA referred to the French African Community; after 1960 it refers to the African Financial Community (Communatí financìere africaine) of the franc monetary zone. Although it is based on a colonial relationship—all but the most recent zone member (Equatorial Guinea) were former French colonies—the CFA zone goes beyond the traditional trade-and-aid links between other European countries and their former colonies. Instead, the CFA zone is a monetary arrangement. It consists of two currency unions (one of the Western, the other of the Central African states) whose rules of operation are connected with France. The common currency of the two unions, the CFA franc, is freely convertible and guaranteed by the Bank of France. In turn, CFA members are required to deposit 65 percent of their foreign exchange reserves in French francs with the Bank of France. Perhaps the most significant aspect of the relationship is the fact that the exchange rate between the CFA and French franc is fixed and has remained unchanged since 1947. Any change in parity requires the unanimous consent of the zone members, including the French government. In sum, the relationship between France and these thirteen African countries explicitly affects the conduct of economic policy within those countries.

In this chapter, we ask whether this distinction has led to any differences in the performance of CFA zone countries vis-à-vis their counterparts elsewhere. One reason for asking this question is that changes within Europe in 1992 may trigger some changes in France's relationship with the CFA zone and hence in the zone itself. In our conclusion, we speculate on what these changes may be and how they may affect the members of the CFA zone, but first we compare performance inside and outside the CFA zone.

For most of the thirteen African members of the CFA franc zone, the 1980s have been a decade of slow or negative growth in per capita GDP, worsening balance of payments, debt crises, financial crises, declining competitiveness, and—most distressing of all—an apparent lack of adjustment to the changed external environment they inherited from the 1970s. Of the few recently documented success stories of adjustment in Africa, none involves a member of the CFA zone (World Bank 1989a).

This disappointing performance is curious in light of the cautious optimism about zone membership voiced earlier in the decade by, among others, Guillaumont and Guillaumont (1984) and Devarajan and de Melo (1987a). Their optimism stemmed from the notion that participation in the franc zone would foster growth on the one hand, and reduce the need for adjustment on the other. Guaranteed convertibility of the CFA franc and the fixed exchange rate with the French franc would lead to a stable investment climate for domestic and foreign investors, thereby stimulating economic growth. As for adjustment, the rules of the zone led to monetary and fiscal discipline. By avoiding some of the excesses of their African neighbors, zone members needed to make less adjustment—even though they lacked an important instrument of adjustment, namely, a currency devaluation (see Honohan 1990). Furthermore, as Devarajan and de Melo (1987b) have pointed out, CFA countries had enough instruments with which to depreciate the real exchange rate that was, after all, the relevant signal for structural adjustment.

In this chapter, we reassess the benefits and costs of the CFA zone in light of the poor performance of its members in the 1980s. Addressed first is whether on average CFA countries fared worse than a group of "comparator" countries. Because there is no clear-cut group of comparators, we look at three: other sub-Saharan African countries, other low- and middle-income countries, and other primary and fuel exporters. Recognizing that a comparison of averages neglects differences within a group of countries, next we use some statistical estimations to examine this question: If we assume that year-to-year GDP growth rates for all countries are drawn from a random distribution, is there evidence that the distribution of CFA countries' growth rates is significantly different from that of the comparators? Finally, we take a closer look at the adjustment experience of CFA countries vis-à-vis their comparators. Did CFA countries adjust less, controlling for the size of the external shock, than other countries? Did they adjust differently? One argument we explore is that because CFA countries cannot devalue their nominal exchange rate, they cannot levy an "inflation tax" to finance a fiscal deficit. We ask whether this led to lower inflation and higher current account deficits. Another argument we test is that the fixed exchange rate makes expenditure switching more difficult, so that CFA countries rely more on expenditure reduction as a means of adjustment. Our concluding remarks include a discussion of the future prospects of the zone in light of our empirical results and the proposed changes in Europe after 1992.

■ Growth and Adjustment in the CFA Zone: An Overview

In this section, we compare the average performance of CFA members with that of the three groups of comparator countries. Rather than undertake a detailed analysis, we look for broad patterns that will suggest the statistical evaluations of subsequent sections. This approach is based on simple, unweighted averages of countries' performance indicators over different periods. The approach does not recognize that during the last two decades, countries have been subjected to external and internal shocks that have varied in timing and magnitude across countries. Our method of aggregation by country groupings implies that the shocks were uniform within each group. Later, we allow for some diversity in comparisons based on an error-components model. Nevertheless, these preliminary comparisons are a useful starting point for further analysis.

The most important of the three comparator groups is other countries of sub-Saharan Africa (SSA). These countries have the most in common with zone members in terms of economic structure, history, and culture. Furthermore, being their neighbors, they provide zone members with the best perspective on life outside the CFA zone. We also compare CFA countries with other low-income countries and other primary exporters. Except for Gabon, all CFA countries had a per capita income in 1980 below $1,200. We use this figure as the cutoff for low-income countries; higher-income countries, such as those in Latin America and East Asia, tend to have very different economic structures and human capital endowments and thus are excluded from the comparator set. In the same vein, there is some evidence that countries producing and exporting primary products have adjustment histories that differ from those of countries that emphasize manufactured goods (Faini and de Melo 1990a).[1] Because every CFA country is either a primary or fuel exporter, we also compare them with other primary/fuel exporters.

Table 8.1 displays the averages for our different indicators of CFA countries and their comparators during the period 1973–1988. We divide the period into two subperiods, corresponding (roughly) to the pre- and postadjustment periods for most countries. The results broadly confirm our earlier results (Devarajan and de Melo 1987a) derived from the sample period 1960–1982. There, we showed that CFA countries' average GDP growth rate was slightly higher than that of other sub-Saharan African countries but lower than that of other developing countries.[2] Furthermore, we found that the relative performance of CFA countries improved after 1973. We attributed the differences to the benefits from

Table 8.1 Comparison of Indicators for CFA Countries and Comparator Groups, 1970s and 1980s (percent)

	1973–1981		1982–1989	
Average annual real GDP growth rate (percent)				
CFA	3.7		2.6	
Other:				
SSA	2.7		2.0	
Low-income	4.4		2.9	
Primary	4.6		3.9	
Real total investment/real GDP				
CFA	24.3		18.9	
Other:				
SSA	20.3		17.8	
Low-income	21.6		19.8	
Primary	22.5		19.4	
Debt/GDP (debt service/exports in parentheses)				
CFA	30.6	(7.7)	62.5	(19.2)
Other:				
SSA	28.6	(9.7)	70.5	(20.9)
Low-income	26.0	(13.0)	58.4	(22.3)
Primary	24.9	(15.2)	56.4	(25.2)
Average annual inflation				
CFA	12.0		4.3	
Other:				
SSA	24.3		29.7	
Low-income	18.4		33.3	
Primary	24.4		44.9	
Real exchange rate (1980 = 100)				
CFA	107.0		108.0	
Other:				
SSA	115.0		147.0	
Low-income	103.0		121.0	
Primary	103.0		119.0	
Average annual export growth				
CFA	6.8		1.5	
Other:				
SSA	1.9		2.6	
Low-income	4.9		5.0	
Primary	4.8		7.6	

Source: World Bank figures from various sources.
Note: Unweighted averages. Number of countries in each group: CFA, 11; SSA, 20; low-income, 41; primary, 52.

stability of a fixed exchange rate regime, especially in the turbulent post-1973 era of floating exchange rates.

The pattern we discerned using data up to 1982 appears to have persisted through the late 1980s. As indicated in Table 8.1, CFA countries enjoyed an average annual growth rate over half a percent higher than their African neighbors. Their performance relative to other low-income and primary-exporting countries continued to be inferior. The basic trends established up to 1982 appear to be sustained, but the gap between CFA and other African countries seems to be narrowing. The difference in GDP growth rates was a full percent in the 1970s.

As for other indicators in Table 8.1, the gap in investment-to-GDP ratios between CFA countries and their African counterparts narrowed much further during the 1980s. Whereas in the 1970s zone members had a higher investment ratio than any of the comparators (and 4 percent higher than other African countries), in the 1980s they were all clustered around the same number. The decline in investment and the narrowing of the gap between CFA and other countries constitute a two-edged sword. On the one hand, lower investment ratios could be associated with an increase in the efficiency of investment, as various "white elephants" are abandoned. On the other hand, if there is no improvement in the marginal efficiency of investment, the shortfall would signal a further slowdown in GDP growth in the future. As we will see, the latter possibility appears more likely when we look at the 1982–1989 period more closely.

The next two indicators, debt and inflation, highlight the particular aspects of the CFA zone rather sharply. Having a fixed and rigid nominal exchange rate with the French franc effectively limits the seigniorage tax that CFA countries can levy. Consequently, the countries have experienced dramatically lower inflation rates than their African counterparts, let alone than other low-income and primary-producing countries. In fact, whereas average inflation rates have risen in other parts of the developing world, the deterioration in the external environment starting around 1982 caused them to fall in the CFA zone: The average rate in the 1980s was under 5 percent.

At the same time, CFA countries have had, until recently, an unlimited line of credit, known as the compte *d'opérations*, from the French treasury. This enabled them to have an average debt-to-GDP ratio in the 1970s that was higher than all of the comparator groups' averages. As it did for other low-income countries, this ratio doubled for the CFA zone in the 1980s. However, the debt-to-GDP ratio rose less rapidly than in the SSA group. Thus, although the fixed exchange rate may have exerted some monetary discipline in the CFA zone countries, it did not decrease their reliance on external finance.

The two indicators of debt service/exports and the real exchange rate should be examined jointly, along with the debt-to-GDP ratio, because a real exchange rate depreciation should help lower the debt-service ratio if there is an export supply response—although it will also raise the debt-to-GDP ratio (e.g., Rodrik 1989). CFA countries' average debt-to-GDP ratio over the 1982–1989 period was lower than that of their African counterparts, but their average debt-service ratio was almost the same. In other words, the debt-servicing needs and, implicitly, the creditworthiness of these two groups of countries are roughly comparable. Whereas the real exchange rate of the other African countries depreciated almost 30 percent between the 1970s and 1980s, that of the CFA zone, however, stayed the same. This may provide a clue to the debt-service puzzle mentioned earlier. By depreciating their real exchange rates, the other African countries have been able to raise exports so that their ratio of debt-service payments to exports is comparable to that of CFA countries, although at the expense of their debt-to-GDP ratio. Put another way, by not depreciating their real exchange rate, the CFA countries have probably not generated a comparable export supply response, and thus their debt-service ratio is the same as that of other African countries, although their debt-to-GDP ratio is lower.

Some of the preceding speculation is vindicated by a comparison of export growth of CFA countries vis-à-vis their comparators. Zone members experienced faster growth in their exports than all of their comparators during the period 1973–1981; in the second period, 1982–1989, their average export growth rate was the slowest, perhaps because of the lack of real exchange rate depreciation.

This comparison between the 1970s and 1980s masks the evolution of adjustment throughout the 1980s. When we break the period up into two subperiods, 1982–1985 and 1986–1989, the deterioration in the CFA zone's position becomes clearer. From the results (Table 8.2), several striking patterns emerge. First, the CFA countries' average GDP growth was higher than that of other African countries in the first subperiod, but it was actually lower in the second. When the growth rate in the rest of Africa accelerated after 1985, that in the CFA zone declined. Second, the investment rate in the zone fell sharply during this period, to the point where it is (marginally) lower than that of all its comparators (recall that in the period 1973–1981 it was the highest). Third, whereas the real exchange rate in other African countries depreciated even more sharply in the second period, it appreciated in the CFA zone, partially a reflection of the depreciation of the dollar vis-à-vis the French franc.

One interpretation of this change in relative positions is that by undertaking adjustment programs that emphasized a real exchange rate depreciation, the other African countries were able to benefit from the improvement in world commodity prices and demand after 1985. In particular, they were able to enjoy export growth that translated into faster GDP growth. Another interpretation would emphasize that the competitiveness of CFA countries was undermined by the continued depreciation of their neighbors' currencies.[3] There is also some evidence that after 1982, the line of credit from the *compte d'opérations* was no longer completely open. Zone members needed to cut back their current account deficits. Given the lack of real exchange depreciation, this must have come through expenditure reduction. In particular, they reduced investment sharply, which led to a fall in GDP growth rates that may continue into the future.

Table 8.2 Breakdown of 1980s Indicators for CFA Countries and Comparator Groups (percent)

	1982–1985	1986–1989
Average annual real GDP growth rate		
CFA	3.5	1.8
Other:		
SSA	1.0	3.0
Low-income	2.4	3.4
Primary	4.8	2.9
Real total investment/real GDP		
CFA	21.3	16.6
Other:		
SSA	18.4	17.1
Low-income	20.7	18.8
Primary	20.6	18.2
Debt/GDP (debt service/exports in parentheses)		
CFA	58.0 (16.1)	67.1 (21.5)
Other:		
SSA	57.1 (17.1)	83.5 (24.9)
Low-income	49.3 (19.5)	67.6 (25.0)
Primary	47.1 (22.4)	65.9 (27.9)
Average annual inflation		
CFA	8.6	1.0
Other:		
SSA	26.2	35.7
Low-income	19.5	50.4
Primary	28.9	64.6
Real exchange rate (1980 = 100)		
CFA	115.0	100.0
Other:		
SSA	124.0	177.0
Low-income	109.0	136.0
Primary	106.0	136.0
Average annual export growth rate		
CFA	3.0	0.1
Other:		
SSA	0.1	5.0
Low-income	1.2	8.8
Primary	7.6	7.7

Notes: Unweighted averages. Number of countries in each group: CFA, 11; SSA, 20; low-income, 41; primary, 52.

■ Are CFA Zone Growth Rates Different?

As mentioned earlier, a comparison of averages assumes implicitly that all countries within a group are uniform. We now relax that assumption. Specifically, we assume that the GDP growth rate for each country in each year is drawn from a random distribution. We then ask whether the distribution from which CFA countries' growth rates are drawn is significantly different from that of the comparators. Note that this, too, is a strong assumption because it ignores the role of a host of other factors that influence growth.

A common method for answering the question about differences in growth rates is to pool the cross-section and time-series data and use least-squares regression with dummy variables. To control for country-specific differences, this method requires a dummy variable for each country, which severely restricts the number of degrees of freedom. Instead, we use a modified approach, known as the "error-components framework," which assumes that the intercept term in the regression of the logarithm of GDP on the time trend (and a dummy variable) is also a random variable. This random variable is assumed to pick up the influence of omitted variables in determining growth. The error-components method requires the use of a generalized least squares estimator to get efficient estimates (Fuller and Battese 1974) but results in greater degrees of freedom.[4] Because this was also the model estimated in our previous work on the CFA zone (Devarajan and de Melo 1987a), it also has the advantage of providing a basis for comparison.

Table 8.3 presents the estimates of growth rates for CFA and comparator countries.[5] The regression results confirm the pattern suggested by the comparisons of averages previously described. Although they enjoyed significantly higher growth rates than their African counterparts in the 1970s, CFA countries fell behind in the 1980s. In fact, the estimated growth rate for CFA countries was lower than that for other sub-Saharan African countries for the 1982–1989 period as a whole. Our comparison of means showed this to be true only for the second subperiod, 1986–1989. Further-

Table 8.3 Estimated CFA and Comparator-Group Growth Rates from Error-Components Model (standard errors in parentheses)

	1973–1981	1982–1989
CFA	3.9	2.1
	(0.33)	(0.43)
Other:		
SSA	2.5	2.3
	(0.25)	(0.33)
Low Income	4.2	3.0
	(0.19)	(0.23)
Primary	4.5	2.8
	(0.17)	(0.20)

Note: All of the coefficients are significantly different from zero at the 95 percent confidence level.

Table 8.4 Comparator-Group Growth Comparisons by Subperiod

	1973–1981	1982–1989
Other:		
SSA	+	NS-
Low-income	NS-	-
Primary	-	NS-

Notes: +(-) indicates that growth in the CFA zone was significantly higher (lower) than in the comparator group; NS+(NS-) indicates the growth rate in the CFA zone was higher (lower) but not significantly so.

more, the gap between CFA countries and other low-income countries and other primary exporters appears to have widened.

Table 8.3 shows that the growth rates of CFA countries and their comparators were all significantly different from zero, and that the growth rate of CFA countries fell more in the second subperiod than did those of the others. It does not, however, answer the question of whether the CFA growth rate was significantly different from that of the comparators. To answer this, we need to test whether the difference in the coefficients is significantly different from zero. Table 8.4 reports the results of such a test, for which "significantly different from zero" is defined at the 95 percent confidence level.

Once again, the results corroborate the fact that the CFA zone's performance declined in relative terms during the 1980s. The members' growth rate was significantly higher than that in sub-Saharan Africa in the 1970s. In the 1980s, it was lower but not significantly so. If we think of economic growth as a running race, CFA countries in the 1970s were clearly ahead of the pack of all African countries; by the 1980s, they were indistinguishable from the rest of the pack. Similarly, although CFA members' growth rate was not significantly different from that of other low-income countries in 1973–1981, it became significantly lower in 1982–1989. That is, in the race with other low-income countries, CFA zone members fell behind the pack in the 1980s.

■ A Control Group Approach to Adjustment

The statistical approach in the previous section suffers from the fact that it does not control for factors that are likely to affect performance. In particular, developing countries were differently affected by external shocks during the 1970s and 1980s. Could the differences in growth rates between the CFA zone and its comparators be attributable to these omitted factors? In this section, we attempt a partial answer to that question by relying on a statistical approach often used in the evaluation of adjustment programs, namely, the modified control-group approach (e.g., Faini et al. 1990). In terms of our evaluation, this method amounts to looking for a fixed effect (in this case, belonging to the CFA zone) in explaining performance after controlling for changes in the external environment facing each country. As before, our comparisons are for the two periods 1973–1981 and 1982–1989. Adding some structure to our model, we now specify that the change in performance between the two periods—with performance measured by the average value of selected indicators during each period—is a function of autonomous policy changes after controlling for changes in the external environment between the two periods.[6]

Because autonomous policy changes are difficult to observe, we postulate that they are a function of the difference between the realized value of a performance indicator and some target value. Hence, we use lagged values of the performance indicators as proxies for the changes in policy (see Faini et al. 1990 for details). The statistical results reported in the following discussion show the coefficients for a model where each observation is an average over the first or second subperiods.

The shock variable (SH) is a weighted average of changes in the world real interest rate (R), export price index (PX), and import price index (PM) for each country. The weights are the ratios to GDP (Y) of debt (D), exports (X), and imports (M), respectively. By "changes," we mean the difference in the average value of these variables between the periods 1973–1981 and 1982–1989.[7]

The estimate of the shock variable turns out to be lower for CFA countries than for any of the comparator groups. Indeed, the shock faced by other sub-Saharan African countries was over twice that facing CFA countries. Hence, some of the lack of adjustment in the CFA zone may be explained by a reduced need for adjustment. The question is whether, given the reduced need for adjustment, the observed adjustment was still "too little."

The results are presented in Table 8.5. The CFA dummy variable has a negative coefficient for all comparisons. The two coefficients that are consistently significant for the CFA zone are those in the inflation and current account equations. The interpretation is that CFA countries, after we control for differences in the shocks they faced between the two periods, had lower inflation and less current account improvement in the 1980s relative to the 1970s. The coefficients on the dummy variables for the GDP growth and investment equations are also lower, but not significantly so. The overall impression from this set of regression coefficients is that although average GDP growth and investment-to-GDP ratios may have been lower in the 1980s in the CFA zone, the more significant differences appear in the average inflation rates and current account

Table 8.5 Comparative Performance in the CFA Zone and Comparator Groups

Dependent Variable	Y₋₁	I/Y₋₁	INF₋₁	CA₋₁	CFA	SH
SSA Countries						
Y	-.889*	.094	.021	.057	-.009	.049
	(-4.73)	(1.47)	(.80)	(.54)	(-.82)	(1.01)
I/Y	1.032*	-.656*	.010	.061	-.022	.235
	(2.37)	(-3.72)	(.09)	(.27)	(-.89)	(1.70)
INF	-2.151*	-.012	.212	-1.397*	-.138*	.135
	(-2.47)	(-.05)	(.67)	(-4.24)	(-3.01)	(.63)
CA	.282*	.052	.021	-.661*	-.032*	-.106*
	(1.73)	(.85)	(.95)	(-5.84)	(-3.24)	(-2.18)
Other Low-Income Countries						
Y	-.433*	.035	.039	-.093	-.021	.014
	(-2.63)	(.58)	(1.27)	(-.95)	(-1.58)	(.37)
I/Y	.457*	-.36*	-.004	.185	-.01	-.078
	(2.07)	(-3.74)	(-.06)	(1.54)	(-.77)	(-1.28)
INF	-1.70*	-.276*	.163	-.827*	-.134*	.081
	(-4.4)	(1.75)	(.65)	(-4.64)	(-3.85)	(1.17)
CA	.111	-.025	.015	-.765*	-.024*	-.056
	(.76)	(-.48)	(.62)	(-6.87)	(-2.48)	(-1.40)
Primary Exporting Countries						
Y	-.63*	.069	.025	.01	-.015	.02
	(-5.1)	(1.60)	(1.58)	(.16)	(-1.30)	(.66)
I/Y	.55*	-.391*	-.027*	-.091	-.005	-.116*
	(2.77)	(-5.41)	(-1.85)	(-.63)	(-.36)	(2.00)
INF	-.75*	-.003	-.123	-.537*	-.106*	.046
	(-1.72)	(-.002)	(-.59)	(-2.74)	(-2.58)	(.59)
CA	-.033	.032	-.001	-.781*	-.026*	-.068
	(-.23)	(.58)	(-.06)	(-7.01)	(-2.40)	(1.51)

Notes: The constant term is omitted from the results. Asterisks denote those coefficients that are significant at least at the 90 percent level. Y = GDP growth; I/Y = investment/GDP; CA = current account/GDP; INF = inflation rate. The subscript (-1) denotes lagged values. Results are corrected for heteroskedasticity by weighing each observation by the inverse of its estimated standard error. Extreme influential observations are excluded.

improvement. The former is not surprising. As mentioned earlier, the rules of zone membership prevent CFA governments from levying an inflation tax, so that the fixed effect on inflation for CFA countries would be lower. The current account coefficient is much more troubling. It implies that in all of the comparator groups, CFA countries are conspicuous for their inability to reduce their current account deficits, even if we take into account the fact that the shocks they face (i.e., the need to adjust) may have been different.

This observation is consistent with our earlier result about the lack of real exchange rate depreciation in the CFA zone. While the rest of sub-Saharan Africa depreciated its real exchange rate by an average of 25 percent in the 1980s, the CFA zone's real exchange rate appreciated. Such a result would not have been a problem by itself had the CFA countries not needed to depreciate their real exchange rate. However, the coefficients in Table 8.5 show that need. Controlling for differences in shocks they faced, we find the amount of current account improvement in the CFA zone was systematically lower than in the comparator groups.

Note that the coefficients of the lagged variables are usually significant with the expected sign. The higher the value of the own-lagged variable, the lesser the change in performance between the two periods. For example, other things being equal, the higher the average growth in the period 1973–1981, the less the increase in average 1982–1989 growth compared with 1973–1981. The external shock variable has the expected sign for the inflation and current account equations, but it enters positively with the change in growth and investment, which is unexpected. Although in most instances these coefficients are not statistically significant, the low explanatory power of the proxy measure for external shocks suggests some measurement inaccuracies.

Another problem with the results in Table 8.5 is that we may have misspecified the model. In particular, by controlling for autonomous policy changes separately from CFA zone membership, we may be neglecting those aspects of membership that are associated with policy. An alternative formulation would be to omit the independent variables for autonomous policy changes or, their proxy, the lagged dependent variables.[8] Unfortunately, this specification only yielded significant coefficients for the CFA variable in the inflation equation. The effect of CFA membership on current account improvement was not statistically significant. Thus, isolating autonomous policy changes sharpens our estimates of the fixed effects resulting from zone membership, possibly because there was no systematic relationship in the use of these policies among zone members.

Despite these qualifications, there is some evidence that adjustment in the CFA zone has been insufficient in the 1980s, arguably the era when almost everybody else in Africa was undertaking major adjustment programs. We have suggested one reason for the zone's lack of adjustment—namely, the inability of zone members to effect a nominal devaluation. But the nominal exchange rate is but one instrument of adjustment. In principle, CFA zone members have enough instruments with which to adjust their economies (Devarajan and de Melo 1987b). In practice, they have been reluctant to use these other instruments, and when they have chosen to use them, the results have been disappointing.[9] The advantage of a nominal devaluation is that it permits "expenditure switching" to accompany the necessary "expenditure reduction" of an adjustment program. In this case, the amount of expenditure reduction required would be less (Corden 1988). It follows, therefore, that CFA members would have had to rely more on expenditure reduction as opposed to expenditure switching in reducing their current account deficits. We now test this hypothesis.

Using the data from the two periods, 1973–1981 and 1982–1989, we estimate an equation that links the target of adjustment—the resource balance expressed as a ratio to GDP—with the investment rate and the real exchange rate. The investment rate is used here as an instrument for expenditure-changing policies. Of course, there are other such instruments, including government consumption expenditure. However, it is easier to cut investment first, especially in a slowly growing economy. Therefore, it is worth examining the extent to which improvements in the resource balance reflected declines in investment.

The regression linking the resource balance with investment and the real exchange rate also contains a dummy variable for each country, to capture country-specific effects, and a time trend. The results of the regression yield a negative—and highly significant—coefficient on the investment variable for both CFA and non-CFA countries. By contrast, the coefficient on the real exchange rate variable is small and indistinguishable from zero. This is consistent with other studies that have attempted to link the real exchange rate to the resource balance or the trade balance. For example, Pritchett (1990) found only a weak relationship between the merchandise trade balance and the real exchange rate, even when controlling for terms of trade movements. His reasoning, which may also apply here, was that although exports may respond to changes in the real exchange rate, imports are determined by foreign exchange availability (i.e., exports) and hence may move perversely.

Undaunted by the insignificance of the real exchange rate variable, we used the estimated regression coefficients to compute the predicted resource balance in 1978–1979 and 1987–1988. For both CFA and non-CFA countries, the resource balance improved between the first and second two-year periods. This is a reflection of the cutback in foreign lending in the 1980s and the simultaneous need for these countries to make increasingly higher debt-service payments. We can then ask the questions: How much of the improvement in the resource balance between 1978–1979 and 1987–1988 resulted from investment reduction, and how much from depreciation of the real exchange rate? Were the relative proportions different between CFA and non-CFA countries? The results are reported in Table 8.6.

First, although the improvement in the ratio of resource balance to GDP was roughly comparable for the two groups of countries, the investment components were quite different. CFA countries relied more heavily on cutting investment than did other low-income countries. Second, the real exchange rate component even has the wrong sign for CFA countries. That is, instead of contributing to the reduction in the current account deficit, the real exchange rate may have worked against it in the CFA zone,

Table 8.6 Changes in Resource Balance, Investment, and the Real Exchange Rate Between 1978–1979 and 1987–1988

	Resource Balance/GDP (1)	Investment Component (2)	Real Exchange Rate Component (3)
Average Predicted Change in			
CFA	.046	-.071	-.033
Other low-income	.050	-.053	.232

Note: Column 1 is equal to the sum of columns 2 and 3 plus the intercept term.

though the lack of statistical significance of the coefficient on the real exchange rate variable calls for caution in interpreting this result. Finally, and most important, the relative contributions of investment reduction and real exchange rate depreciation (column 2 divided by column 3) are very different between the two groups of countries. For other low-income countries, it is about one quarter, whereas for CFA members, it is over 2 (and with the wrong sign).

■ **Conclusions**

In this chapter we have assessed whether the particular institutional arrangement of the CFA zone has aided or hurt its members. It has been argued that the convertible currency with a fixed exchange rate results in monetary and fiscal discipline that in turn benefits zone members. Just as Ulysses tied himself to the mast, CFA governments abdicated the right to levy an inflation tax so that they will never be tempted to do so. The evidence of the relative performance of CFA countries' economies vis-à-vis those of their comparators shows that this argument was persuasive until the early 1980s.

After 1981, changes in the world environment and persistent current account deficits meant that CFA countries needed to adjust their economies along with most other developing countries. Our statistical results show that they did not adjust as much as they needed to. Furthermore, their growth performance was disappointing. Under every estimate, zone members' GDP growth rates fell behind those of their counterparts, including the other African states. Finally, the burden of adjustment appears to have fallen disproportionately on expenditure reduction in general and investment reduction in particular—an ominous sign for future growth.

Of course, a change in external circumstances does not necessarily mean that the original commitment to a fixed exchange rate was unwise.[10]

It is possible that CFA zone members took all these contingencies into account in making the original decision to join the zone and hence forgo the opportunity to devalue their nominal exchange rate in the future. In this case, there are no policy implications from the recent deterioration in the zone's economic performance. The members may have drawn a bad hand, but not one that renders their original decision suboptimal.

An alternative interpretation is that the current circumstances facing the CFA zone lie outside the set of events considered when the original decision to join the zone was made. In particular, the adverse terms of trade shocks of the 1970s and 1980s and the attendant need to shift resources from nontradables to tradables may not have been expected in the 1960s. Such an argument is compelling because the exchange rate is both an instrument for transforming resources from nontradables to tradables as well as an inflation-creating (or -controlling) tool. It could be that the founders of the zone calculated the inflation-controlling benefits of a fixed exchange rate without anticipating the costs in terms of the countries' inability to adjust to unfavorable external circumstances. Thus, the very institutional arrangement that enabled these countries to enjoy faster and more stable growth in the 1970s prevented them from adjusting to the external and internal shocks of the 1980s. What began as an Odyssean journey may have turned into a Trojan horse.

What are the implications of these conclusions for the future of the CFA franc zone after Europe 1992? Our analysis has drawn attention to one aspect of the zone—the fixed exchange rate—as being responsible for the deterioration of the CFA zone's relative performance. This is also the institutional arrangement that is most vulnerable to changes in the European Community: As the French franc becomes increasingly tied to other European currencies, so does the CFA franc. If the Delors Plan is adopted, the CFA franc will be pegged to the single European currency (Cosgrove and Laurent, 1991). In either case, the parity of the CFA franc will have to be reestablished. This may be an opportunity to effect the devaluation that until now has been resisted. Alternatively, if the other European partners are unwilling to support the CFA franc, the outcome may be a severing of its link with the French franc.

Any alteration of the current arrangement will have significant long-term implications for the CFA zone economies. A change in parity is equivalent to abandoning the fixed exchange rate. The reason is that the credibility, which made the original arrangement tenable for so long, is now lost. Once it is known that the CFA franc *can* be devalued, pressures will mount for it to be devalued again and again. For example, an unfavorable terms-of-trade shock could cause so much capital flight that a devaluation would be inevitable. The net result is that the CFA franc will be subject to periodic devaluations, just as other African currencies are. Once this process is set in motion, the convertibility of the currency and the guarantee from the Bank of France become less tenable and could also be abandoned.

How will these changes affect the performance of CFA zone economies? Predictions are always subject to uncertainty, but some insights may be obtained by looking at the behavior of the non-CFA countries in our sample. There is no reason to think that the outcome for CFA countries after 1992 will be any different from that for the non-CFA African countries up to this point. In concrete terms, the CFA countries will experience significantly higher inflation, but they will be able to adjust more effectively to adverse external and internal shocks.

One other possible outcome of the change in parity deserves mention. The countries within the CFA zone are not identical. The degree of exchange rate overvaluation varies considerably across countries (El-Badawi and O'Connell 1990). If as a result of Europe 1992 the CFA franc is devalued, the impact will not be uniform around the zone. This could lead to calls for different parities for different countries within the currency union. Although such a scheme is sustainable in principle (witness the current Exchange Rate Mechanism system in Europe), it will almost surely weaken the currency union. It is not inconceivable that the change in parity will lead to the dissolution of the two currency unions that make up the CFA zone.

■ Notes

1. The definition of a manufacturing exporter is a country whose share of manufactured goods in total exports exceeds 30 percent and whose share of manufacturing in GDP exceeds 13 percent. All other developing countries are in our comparator group.

2. A complementary study by Guillaumont and Guillaumont (1988a) reached the same conclusion using a broader set of indicators. See also Guillaumont and Guillaumont (1988b).

3. Lest we read too much into the real exchange rate figures, we should clarify how they are constructed. The figures represent the ratio of the trade-weighted average of the wholesale price indexes of each country's trading partners to the consumer price index of that country. Hence, they represent only a partial index of competitiveness. In particular, a sudden increase in a country's export price will not be captured in the real exchange rate index. Nevertheless, to the extent that African countries face similar commodity prices, the index presented here reflects the differences in competitiveness across groups of countries.

4. The maintained hypothesis is that the random component is uncorrelated with the time trend.

5. More precisely, we estimate the coefficients for β and β' in the following model:

$$Y_{it} = \alpha_i D_i + \alpha'_i D'_i + \beta D_i T + \beta' D_i T + u_{it},$$

where
Y_{it} = logarithm of GDP of country i in year t
D_i = dummy variable for CFA members

D'_i = dummy variable for comparator group members
T = time trend
u_{it} = composed error term

Given the definition of the variables, the estimates of β and β' represent the growth rates for CFA and comparator countries, respectively.

6. Specifically, we denote the set of performance indicators j for country i by y_{ij}. We postulate that changes in the value of each performance indicator depends on the vector of autonomous policy changes, x_i, on changes in the external environment, SH_i, and on membership in the CFA zone:

$$y_{ij} = \alpha_{oj} + x'_i \alpha_i + SH_i \alpha_{2j} + \alpha_{3jd} + \epsilon_{ij},$$

where a prime denotes a transpose and d is a dummy variable that takes the value 1 for countries that belong to the CFA zone and 0 otherwise.

7. The concept expressed in symbols is:

$$SH = (R_2 - R_1)(D/Y)_1 - (PX_2 - PX_1)(X/Y)_1 + (PM_2 - PM_1)(M/Y)_1,$$

where the subscripts refer to averages over the first and second sub-periods, and country subscripts have been omitted.

8. We are grateful to Stanley Fischer for this suggestion.

9. For a discussion of Côte d'Ivoire's attempt at simulating a devaluation by a uniform tariff-cum-subsidy scheme, see O'Connell (1989).

10. We are grateful to Ravi Kanbur, whose comments helped us sharpen this argument.

9
Aid Performance and Prospects
Roger C. Riddell

My object in this chapter is first to give an overview of recent trends in foreign aid to sub-Saharan Africa (SSA) and then to discuss the prospects for aid to the subregion to the mid-1990s, placing particular emphasis on European-African relations. The discussion not only highlights broad quantitative trends, but it also provides a commentary on the impact and effectiveness of foreign aid on African economies. Although greatest attention is focused on official development assistance (ODA), mention is also made of the rise and growing importance of voluntary aid and the role played by nongovernmental organizations (NGOs) in contemporary African development initiatives.

One initial word of caution or concern is necessary. The international financial institutions, bilateral and multilateral donors, and the international community as a whole have for some time now grouped together the forty-seven countries of Africa south of the Sahara into a subregion called sub-Saharan Africa.[1] Aggregate data for the region conceal a rich and complex diversity of achievement and performance among countries and across sub-subregions, and it needs to be stressed continually not only that conditions, problems, and prospects differ markedly among countries, but that general trends for the whole subregion do not necessarily reflect the situation in particular countries.

■ Aid to Sub-Saharan Africa in the 1980s

☐ Quantitative Trends

As the economic crisis of many of the countries of SSA worsened during the course of the last decade, the international community responded by providing more aid to the subregion. In the post-1985 period, especially, there was an acceleration of official aid funds committed to SSA. The share of global ODA from individual OECD Development Assistance Committee (DAC) donors, Arab donors, and multilateral agencies channeled exclusively to SSA countries rose from 19.5 percent in the mid-1970s to 22 percent at the start of the 1980s and to 32 percent by 1989 (OECD 1990a, 224ff).[2]

Official aid to SSA has not only increased in proportionate terms, but it has also expanded in real terms. During the 1980s, the real increase in ODA to SSA averaged 3–4 percent a year. From 1980–1981 to 1988–1989, total ODA to all developing countries fell by $774 million; for the SSA region, however, total ODA, at 1988 prices and exchange rates, rose from $11.8 billion in 1980 to $15.3 billion by 1989, a rise of one-third (OECD, 1990a, 1286–1287, 228).

What is more, aid funds have grown to be the single most important source of external financial flows for SSA. Between 1980 and 1987, the share of ODA to total resource inflow increased from 57 to 67 percent for all countries of SSA, and from 60 to about 85 percent for the low-income countries of the subregion. For all lower-middle-income and upper-middle-income countries, the ODA to total resource flow ratios in 1988 were, respectively, 53 percent and 30 percent (OECD 1989a, 218; OECD 1989b, 32).[3]

A further feature of official aid to SSA is the greater importance of multilateral allocations in comparison with other regions of the world. For all developing countries, almost 80 percent of all ODA consists of bilateral assistance, a figure that remained fairly constant throughout the 1980s. For SSA, however, bilateral aid accounted for just 70 percent of the total, and the share of bilateral to total aid fell (slightly) during the course of the decade: Just over 40 percent of all the multilateral official aid provided to developing countries went to the SSA subregion in the second half of the 1980s.

Table 9.1 provides data on the trends of European[4] to total ODA to SSA from 1978 to 1988. The table shows that European Community (EC) countries as a whole are the major source of official aid funds, and that the share from this source has risen, from about half of the total at the start of the 1980s to 57 percent by 1988. Most rapid has been the expansion of European Development Fund (EDF) aid, which by 1988 accounted for 10 percent of total ODA funds (second only to France as a source of aid) and for 34 percent of all multilateral funds.

Yet it is also important to note that funds from the International Development Association (IDA) rose more than twice as rapidly as the expansion of EDF funds, and by 1988, they, too, accounted for over 30 percent of SSA's official multilateral aid receipts. Although bilateral aid from EC countries rose by 79 percent in real terms over the period 1978–1988, it fell as a proportion of all bilateral aid, from 70 percent in 1978 to 67 percent by 1988. This was due largely to a more rapid expansion

Table 9.1 Net Disbursements of ODA: Totals and European Sources of Funds (in millions of dollars at 1987 prices and exchange rates)

ODA and Source	1978	1985	1988	Percent Increase 1978–1988
Total bilateral	5,114	8,692	9,460	85
EC bilateral	3,582	5,465	6,401	79
% of total	(70)	(63)	(67)	
Total multilateral	2,711	4,236	4,112	52
EDF	777	1,053	1,385	78
% of total	(29)	(25)	(34)	
Total ODA	8,644	13,805	13,757	59
Total EC[1]	4,359	6,518	7,786	79
% of total	(50)	(47)	(57)	

Source: OECD 1989a, 242.
[1] Includes EC bilateral plus EDF funding.

in bilateral aid from the Scandinavian countries and Japan. However, trends in EC bilateral aid themselves conceal differences among EC countries. Most remarkable has been the growth of the Italian bilateral aid program, which rose from $27 million in 1978 (at 1987 prices) to $1.3 million by 1988 (also at 1987 prices). When we exclude Italy and Denmark (whose bilateral aid to SSA rose by just over 100 percent in the eleven-year period), bilateral EC aid rose by only 41 percent from 1978 to 1988; German, Belgian, and Irish bilateral aid flows fell in real terms from 1985 to 1988.

For some countries, there has been a link between the lower than average rise in bilateral aid from leading European donors and the more rapid expansion of the EDF. In 1977, for instance, UK aid contributions to the EC amounted to 10 percent of total official British aid; by 1987, the share had doubled to 20 percent. A significant factor in this shift has been the desire to reduce the administrative costs of the aid program (in line with similar policies throughout the British civil service).[5]

This analysis of quantitative trends has been based almost exclusively on data from the OECD—as are nearly all discussions of international aid trends.[6] It is important to understand how these data are gathered and as a result to be aware of possible inaccuracies and errors in interpretation.

The OECD data are based on submissions reported by the donors. The most accurate data are the bilateral flows provided by the member countries of the OECD and those from the multilateral agencies. Because the figures are donor-based, they include all funds considered by the donor to be aid funds (providing they comply with the DAC's definition of concessional assistance). They thus include all technical assistance paid to donor-based consultants and consultancy firms, the value given being the donor-originating cost of goods shipped and services provided to recipient countries. In some countries, the figures also include the costs of administering the aid program in the donor country. As a result, the figures clearly exceed the amounts of aid that cross the border into the recipient country and that are recorded in its balance of payments. From the point of view of analyzing aid amounts to developing countries, the OECD figures are probably inflated by a factor of at least 20 percent.

Another major area of data inaccuracy occurs if recipient countries receive a significant proportion of aid from non-DAC bilateral donors, because these figures are either unreported or underreported in the OECD database, even though in recent years coverage of some Arab and CMEA (Council for Mutual Economic Assistance) sources have improved. Clearly, it is not known with any accuracy precisely how important these particular funds are to total flows; however, the case of Uganda illustrates the scale of the problem for one country in Africa. Data provided by all aid donors to the Ministry of Planning and Economic Development in Uganda for the financial years 1987/88, 1988/89, and 1989/90 show that bilateral aid from seven communist or developing countries amounted, respectively, to 17, 5, and 10 percent of all recorded official aid and 34, 14, and 21 percent of all bilateral aid flows.[7] None of these aid funds—totaling $170 million over the three-year period—appeared in the OECD figures. Clearly, Uganda has been in receipt of official aid substantially in excess of that recorded in the official aid figures of the OECD and the UNDP and reproduced by the World Bank.[8]

☐ *Issues*

Analysis of trends in total aid flows is of importance to policy debate to the extent that they are relevant to belief in the principle of "the more aid the better." Many debates about the adequacy of aid, in conventional wisdom, tend to assume that the aid channeled to SSA in the 1980s—and on into the 1990s—has been used and will be used effectively. There are, however, a number of doubts on this score. Most important, there does not seem in the recent past to have been any strong association between aid flows and economic growth. Indeed, the increase in ODA to SSA during the 1980s occurred at a time when the economies of the subregion were experiencing minimal growth and a contraction in gross domestic product (GDP) per capita. Even some analysts from within African recipient countries have gone so far as to argue that from a macroeconomic point of view, the aid they have received has had little to no impact.[9]

In a recent overview of the evidence on the impact of aid across Africa, particularly in the 1980s, Killick (1990, 41) came to this conclusion:

> The evidence presented in this paper points clearly to the conclusion that, taking the region as a whole, much of the proportionately large amounts of aid received by SSA has been ineffective in developmental terms, even after due allowance for all the difficulties of assessing this and for the fact that poor performance is often seen as a reason for aid.

Furthermore, Killick's analysis suggests that "the distribution of aid ... seems to have paid scarce regard to ability to use it well" (1990, 15). This pessimistic conclusion has also been drawn from what has probably been the most comprehensive study of aid worldwide (Cassen et al. 1986).[10] Sectoral studies of aid to Africa have been even more critical of impact. Both integrated rural development and livestock projects appear to have been particularly disastrous in Africa, leading in the case of the first to a radical rethinking of approach and in the case of the latter to a substantial withdrawal from the sector. As for technical assistance projects in Africa, these have proved to be extremely costly and have made little impact in relation to creating a cadre of skilled Africans to replace the tens of thousands of foreigners working on the continent.

This pessimistic assessment of impact is worrisome not only because of the poverty of the region but because of the importance of official aid to the economies of SSA. Surprisingly, in the period 1984 to 1987, only 7 percent of all aid to Africa consisted of food or emergency assistance; the rest went into economic, social, or infrastructural projects and programs. Thus in 1988, ODA accounted for a full 60 percent of gross domestic investment and for 41 percent of total imports to SSA. Aid not only has been rising in absolute terms, but it has accounted for an increasing share of GDP. In 1988, the ODA/GDP ratio stood at nearly 9 percent, compared with 3.2 percent in the 1960s and only 3.6 percent in the 1970s (Culagovski et al. 1990, 5).

The poor performance of aid in Africa, however, provides only a partial picture. As Mosley (1987) argues, in many cases (he details fully the case of Kenya) aid is often provided and increased precisely because a country is experiencing problems: In these cases it is not aid that causes or leads to poor economic performance but poor economic performance that induces donors to provide more aid. Further, the fact that increased aid flows have not been associated with better economic performance tells us nothing about what the situation would have been without aid, nor is it necessarily a good guide to future aid requirements.

Important, too, is the need to assess flows of concessional assistance in relation to other flows. During the 1980s especially, growing quantities of debt interest and principal constituted major outflows. Indeed, for most years of the decade, the net inflow of foreign aid was insufficient to meet funds used for the repayment of previously accrued foreign debt: From 1982 to 1987, SSA's debt repayments totaled $63 million; net official aid disbursements were $10 million lower, at $53 million.[11] Finally, in this context, it needs to be remembered that although economic theory argues that foreign aid has a dual positive effect through filling both a foreign exchange and a savings gap, it also asserts that aid will not be effective unless the conditions are right. Particular reference is made to the levels of skill, organizational competence, and ability to use the funds made available.[12]

Undoubtedly in the late 1970s and early 1980s, concern about the effects of aid and worsening economic performance had an important influence on the form and type of aid that donors provided to Africa. Severe balance-of-payments problems and disillusion about project assistance, particularly to the agricultural sector, led the international institutions to shift attention away from project aid and toward program aid. Initially, however, this was not the traditional form of program aid.[13] Rather, the form of aid provided in the 1980s was increasingly associated with what became known as structural adjustment programs (SAPs), which today have become so dominant in Africa. As the 1980s progressed, more and more countries in Africa were forced to adopt some sort of SAP, with greater shares of official aid becoming tied to the adoption of such policies. Countries like Côte d'Ivoire, Togo, and Ghana received massive amounts of assistance once they adopted World Bank–initiated SAPs; countries like Zambia and Zimbabwe received far less during the times they resisted these types of conditionality.[14] Of more than passing interest was that SAP-linked aid flows were tied more to the adoption of SAP policies than to economic performance. Further, preliminary analysis of recent economic performance in Africa suggests that those countries that adopted SAPs performed no better on a range of criteria than those that did not adopt the orthodox aid-linked approach (see Harrigan and Mosley 1990).

It was not only the Washington-based institutions that increasingly came to link their concessional lending to the adoption of SAPs; many of the bilateral donors also pursued the policy of "linkage." Prominent among these were the major European donors—the UK, Germany, the Netherlands, and in some respects, Italy. The linkage of growing amounts of bilateral aid to Africa to SAP conditionality was also related to disillusion about bilateral project assistance, but it also came about partly as a result of greater interchange among donors; it was only in the 1980s that roundtable aid meetings among major donors became institutionalized and greater attempts were made to provide consistency in approach.[15] For its part, the EC (through the EDF) continued throughout much of the 1980s to distribute EDF money in terms of agreed indicative country programs under Lomé II and Lomé III, with emphasis laid on agricultural and infrastructural projects; a special SAP component of EDF aid was to wait until the signing of the Lomé IV Convention. Part of the reason for the EDF's slower adoption of SAP linkage (it could have been formally institutionalized into Lomé III aid programs) was the long periods between different EDFs. A more practical issue, however, has undoubtedly been the slowness of commitment and disbursement of EDF funds.[16] Yet the EC, like the leading European bilateral donors, did make a shift to increased balance-of-payments support during the second half of the 1980s. Commodity import programs, under which lines of credit were set up usually for the purchase of goods tied to the donor,[17] became commonplace, with the French, British, Italians, and Germans prominent European promoters of this form of aid.

But this was not the only innovation in the EC's program of assistance to Africa. In a unique initiative after the Venice summit of industrialized nations in 1987, the EC launched a special program for SSA. A total of ECU 600 million was allocated for disbursement to debt-distressed countries of SSA.[18] Although a nominal condition for use of these funds was that recipients had to be committed to "adjusting their economies," no linkage with Washington-initiated SAPs was required.

A final important change in the 1980s was the rise in importance of NGOs to become if not major then at least significant actors on the aid scene. Dominant among foreign-based NGOs have been those from Europe. Grants by NGOs to developing countries amounted to about $4.2 billion worldwide in 1988, just over 7 percent of total official aid flows. For SSA, accurate data are unavailable; however, unofficial assessments suggest that voluntary contributions from abroad (including those provided by church organizations) probably account for some 15 percent of net official disbursements. Although this is a significant monetary contribution, the importance of NGOs lies probably more in the manner in which their role has increased in recent years. They are not only supported by voluntary contributions, but increasingly in the 1980s, donor agencies (bilateral and multilateral) have channeled official aid money to and through them. Thus, official DAC donors channeled $2.6 billion through NGOs in 1988–1989 (OECD 1990a, 19). Besides funds allocated for emergency relief, most funds used by NGOs in Africa go into particular projects, predominantly rural-based and with emphasis on agriculture, health, water, and sanitation. Indeed, the retreat of official aid from rural development projects was in some measure compensated by the official funding of NGOs whose work in this field has expanded substantially. A related area of NGO expansion has been in what are termed "income-generating" projects, whose purpose is to enhance the incomes of recipients.[19] Besides European bilateral agencies providing funds to support such initiatives, a major funder of these types of projects has been the EC through the EDF. In this context, it should be noted that EC initiatives have not been confined to the financial support of NGOs from Northern countries. In most countries of SSA, the EC is the major funder of a range of microprojects sponsored and operated by local community groups.

In summary, therefore, the 1980s brought not only a substantial increase in foreign assistance to SSA, boosted especially in the second half of the decade by the creation of special funds, but also a change in the form in which aid is provided. Greater attention has been paid to the macroeconomic context and climate, and there has been a retreat by the official donors away from project aid, with NGOs in some measure moving in to fill this particular gap. The decade also saw greater cooperation and consistency among especially the European bilateral donors, the United States, and the Washington-based institutions that in many ways took and maintained the initiative in regard to new approaches to aid. Only in the closing years of the 1980s, with the conclusion of the Lomé IV agreement, did the EC officially adopt this type of approach.

■ Aid to Sub-Saharan Africa in the 1990s

□ Quantitative Trends

It is difficult, if not impossible, to forecast what SSA's aid needs are likely to be in the 1990s because of the wide array of variables involved in making such an assessment.[20] One starting point, however, might be an influential study by the World Bank (1989a). Based on a "required" growth rate for the subregion of 4-5 percent a year, the study judges that the subregion's gross aid requirements will rise from $15 billion a year in 1990 to $22 billion by the year 2000, at 1990 prices (1989a, 179). This implies that "the momentum of aid generated in the past few years will have to be maintained during the 1990s" (1989a, 176). One implication of such a scenario would be that the ODA/GNP ratio will continue to rise, making SSA still more dependent upon aid at the end of the century than it was at the start of the 1990s.[21]

Clearly, required aid flows will depend critically upon what happens to other key variables. A major factor will be foreign debt obligations. The World Bank (1989a, 176) maintains that

> the external resource requirement of Sub-Saharan Africa during the 1990s could be met if donors achieve two related targets. First, during the 1990s, gross ODA continues to increase at about 4% a year in real terms. Second, debt relief mechanisms are put in place so that actual debt service payments for countries with strong reform programs are kept within manageable limits.

However, the World Bank is by no means optimistic that this rate of expansion will be maintained. It argues that the 4 percent annual growth rate of ODA (1989a, 179) may not be realised in the 1990s unless the share of low-income countries in ODA can be increased, since reallocating ODA from poor countries in other regions would seriously hamper their development efforts. If adequate funding for Africa is not forthcoming, Africa's decline is likely to continue in the 1990s.

Toward the end of the 1980s, the DAC suggested that the rate of increase of ODA from DAC members would be unlikely to be more than 2 percent a year, compared with between 3 and 4 percent achieved during the 1980s. Late 1990 World Bank projections for the first half of the 1990s are for a growth rate of only 2.5 percent. In its most recent report, the OECD's coded language bears the hallmarks of rising pessimism (OECD 1990a, 137):

> No firm ODA projections are possible given the uncertainties in future aid prospects for some of the larger donors. Taking account of past longer-term trends and of the available indications for the aid volume prospects of individual DAC countries . . . , ODA can be expected to continue to show a modest upward movement in real terms over the next few years.

For SSA, a crucial question is not whether aid levels will expand (they almost certainly will) but whether the 1990s will be a repeat of the 1980s, when the subregion received a rising share of global ODA. The prospects would appear to be particularly gloomy especially in relation to both European donors and to the major components of multilateral aid. The World Bank has suggested on the issue of Africa's 1990s financing needs that bilateral ODA is only likely to grow in line within nominal GNP in the OECD countries, and that with the share going to SSA remaining constant rather than increasing, there will be a leveling off of what in the 1980s was a steady increase in Africa's share of global ODA (Culagovski et al. 1990, 31).

Much apprehension has been expressed within Africa, especially, about the extent to which changes occurring within Europe are likely to affect bilateral aid flows to SSA in the 1990s. Little fear has been voiced in relation to the formation of the single market—the greater concern has been about the effect on African aid volumes of a possible diversion of funds to what was termed "Eastern Europe." In response to these fears, all European bilateral donors have stated that the support and assistance they are giving and are planning to give to these countries will not lead to any reduction in the assistance they provide to Africa. This, however, provides little but short-term reassurance: The main issue for the 1990s (as the World Bank statements set forth earlier indicate) is whether bilateral donors will continue to provide increasing amounts of aid to SSA as the 1990s unfold. Overall, there is little to suggest that they will—already, European and other Western donors have pledged substantial aid to both the Eastern European countries and the republics of the former Soviet Union that will run into tens of billions of dollars.

Yet the main influences on the level of European bilateral support to SSA would appear to lie outside the Eastern Europe aid-diversion question, with the principle exception of Germany. For Germany (which accounted for just under 10 percent of bilateral aid to SSA in 1989), the financial pressures on public expenditure flowing from unification are already substantial and are going to increase, which suggests that expansion of its bilateral aid program to Africa is unlikely to occur.[22] German bilateral aid to SSA had already fallen by 5 percent in real terms from 1985 to 1989, before these pressures became apparent. The larger Italian bilateral aid program to Africa (14 percent of total bilateral aid) has already peaked at $1.36 billion in 1988; it fell in real terms by 25 percent in 1989 and is unlikely to recover again in the near future. The root cause of this contraction, however, lies only minimally with broader developments in Europe; far more important are domestic, especially budgetary, pressures within the country. In the 1980s, the Italian bilateral aid program to Africa experienced the most remarkable expansion of any official program, though Italy also provided significant funds to a number of multilateral institutions, including those based in Italy. Indeed, it has been Italy's growing inability to maintain efficiency of its bilateral aid program together with domestic financial constraints that together are likely to lead to further contraction in the bilateral program in the 1990s.

Pressures for France and Britain to commit funds to Eastern Europe in preference to their traditional recipients in Africa are likely to have the least impact, not only because of history but also because of the existence of influential groups within both donor countries lobbying for Africa. Of all bilateral donors to Africa, France is most likely to maintain steady increases in aid to Africa; it was responsible in 1988 for almost 30 percent of bilateral aid to Africa.[23] If this occurs, however, it will relate not so much to wider events in Europe as to what is going on in French Africa and in France: support to present leaders of former African countries, support to former French colonies suffering from coffee and cocoa price collapse, support for and possible reorganization of the franc zone, and finally, support for French investors if and when devaluation of the CFA franc occurs.[24]

For Britain, the level and direction of aid flows are going to be determined crucially by the results of the forthcoming general elections. If the Conservatives win another election, bilateral aid to Africa is unlikely to see any marked acceleration; indeed, approval by Britain for the shift in the aid parameters of Lomé IV would suggest a continuation of greater British contributions to the EDF.[25] Were the Labour Party to win at some point, however, bilateral aid to Africa would increase rapidly: A commitment was made before the 1992 elections to reach the 0.7 percent

ODA/GNP ratio target in the life of the first parliament. However, even a doubling of British bilateral aid to Africa (equivalent to under 4 percent of total ODA to SSA) will not make a major difference to total aid flows. Similarly, although the Danish government has committed itself to a more rapid expansion of aid to Africa, this will not make a major difference (Danish aid was less than 2 percent of the total ODA to SSA in 1989), even if the wider events in Europe will have minimal impact on Denmark's expanded program.

Although to date there has been little publicity on the issue, the major effect the single market in Europe is likely to have on bilateral aid flows relates to current aid-tying arrangements. Although most individual European donors have been reluctant to comment on the matter, it is the view of senior EC Commission and OECD officials that as a result of the creation of the internal market, individual donors within the EC will no longer be able to tie the provision of goods and services in their bilateral aid to their own nationals and their own products. The implication is that individual European donors in their bilateral aid programs will not be permitted to link the aid they give exclusively to the services provided by their own nationals (in the case of technical assistance); the supply of their own goods (in the case of commodity aid and other product purchases); and the finance offered by their own banks, finance houses, export credit agencies, and shipping and insurance firms (in the case of these aid-related services). These donors will have to widen their tendering procedures to encompass all twelve EC member states. In effect, this would bring them in line with the EC's own EDF procedures.

The potential gains could be substantial. Those European countries reporting on the issue to the OECD stated that some 57 percent of their aid was tied or partially tied to imports from their countries, and analysis of price differences suggests that tied-aid goods are on average 20–25 percent higher than the lowest cost-competitive market prices. Simple arithmetic would suggest that on the basis of 1988 bilateral ODA flows from EC countries to SSA, overall purchases of tied goods could be "costing" SSA in excess of $730 million over the lowest competitive price.[26]

This of course raises the question of whether the level of bilateral aid would be maintained at current trend rates if the direct benefits to the donor countries of tying are threatened. Certainly there are several informal tying mechanisms that could continue to operate if formal tying arrangements are prohibited, which would offer a means of supporting the maintenance of aid flows at current levels.[27] Whatever the actual outcome, it is apparent that the issue of tied aid and procurement is likely to receive increased attention in the lead-up to and following the creation of the single market.

The ambiguity in likely trends in European bilateral aid to Africa just discussed is not as pronounced in the area of multilateral aid. Here it is much easier to indicate the likely pattern of flows at least in the first half of the 1990s, because major funding commitments have already been made. To be noted immediately is a difference with the situation in the second half of the 1980s: There are no indications that the special funding arrangements brought in then will be repeated in at least the first few years of the 1990s. For the EDF in particular, increased EC attention eastward is likely to be a major restraint in any attempt that might be made (none is currently on the agenda) for providing funding for Africa in addition to that provided under Lomé IV. It might, too, affect the quantity of aid that will be provided under the eighth EDF (1996–2000). Growth in multilateral aid flows to SSA are only expected to grow at a rate between 2.5 percent and a maximum of 4 percent to the mid-1990s.

It is useful to look briefly at funding for SSA from IDA and EDF, which together in 1988 accounted for 65 percent of all multilateral aid received. World Bank analysis indicates that SSA will receive a slightly smaller share of total IDA9 funds (47.2 percent) for the period 1991–1993 than it did for IDA8 (48.9 percent), which means that overall the subregion will receive only about a 2 percent rise in commitments for the 1991–1993 period. In real terms, this will mean much the same level of IDA funding as for the period up to 1991.

The seventh EDF under Lomé IV (1991–1995)[28] is valued at ECU 10.8 billion, a nominal rise of 46 percent over the sixth EDF but a real increase of only some 23 percent over Lomé III's aid resources, or an annual increase of about 4 percent a year.[29] This is far less than the ECU 15.5 billion requested by the African, Caribbean, and Pacific (ACP) negotiators, who based their figure on population increase, commodity price falls, and general economic decline. Of importance, however, is that commitments should be disbursed faster than under the sixth EDF both because of the new structural adjustment support (SAS) facility (11 percent of the total EDF) and the increase in the STABEX fund (14 percent of the total).

It is probably too early to speculate on the size of the eighth EDF, the bulk of which is to be used in Africa. However, one of the major beneficial economic effects of "Europe 1992" outlined in the Cecchini (1988) report is the higher rates of growth of the EC member countries. The voluminous Cecchini report was sponsored by the Commission to demonstrate the benefits that could accrue to the EC from removing barriers. To the extent that this does happen, it is tempting to argue that this could lead to more favorable amounts of aid that could be forthcoming from the EC Commission for the eighth EDF. But this optimism ignores the fact that aid funding by the commission is of minimal interest in comparison with other issues such as agricultural subsidies, trade arrangements and regional subsidies, and increasing pressures to commit further funds to Eastern Europe. It therefore seems safer to suggest that the formation of the single market is unlikely to have a significant impact in stimulating a further significant real rise in EC aid levels to SSA.

Finally, brief mention should be made of NGOs. In the first half of the 1990s, there is likely to be a continuation of the acceleration of funds channeled through and to NGOs, with both Northern-based and, increasingly, Southern NGOs benefiting, the latter especially through further expansion of the microprojects scheme.[30] As for funding sources, official contributions of NGO programs are likely to continue to expand, both under the terms of Lomé IV and through direct bilateral funding. What remains less certain is the extent to which the level of voluntary contributions for African development will respond to media coverage of events as they unfold. It is possible that the "oversaturation" by the media of Africa's development problems in the 1980s will lead to some sort of backlash, such that if the problems are repeated in the 1990s, the response from the public is not likely to be so great.[31] This is likely to be a more important reason for any potential decline in private funding of Africa in the 1990s from European sources than will any radical shift of funds from private sources from Africa to Eastern Europe.

□ *Issues*

The 1990s raise a number of policy issues that are likely to feature prominently in the Africa-Europe aid relationship as the decade unfolds. A key question is the extent to which the linkage of aid with structural adjustment will continue to dominate policy debate and implementation. A number of differing trends are apparent. Of more than passing interest is that the closer alignment of EC aid to structural adjustment has been evolving at a time when the World Bank, in particular, appears to have become somewhat disenchanted with at least the dominance of structural adjustment lending. As Hewitt (1990, 8) observes: "The latest (1990) World Bank Annual Report shows its adjustment lending (structural and sectoral) down from 30% in FY 1989 to 19% in 1990 on an IBRD commitment basis. This is a massive one-year fall." Under the influence especially of UNICEF, some bilateral agencies, and leading NGOs, the World Bank is expanding its funding of programs that address the "social dimensions" of adjustment through a type of targeted intervention not far removed from the basic needs-types of intervention dominant since the mid-1970s.[32] It is quite possible there will be a further shift toward project-specific funding in the coming decade.

This does not necessarily mean that the EC is going to find itself out on a limb, independently executing policies that Washington was vigorously promoting ten years ago but is now pushing less vigorously. The SAS programs are to be part of the national indicative programs and, given the shortage of foreign exchange in Africa, could continue to be little more than the balance-of-payments support initiatives that became commonplace in the second half of the 1980s. The EC has recently commenced a substantial research project (DIAL) that is attempting to provide policy guidelines for integrating structural adjustment initiatives into a longer-term framework of development. It is likely that the results of this initiative will steer the EC Commission away from the early orthodoxies of structural adjustment programs.

What appears to be new from Washington is a greater focus on some of the basic conditions upon which aid efficiency is predicated. Uppermost are issues such as the institutional framework, the efficiency of delivery systems, and more generally, the broad area of governance. The World Bank, in particular, is already investing considerable time, human resources, and money (hundreds of millions of dollars) into "capacity-building" initiatives in Africa. The purpose of such approaches is to enhance—often to create—a local capacity within government and key public institutions to assist administrations to manage effectively their economies and, in the process, to reduce their dependence upon external technical assistance. What remains to be seen is the extent to which this type of initiative will come to dominate the aid relationship in the 1990s and how far individual donors are willing to support it. In private, many of the leading European donors to Africa remain skeptical, at least of the ambitious nature of the initiative, although this does not necessarily mean either that their own programs will escape influence by the initiative or that they will refuse to contribute to funding World Bank programs. Some have already indicated their willingness to support these projects.

A related issue likely to receive increasing prominence in the 1990s is the linkage of aid provision with political reforms and human rights. Although donors have maintained that human rights issues have always had a place in aid decisions, the changes taking place in Eastern and Central Europe have played a major role in raising this issue on the agenda for African aid and perhaps altering its importance.33 Thus, for instance, the Lomé IV Convention incorporates a new article linking development cooperation with human rights performance, a connection that mirrors increasing concern over the issue by bilateral European donors (such as France and Britain), even if little is specifically spelled out in terms of action and practical policy implication in the new convention. One indication of the manner in which the linkage of human rights and aid questions might evolve in the 1990s comes from comments that bilateral European donors have increasingly been making on the subject. For instance in June 1990, British Foreign Secretary Douglas Hurd stated that British aid to Africa in the 1990s would be linked to the same political criteria as for Eastern Europe: "Those who persist with repressive policies, with corrupt management or with wasteful and discredited economic systems, should not expect us to support their folly with scarce aid resources which could be better used elsewhere" (*African Economic Digest,* July 2, 1990).

Such statements (and the human rights clause in the convention) are strong on rhetoric. What remains unclear is precisely what difference in practice such a concern will make to traditional recipients of European aid. In particular, one still has little sense of the extent to which human rights considerations will override broader or different political, economic, or even military objectives of donor governments. Thus, an October 1990 report on political repression in Malawi by the human rights group Africa Watch challenged Britain to reduce its aid to Malawi because of widespread human rights abuses.[34] No comment from the British government was forthcoming. For their part, African governments have expressed their concern about the extent to which donors might wish to condition aid flows upon Western concepts of democracy.

Besides highlighting the human rights issue, the British foreign secretary in his statement also added that aid programs in Africa in the 1990s would favor countries that adopted market economies. Support for and promotion of private-sector initiatives by all Western donors (multilateral and bilateral, European and non-European) became increasing features of donor approaches to African aid, especially of most European bilateral donors, as the 1980s developed. This trend is likely to continue well into the 1990s—indeed, it will probably intensify. Conditionality related to the retreat of the state and support for nascent private-sector development is likely to become more widespread and probably more specific in nature. For instance, the funding of packages of joint-venture agreements with, for instance, the International Finance Corporation (IFC), the Commonwealth Development Corporation (CDC), and the European Investment Bank (EIB) is likely to expand rapidly, together with those supported by European bilateral agencies such as the Danish Industrialization Fund for Developing Countries (IFU).

Projections of future multilateral and bilateral official aid to SSA suggest that the balance between bilateral and multilateral funding is unlikely to change much, at least in the early part of the 1990s. This leaves open the question of whether European donor preference is tilting toward or away from the shift to multilateral aid. To the extent that individual member states of the EC perceive 1992 as beneficial to their national interests and that EC-wide initiatives on Eastern Europe appear to "work," one might expect to see a relative shift in favor of EC aid initiatives in Africa. Yet such a trend needs to be counterbalanced by the exposure of some major problems of EDF projects and programs (frequently described in detail in the annual reports of the Court of Auditors) and the knowledge that EDF funds usually follow a tortuously long and drawn-out route from indicative program plan through to commitment and finally to disbursement. By the end of 1988, for instance, only 16 percent of the sixth EDF funds had been spent; funds as yet unspent for the fourth and fifth EDFs were 6 and 29, respectively. What remains uncertain is whether member states concerned with what is perceived as the overly bureaucratic nature of aid administration in Brussels see their best interest in continuing to attempt to reform the system or in retreating to the more direct gains that can be made from expanding their bilateral programs.

A final new feature of Lomé IV with important implications for SSA needs highlighting—namely, a change in the eligibility of countries to make claims under STABEX. Under the provision of Lomé III, countries qualified for receipt of STABEX funds for relevant primary agricultural commodities if there had been a qualifying drop in export earnings, but the contraction of earnings was calculated not in relation to current exchange rates but to a 5 percent (10 percent for least-developed countries) band averaged from the previous five years' rates of exchange. The effect of this so-called tunnel mechanism was that countries that suffered sharp falls in their export earnings and sharp falls in their exchange rates consistently failed to qualify for STABEX payments. Generally, CFA franc countries that experienced rapid falls in the value of their coffee and cocoa exports tended to benefit, whereas non-CFA franc countries did not.

Under Lomé IV, qualification for STABEX payments will be made in reference to ECU values of export earnings, and at CIF (cost, insurance, freight) European values rather than FOB (free on board) the country of shipment. This means that all African countries that experience the required fall in the export earnings of qualifying products will qualify for STABEX payments in the 1990s. Because of the "tunnel" calculations of exchange rates, some African countries, such as Uganda, have not received STABEX payments for over fifteen years, despite massive drops in export earnings.[35] Now they will start to do so. Although this is certainly a welcome move, doubt has been expressed about whether even the increased amount of STABEX funds under Lomé IV—ECU 1.5 billion, compared with ECU 950 million for Lomé III—will be sufficient to meet all claims, especially if the downward trends in coffee and cocoa prices persist.[36]

■ Conclusions

Europe will continue to be a major donor to SSA in the 1990s. Indeed, although the pace of growth of official aid to the SSA subregion is unlikely to match that experienced in the second half of the 1980s, aid levels are set to grow. By the end of the 1990s, SSA will be even more dependent upon aid than it was at the start of the present decade.

The changes within Europe resulting from both 1992 and the opening up of Eastern Europe are likely to bring only marginal changes to the Africa-Europe aid relationship in the short term. Yet the manner in which the EC is addressing the twin issues of democracy and economic development in Eastern Europe is likely to affect its relations with Africa in three ways: First, initiatives to support the private sector in Africa, indigenous and external, are likely to be expanded. Second, human rights issues will certainly form an important part of the rhetoric of aid to Africa in the 1990s, though the manner in which these concerns by donors will be fleshed out in practice remains unclear. Third, in the short term there is likely to be little rechanneling of European official aid flows earmarked for Africa into Eastern Europe.

The expanded financial commitments of the EC and its members to support the new democratic movements in Europe and to encourage the forces of democracy and openness in the former Soviet Union are likely to produce two adverse effects. First, any calls for further aid in the period up to 1996 (in the form of new facilities) are far less likely to receive a positive response, or at least a level of response similar to what was forthcoming in the second half of the 1980s. Second, if the problems in Eastern Europe and the former Soviet Union upon which current (large) aid commitments are based persist (and even intensify), the funding of the eighth EDF, from 1996 to 2000, is likely to be additionally constrained.

The form that aid to SSA will take is likely to shift during the 1990s, as it did in both the 1970s and the 1980s. Although the macroeconomic context of aid insertion will continue to be important, greater concern will evolve about longer-term development issues, programs targeted to those marginalized by adjustment-linked lending, and a series of institutionally related factors inhibiting efficiency of aid programs and projects. Issues such as these will all lead to a broadening of the focus of aid and to even greater financial support to the projects of NGOs.

Lomé IV has brought some changes to African-European aid relations. There has been both a nominal and real increase in EDF funds, together with the IDA9 funds and projections of European bilateral commitments, but these are unlikely to provide aid in quantities sufficient for significant rises in per capita income to be sustained into the 1990s. The new SAS facility is being introduced at a time when other influential donors are placing less emphasis in their programs on structural adjustment linkages, although there is sufficient flexibility in the EDF scheme to prevent this particular mechanism from being fixed in an outdated time warp. At least the rate of disbursement of EDF funds is likely to be slightly more rapid than the dismal performance achieved during the 1980s.

Much of the literature on aid to Africa highlights the large and growing gap between external resource requirements and the likely level of external flows, of which ODA is the largest component. Impact and effectiveness questions are often set aside in the desire to bridge this gap.

But even if in macroeconomic terms aid to Africa in the 1990s continues to be provided in inadequate quantities, the subregion is set to become increasingly aid-dependent as the 1990s progress, and more and more of the poorer countries will not only be aid-dependent but become aid-driven.

A final—and perhaps more speculative—thought arises from a different attitude to foreign aid that some of the new Eastern European recipients are projecting. There is in some of these recipients a wariness about receiving large quantities of aid money, not only because of a fear of the costs of aid-dependency but also because of a belief that this could lead to lessened concern about other equally, or even more important, economic issues—such as investment, technology transfer, patent sharing, and export-promoting initiatives—the careful nurturing of which might well better provide them for a future in which the economies are internally rather than externally driven and are therefore more internationally interdependent. Could it be that as links develop between African countries and the new democracies of Europe, one will begin to see a more extensive questioning by African aid recipients of the merits of having their own economic growth and development wedded ever more tightly to dependence upon donor handouts, not least from Europe?

■ Notes

1. For a fuller discussion of the classification and anomalies in the country grouping, see Riddell (1990a, 23–32).

2. The share of total ODA going to South Asia fell from 21 percent in the mid-1970s to 17 percent by the end of the 1980s; the share going to the Middle East and North Africa fell even more sharply, from 30 percent to 16 percent, respectively. The shares going to Latin America and the Caribbean remained fairly static, whereas the share going to "Other Asia" and Oceania also rose, from 17 percent in the mid-1970s to 23 percent by the end of the 1980s. (See OECD 1989a, 212–213.)

3. Similar perverse trends are apparent in relation to foreign direct investment (FDI) inflows. According to OECD data, whereas in the three-year period 1980–1982 direct private investment accounted for 9.9 percent of total net resource flows to SSA, the ratio of foreign investment to total external inflows had fallen to just 2.3 percent for the years 1985–1987. In contrast, the ratio of FDI to total resource flow for all developing countries between the same periods rose from 10.8 percent to 14.4 percent. It fell only marginally from 5.3 percent to 4.2 percent for all low-income countries, stayed roughly the same for Asia, and almost doubled for countries of the Western Hemisphere (OECD 1989b).

4. "European" here is used in the OECD sense of both bilateral OECD donors and the funds from the European Development Fund (EDF). It should be noted that the EDF figures differ from the figures on ODA usually provided by the EC Commission. These latter figures are usually higher because they include European Investment Bank (EIB) funds outside the EDF.

5. Ex-post justification for such a shift has been supported by the increasing

influence of Britain in EC aid decisions—for instance, over food aid policy under Minister Christopher Patten, Secretary of State for the Environment.

6. In most countries, the bulk of the data found in the annual reports of development cooperation produced by the United Nations Development Program (UNDP) come from these sources.

7. These countries were China, Cuba, the German Democratic Republic, India, Libya, Pakistan, and Yugoslavia.

8. Not known is the extent to which these non-DAC flows would have qualified as concessionary flows under the DAC definition.

9. Thus a report from the Economic Planning Ministry in Uganda concluded that during the ten-year period 1975–1985, foreign assistance made no positive impact on the economy.

10. In a speech to the Overseas Development Institute's 1990 conference on African development, the executive vice-president of the International Finance Corporation (IFC), Sir William Ryrie, stated boldly that Western aid to Africa over the past decade has been a failure. See also Mosley (1990).

11. The gap would have been even greater had SSA countries not rescheduled significant quantities of debt owed.

12. For a more detailed treatment of this issue see Riddell (1987, 85ff).

13. The traditional form of program aid is unconditional or loosely conditioned balance-of-payments support.

14. Between 1981 and 1988, Côte d'Ivoire received over $2 billion from the Washington-based institutions and from France (Riddell 1990a, 172).

15. We are still very far away from anything resembling serious coordination of aid initiatives among donors in Africa. All major donors assert their support for coordination, but few are willing to let that make a major difference in their own programs.

16. For instance, by October 1988, 70 percent of the time period for Lomé III had elapsed, but only 10 percent of the funds allocated had been disbursed.

17. In the case of EC funds, aid tying was extended to all member countries.

18. Only ECU 300 million of this could be considered "additional" funds: ECU 200 million were from Lomé III reserves and ECU 100 million from a Council of Ministers decision. The remainder was to come from accelerated disbursements of the indicative programs.

19. Many NGOs are reluctant to concentrate exclusively on income-generating initiatives; they wish also to emphasize the social and community aspects of their projects.

20. These relate, inter alia, to investment and saving ratios, export prices, import requirements, debt-servicing obligations, foreign investment inflows, and expected growth rates.

21. Some economies (such as Uganda) could already be described as "aid-driven."

22. Africa is now the largest recipient of German aid.

23. Over 80 percent of French bilateral aid went to French dependencies or former French colonies.

24. Internal pressures from the French business community and the government treasury to trim the aid budget have been opposed by both the president and the Ministry of Cooperation. Some channeling of aid shares away from former French possessions could, however, occur.

25. Note that Britain was not among the European partners to lobby for a sizable increase in the EDF under Lomé IV; this was the prerogative of the French.

26. There is hope, too, that the movement toward greater trade liberalization will also encourage a reduction in aid tied to the use of mixed credits.

27. "For example, a donor country may provide technical assistance so that projects are prepared in such a way that aid funds are allocated to suppliers in this country even though they are not tied. This means that the abolition of informal tying will not necessarily lead to the eradication of this phenomenon" (report of the Netherlands National Advisory Council, 1989, quoted in Davenport and Page 1990, 59).

28. Lomé IV is to run for ten years, but the seventh EDF is to run only for the first five. It remains uncertain on what basis the eighth EDF figures will be based.

29. Total aid under Lomé IV amounts to ECU 12 billion, of which ECU 10.8 billion consists of EDF funds, and the remainder of European Investment Bank (EIB) funds.

30. Of the limited evaluations of the EC's microprojects schemes that have been done, indications suggest that a high proportion (over 25 percent) of projects are developmentally unsound. Greater awareness of problems of the microprojects scheme, however, is more likely to lead to change in rules for accepting projects than in any short-term decline in funding.

31. Some argue that this has already happened. In December 1990, famine was threatening millions in Sudan, Ethiopia, Mozambique, and Angola, and aid workers were predicting more deaths than occurred in the Ethiopian famine of 1984–1985. But the international response has, correspondingly, been minimal (*Financial Times,* December 12, 1990).

32. These would include what is called PAPSCA (Program for Alleviation of Poverty and the Social Costs of Adjustment) in Uganda and, more recently, PAMSCAD (Program of Action to Mitigate Social Costs of Structural Adjustment) in Ghana, the latter valued at over $100 million.

33. A mid-1990 debate among members of the EC's development council unanimously recognized that "it is very difficult to demand very strict conditions from Eastern European countries which are returning to democracy and at the same time not to make aid to developing countries dependent up to a certain extent upon similar criteria" (*EEC Bulletin,* September 1990 [Kampala, Uganda], 4).

34. In 1988, Malawi was the fifth largest recipient of British aid, the third in Africa after Kenya and Tanzania. Between 1986 and 1988, British bilateral aid to Malawi rose from 15 million to 46 million pounds.

35. In 1986, Uganda exported 140,000 metric tons of coffee, for which it earned $400 million; in 1989, it exported 176,000 metric tons, and earned only $263 million.

36. As Stichele (1990, 3) writes: "The new rules basically aim at giving less to more countries. The increased allocation of 1.5 billion ECU will barely cushion certain countries from the blow of the collapse of the International Cocoa and Coffee Agreements."

10

Prospects for North-South Negotiations in a Changing International Political Economy

Eve N. Sandberg
George E. Shambaugh IV

Throughout the post–World War II era, North-South negotiations have failed to provide Southern states with many of the trade and aid benefits they sought. There have been, however, a limited number of successful cases of North-South bargaining. Each of these cases shares a set of common bargaining conditions under which successful outcomes for Southern states were achieved. In this chapter, we identify the conditions under which Southern states were able to bargain successfully with Northern states. Moreover, we demonstrate how probable changes in the international political economy of the 1990s will influence bargaining outcomes in future North-South relations.

Our chapter contains three major sections. The first section identifies the criteria by which we define a "successful" case of Southern bargaining. In the next section, we characterize the conditions under which successful Southern bargaining with Northern states occurs. Finally, we identify changes taking place in the international political economy of the 1990s and the implications of these changes for successful bargaining outcomes for Southern states engaged in North-South negotiations.

We analyze five cases in which groups of Southern states bargained with the North to gain trade and aid concessions. These groups include the Organization of Petroleum Exporting Countries (OPEC); the Group of 77; the African, Caribbean, and Pacific (ACP) countries; the Association of Southeast Asian Nations (ASEAN), and the Latin American debt coalition (LADC) (Argentina, Brazil, and Mexico). In 1973, OPEC provided the first real flexing of muscle by Southern states in the post–World War II period. Both the Group of 77 and the ACP countries built on the OPEC effort, one with more success than the other. ASEAN is an enduring example of regional coordination among Southern states. Although ASEAN was established primarily as a regional security organization, its member states expanded the ASEAN agenda to include economic concerns. ASEAN now negotiates as a regional group with the EC, Japan, and the United States. Finally, the countries of LADC attempted to alleviate their debt problem in the early 1980s.

In addition to traditional primary and secondary data sources, our analysis is informed by a survey we conducted of the ACP and EEC signatories to the Lomé IV accords.

■ Criteria for Evaluating Success

We define success according to both instrumental (goal-oriented) and institutional criteria. Most observers argue that cases of successful Southern bargaining must include the achievement of instrumental objectives. For the purposes of this chapter, instrumental objectives include the achievement of short- and long-term economic and political goals. We believe that, given the power differential between Northern and Southern states, each time the Southern states have been able to achieve even incremental short- or long-term economic and political gains in their negotiations with Northern states, those negotiations can be characterized as instrumental successes.

The achievement of the South's long-term economic and political goals requires the institutionalization of ongoing negotiations with Northern states. Institutionalization is necessary to monitor and safeguard negotiated gains. Hence, we include institutionalization criteria in our definition of success.

Institutional success is defined in terms of six variables: loyalty, voice, exit, maintenance (dues, coordination), membership expansion, and incremental expansion of issue-areas (see Table 10.1). Our criteria of loyalty, voice, and exit are adopted from Hirschman's analysis of institutions (Hirschman 1970). Hirschman argues that the exercise of exit, voice, or loyalty by members of an organization are indicators of organizational performance. Voice refers to attempts by members to change the policies of an organization. The exercise of voice indicates that despite disagreements over specific policies, members consider the institution important enough (successful) to remain affiliated. Alternatively, members may choose to exit from an organization rather than attempt to influence it. Exit by many members is one indicator of institutional failure. Loyalty (maintaining membership) results from one of two factors: the extent to which members are willing to trade off the certainty of exit against the uncertainties of an improvement in the service of the organization; and the members' estimations of their ability to influence the institution.

Institutional maintenance has two components. The payment of dues demonstrates that the services provided by the institution are valued by its members. The ability to coordinate issues demonstrates significant agreement on the value, purpose, and continued functioning of the institution.

Table 10.1 Defining Successful Southern Bargaining with Northern States

	Failure			Success	
	OPEC	Group of 77	L.A. Debt Coalition	ACP	ASEAN
Instrumental Success					
1. Short-Term					
A. Economic	Yes	Yes/No	No	Yes	Yes
B. Political	No	Yes	Yes	Yes	Yes
2. Long-Term					
A. Economic	No	No	No	Yes	Yes
B. Political	No	No	No	Yes	Yes
Institutional Success					
1. Loyalty	No	Yes	No	Yes	Yes
2. Voice	Yes	Yes	No	Yes	Yes/No
3. Exit	Yes/No	No	Yes	No	No
4. Maintenance					
A. Dues	Yes	No	No	Yes	Yes
B. Coordination	No	Yes/No	No	Yes	Yes
5. Membership expansion	Yes/No	Yes	No	Yes	Yes
6. Incremental issue-area expansion	No	No	No	Yes	Yes

Membership expansion indicates nonmember perceptions of institutional success. Finally, the incremental expansion of issue-areas demonstrates the members' calculations that their institution can achieve their goals in new areas.

As Table 10.1 indicates, only two of the five cases we analyzed can be considered successful instances of Southern bargaining with Northern states. Both the ACP and ASEAN groups were successful institutionally as well as in achieving their short- and long-term goals.

☐ *Success Cases*

The ACP Group. As other chapters in this book have described in detail, forty-four ACP countries negotiated with ten EEC states in 1975 to sign the first Lomé (Togo) accords of aid and trade. Lomé II accords were signed in 1980, Lomé III in 1985, and Lomé IV in 1990. Lomé IV, which will have a duration of ten years, includes sixty-nine ACP and twelve EEC countries.

Many Western social scientists have argued that the long- and short-term economic and political gains of the ACP states have not been great enough to consider ACP negotiations with the EC successful. Some of our survey respondents also indicated that they were dissatisfied with various aspects of the Lomé accords. For example:

African Negotiator:
Little progress was made on the questions of debt, commodities, and the financial package, issues which are very important to the economies of the ACP.

Some of the most frequently cited complaints in the survey were slow disbursements from the EC; poor implementation of regional development projects; continued trade problems regarding "rules of origin"; and the use of nontariff trade barriers such as elaborate forms and procedures.

Many of Lomé's critics have cited statistics to demonstrate that ACP countries have suffered both relative and absolute declines in trade with the EC since 1975. Our data confirm this criticism. Figure 10.1 shows that the small increase in total trade (exports plus imports) between ACP and EC states was overshadowed by the rather dramatic increase in total trade between all non-oil-exporting less-developed countries (LDCs) and the EC. Figure 10.2 confirms that the share of ACP exports and imports to the European Community has generally declined relative to other LDCs.

The contraction of the world economy that characterized many of the years that the Lomé accords were in force intensified competition among all LDCs. Many ACP officials acknowledge their countries' inability to compete relative to other LDCs. Yet we argue that in a truly liberalized trade system, without the Lomé accords, the ACP countries' might have suffered even greater relative losses. This argument is supported by our survey results. Despite the relative decline in market share, respondents noted the salience of Lomé in safeguarding ACP market access. As one respondent mused:

Pacific negotiator:
Just think what would have happened without Lomé!

Another respondent hypothesized:

Caribbean Negotiator:
Many commodities and other products would have suffered tremendously in direct competition with products of other non-ACP states.

Our survey of Lomé IV negotiators indicates a keen awareness on their part of the tremendous benefit of the accords despite the criticisms. In answer to our question "Do you believe that the Lomé accords have benefited the ACP countries?" sample responses were as follows:

Caribbean Negotiator:
Unquestionably, they have, whether one looks at gains from preferred market access and prices or whether one looks at direct development assis-

NORTH-SOUTH NEGOTIATIONS IN A CHANGING ECONOMY

Figure 10.1 Total EC-ACP Trade as a Percentage of Total EC-LDC Trade

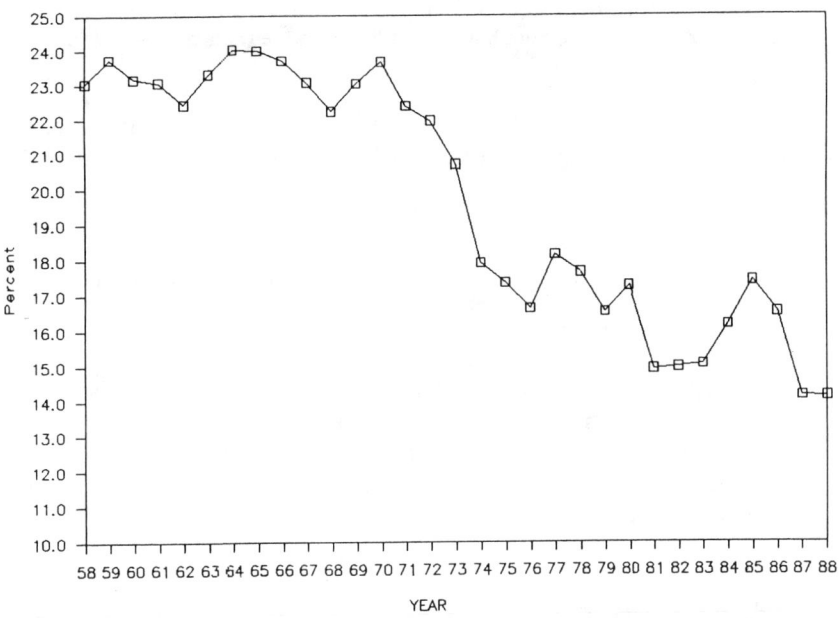

Figure 10.2 ACP-EC *X* and *M* as a Percentage of LDC-EC *X* and *M*

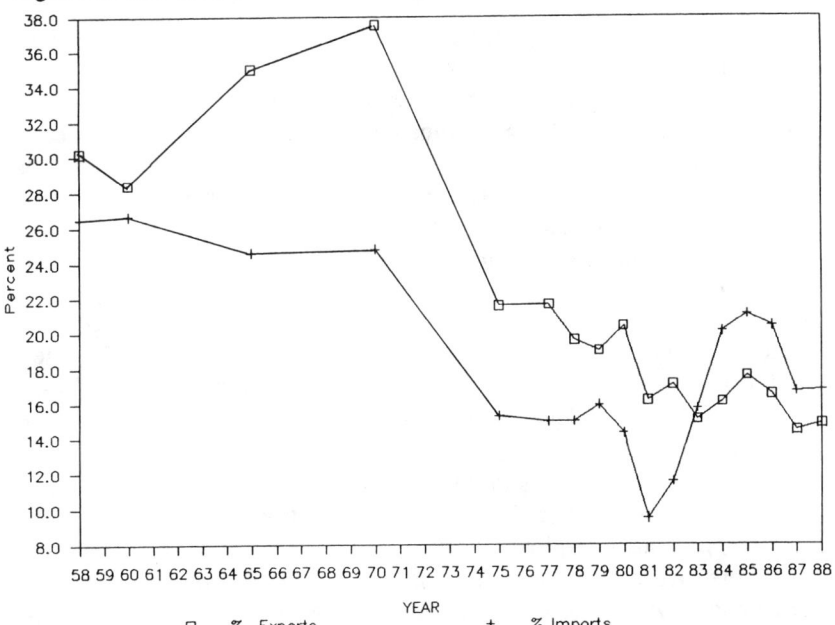

tance. Aid from the EC compares very favorably with that from other multilateral institutions.

Otherwise we would not have benefited from the trade access and foreign aid.

In answer to our question "Why do you believe that the successive accords were negotiated and signed even though some were unhappy with them?" one respondent noted:

Caribbean Negotiator:
I was not aware of [the] claim—even if all countries are not happy with all aspects, their decision to continue reflects, on balance, acceptance of the whole package.

Other respondents indicated support for Lomé, on balance, because particular components of the Lomé package supported important sectors of their economy. Moreover, despite criticisms that Lomé yielded only limited gains, negotiators endorsed successive accords because they considered the institutionalization of negotiations to be an indicator of success.

African Negotiator:
Both parties were committed to cooperation and they believe that where either party may or has found problems, these could be tackled in the next negotiations and hopefully produce a better agreement.

Many negotiators have noted publicly, or in response to our questionnaire, that the short- and long-term benefits of Lomé are substantial. Some of the short-term gains noted by our respondents included increased foreign aid, including EDF grants and EIB funding; greater market access; modest debt reductions; technical assistance; and special programs for particular commodities such as bananas, bauxite, rice, rum, and sugar.

Our respondents also noted what we have characterized as long-term gains: the implementation of measures to increase absorption of financial assistance; administrative assistance; infrastructure support (especially roads and electricity); the initiation of sectoral programs in agriculture, fisheries, forestry, and tourism; increased support for the role of women in development; technical environmental consultation; and the establishment of a trade and development service to develop and promote ACP trade in the EC.

The ACP negotiations with the EC can also be considered successful in terms of our institutional criteria. The institutional success of the ACP group is demonstrated by the loyalty, voice, and exit options. No ACP members have left the group since the first accord was signed; all members remain loyal. As previously discussed, our survey of ACP negotiators who participated in the Lomé IV accords reveals that most Southern members of the ACP group believe that the gains of remaining with the group provide greater benefits than the option of exit provides. Moreover, the successful institutionalization of the ACP group provides its members with the confidence that they can exercise voice and perhaps influence the course of negotiations over time.

The successful institutional maintenance of the ACP group includes the financing of an ACP Secretariat that provides background negotiating support and facilitates coordination of bargaining positions on negotiating issues among member states. Although ACP members may not individually pay dues to support the Secretariat, the members have extracted a financial commitment from the EC states to maintain its operations. Were they not committed to institutional maintenance, members would seek individualized uses for those resources. ACP states bear indirect costs to maintain their institution and continue to use it as a forum to develop and pursue their agendas. This fulfills our maintenance criteria of dues and coordination.

ACP membership has increased by over 50 percent since negotiations were initiated with the EEC. In order to preserve the relative gains derived from the Lomé negotiations, additional states from Latin America and Asia have been denied requests for membership in the ACP group.

Our final category of institutional success is met by the incremental expansion of issue-areas addressed in successive Lomé negotiations. Lomé IV, for example, included new negotiations relevant to the structural adjustment programs, women in development, human rights, opposition to South African apartheid, and environmental concerns.

The ASEAN group. ASEAN originated as a regional security group whose original members included Indonesia, Malaysia, the Philippines, Singapore, and Thailand. Over time, however, ASEAN has evolved as a regional organization used for both economic and security negotiations with Northern states. As one noted Southeast Asian scholar reports, "Overall, it would appear that ASEAN has been able to achieve some solid economic success and greater diplomatic leverage acting as a 'collective-bargaining' force" (Crone 1983, 51). The success of Lomé I, in which the ACP states successfully negotiated new aid and trade arrangements with the EEC, prompted ASEAN officials to request that the EC states also negotiate new aid and trade arrangements with the ASEAN states.

The ASEAN states achieved some of their short-term goals by successfully negotiating foreign aid increases from the EC to their members (see Figure 10.3). The increase in foreign aid from the EC should be considered a short-term rather than long-term success because the levels of aid have been renegotiated intermittently. As Figure 10.3 demonstrates, ASEAN was able to negotiate an enormous increase in Japanese foreign assistance in time for its twentieth anniversary in 1987.

Figure 10.3 EC and Japanese Aid to ASEAN

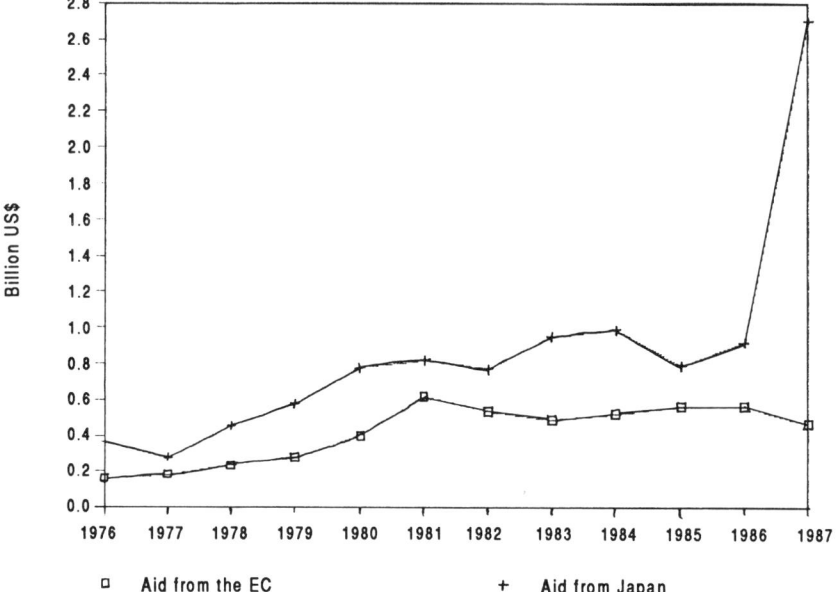

This should also be considered a short-term success. However, ASEAN was less successful in negotiating trade concessions because of intervention from the U.S. trade representatives who feared increased competition from ASEAN within the EC.

ASEAN has made some progress in achieving two long-term economic goals. First, the member states have been partially successful in resisting pressure by the home governments of foreign multinationals operating in ASEAN states. The ASEAN members, and Indonesia in particular, have managed to retain national control of their own manufacturing sectors. Second, the group has secured technical cooperation for several long-term development projects.

The ASEAN group meets our criteria of institutional success in every category (see Table 10.1). Despite the enormous political and ideological differences among the governing regimes of the member states, all states have remained loyal members of the group. Voice is exercised, but exit is not. The fact that ASEAN members have pursued a common negotiating front that parallels their own individual efforts is particularly significant because each of the member states exports similar products and competes with the others for foreign investment, trade, and aid. Each member has supported the financial costs of this regional group, and formal meetings of officials from technical and political ministries of the member states meet on a regular basis. Membership expanded when Brunei joined in 1984. Thus, our criteria for membership expansion, institutional maintenance, loyalty, voice, and exit are met.

Finally, ASEAN has continued to expand its agenda for negotiations with Northern states. Its original focus on negotiating guarantees of regional security has expanded to include issues of aid, trade, and technical assistance. Since the mid-1970s, ASEAN has initiated negotiations with Northern states on a wide range of issue-areas: lobbying Japan to create ASEBEX, an institution to stabilize commodity prices modeled after the ACP-EEC agreement; forming the ASEAN Development Corporation with the support of Japanese banks; promoting conferences with the EC to enhance EC-ASEAN industrial cooperation; and running trade fairs with Australia and Japan.

□ *Unsuccessful Cases*

OPEC. In 1973, the Organization of Petroleum Exporting Countries (OPEC) achieved two short-term goals: raising the international price of oil and nationalizing international oil companies operating in OPEC states. This accomplishment has been characterized as "the most effective exercise of power by the South against the North since the conclusion of the Second World War" (Krasner 1985, p. 108) At the same time, however, OPEC failed to achieve its short-term goal of altering U.S. policy in the Middle East.

Despite short-term increases in oil prices, OPEC has not achieved its long-term goal of autonomous control over the international price of oil. Alternative energy sources, conservation efforts, and changes in the international economy have influenced the international demand for oil as well as its price. Both demand and price remain beyond OPEC's control. In addition, individual OPEC members have resorted to independent behavior that often undercuts OPEC's collective leverage against Northern states.

In 1975, OPEC members believed they could capitalize on their initial success and introduce major changes in the structure of North-South relations. OPEC insisted that broader issues of concern to LDCs be included in the Conference on International Economic Cooperation (CIEC), which Northern states had hoped would focus exclusively on energy topics. Despite two years of negotiations, the CIEC ended in failure. Even with the help that OPEC provided, the CIEC failed to reach agreement on a single issue of importance to either set of participants.

OPEC has endured, but it cannot be judged an institutional success.

Although OPEC members have not exited completely from the organization, they can be characterized as disloyal. Disputes over production quotas and price levels and frequent production cheating among its members prevent OPEC from achieving institutional success. OPEC states contribute to maintain the formal structures of the organization, but the disputes that erupt during its semiannual conferences demonstrate the inability of the member states to coordinate their policy positions successfully. The most extraordinary example of internal conflict and a complete lack of coordination is Iraq's recent accusation of Kuwait's noncompliance with OPEC policies and its resulting invasion and annexation of that country.

OPEC has not expanded membership since its prominence in 1975. And after its failed attempt to tie LDC concerns to a meeting with the International Energy Agency in 1975, there have been no additional attempts to expand OPEC's agenda beyond oil price and supply. OPEC weathered the Iran-Iraq war, but the Gulf War may well mark the end of its ability to coordinate the policies of its members even on this narrow agenda.

The Group of 77. The Group of 77 was organized in 1962 primarily to win a United Nations General Assembly vote to call for the formation of the United Nations Conference on Trade and Development (UNCTAD). The establishment of UNCTAD was the first of many initiatives by the Group of 77 to restructure completely the international trade and financial systems.

The two major achievements of the Group of 77 have been the establishment of UNCTAD as a new forum for debating Southern trade concerns and the promotion of a unified call by LDCs for a new international economic order (NIEO). The Group of 77 has been successful in drawing attention to the concerns of LDCs, but it has failed to achieve concessions from Northern states to address those concerns. On balance, the Group of 77 has failed to attain its economic and political goals in bargaining with Northern states.

The Group of 77 has maintained itself institutionally. Its members have remained loyal, even though they voice disagreement over the priority of issues that must be negotiated with the North. Unfortunately, the Group of 77's inability to set priorities has been a source of frustration to Northern officials who refuse to negotiate a total restructuring of the international political economy. Membership in the group has expanded, but members acknowledge the lack of success by the Group of 77 and frequently choose other means of negotiating with the North. To date, the Group of 77 cannot be considered an institutional success.

The Latin American debt coalition. In 1983, Northern states with large outstanding loans to Southern debtors feared that the presidents of Argentina, Brazil, and Mexico were attempting to form a coalition to deal with Latin American debt. Each of these Latin American countries owed in excess of $80 billion to multilateral, governmental, and private-sector creditors.

Many citizens of Southern states hoped that the enormity of the debt of these three countries would provide leverage by which Northern creditors would be forced to implement programs of debt relief that would become models for all Southern states. The failure to achieve a Latin American debt coalition dashed one of the most recent hopes of Southern states for effective negotiations with Northern countries on the most urgent problem of the South.

The inability of Argentina, Brazil, and Mexico to institutionalize their bargaining with Northern creditors is a major reason for their lack of success in achieving their short- and long-term goals of debt relief. Although it was widely reported that high officials from the three countries met to discuss a common approach when negotiating with the North, no country would publicly acknowledge that such consultations were occurring. Loyalty was nowhere in evidence. If there was such an agreement, exit was opted for by Mexico after the North offered only Mexico a unique package. No other LDC could step forward to replace the bargaining position of Mexico—the country occupied a special status for U.S. policymakers because of its geographic proximity, shared immigration, and energy concerns. Moreover, the enormity of its debt and production capacity placed it in a category shared only by Argentina and Brazil. Thus, there could be no effective membership expansion after Mexico's defection.

■ Conditions That Foster Successful Bargaining

The next step after identifying what composes a "successful" case of Southern negotiations with Northern states is to determine when success is likely. In this section, we discuss four conditions under which successful Southern bargaining occurs. These conditions have been derived by an analysis of the cases we discussed in the first section. As shown in Table 10.2, the conditions necessary for success are to have (1) win-sets for both Northern and Southern bargainers; (2) limits on the scope of the negotiations; (3) selective targeting of Northern states; and (4) routinized North-South negotiations.

First, win-sets for both Northern and Southern bargainers must be present for successful negotiations to take place. The potential for gain is the primary motivation for entering into a bargaining relationship. The potential gains one receives by cooperating must be greater than those received by not cooperating, or no agreement will be reached. This does

Table 10.2 Conditions Needed for Successful North-South Bargaining

Condition Success	Failure			Success	
	OPEC	Group of 77	L.A. Debt Coalition	ACP	ASEAN
1. Win-sets for both North and South	No	No	Yes	Yes	Yes
2. Limited scope of the agenda	No	No	No	Yes	Yes
3. Selective targeting	No	No	No	Yes	Yes
4. Routinized North-South negotiations	No	No	No	Yes	Yes

not necessarily imply that the agreement reached will provide the best possible outcome for both players. As is often evident in North-South relations, the agreement must be perceived to be better than no agreement at all, but the negotiators need not have achieved all of their objectives for the outcome to be perceived favorably, as one respondent noted:

African Negotiator:
   Negotiations by their very nature imply that concessions must be made to accommodate the requests and account of the positions of both the parties concerned. There is naturally a margin of difference, therefore, between the objectives the negotiators set out to achieve and the results achieved. Nevertheless, whatever may have been the final outcome of the negotiations and the failure to attain the initial objectives, the advantages derived from the various [Lomé] Conventions warranted fully their acceptance.

Furthermore, all the costs and gains of an agreement need not be immediately operational. For example, one win (discussed later) by the Southern participants in Lomé IV was protection against the costs of future industrial competition and market access to the EC.

Critics of the Lomé accords and other North-South bargaining efforts have argued that any wins for the North are out of place and merely maintain dependency relations. Our findings, however, support arguments made by Zartman (1987) and Ravenhill (1985b) that negotiations must be "positive sum." We find that the absence of gains for the North will preclude bargaining with the South and, therefore, gains for it. Win-sets for both players are necessary for successful Southern bargaining with Northern states.

Our second condition is that the scope of the negotiations must be limited. Our cases demonstrate that Southern states will be successful more often when they negotiate a subset of priority issues instead of presenting all-encompassing demands. The range of change attempted alters the potential costs and payoffs of cooperation and as a result can greatly affect the outcome of negotiations. As a result, actors will be far less willing to negotiate for drastic change than incremental or piecemeal change. As Lindblom (1980) and Zartman (1987) have argued, successful change within a bargaining relationship is far more likely to take place at the margins of an agreement than at its roots.

Our third condition is the selective targeting of Northern states by the South, a tactic that enhances the South's bargaining position. Selective targeting allows Southern states to use bonds resulting from historical contacts and unique economic and social ties. In our cases of successful Southern bargaining, both Northern and Southern negotiators cited the existence of such ties as a key factor in garnering Northern domestic support for concessions to the South.

Respondents from our survey argued that the Lomé negotiations occurred because of "the unwillingness of Europe to forego postindependence links," and "ACP insistence that the EEC has a historical and moral duty to be of assistance to the ACP" (Caribbean negotiator and African negotiator, respectively). Along these lines, several respondents also voiced concern that the expanding size of the EC will "dilute its historical and moral commitment" to their concerns (Caribbean negotiator). These responses track well with Ravenhill's analysis (1985b) of the strategy of "collective clientelism" in which Southern states combine in an effort to exploit the special ties that link them with more powerful Northern states.

Our fourth condition is the routinization of North-South negotiations. Routinized North-South negotiations increases the potential for successful outcomes for Southern states. Repeated interactions, or what Axelrod (1984) has called "iterated games," can greatly increase the potential for cooperation. Cognizance of future interactions can facilitate cooperation by creating a reputational incentive for cooperation to take place. Historical and ongoing ties between a group of actors extends the "shadow of the future" of the bargaining relationship and makes continued cooperation more likely.

In cases of North-South bargaining, there also appears to be a "shadow of the past." Negotiators who return to successive rounds of bargaining promote the institutionalization of negotiations and bring to the bargaining table a vested interest in successfully concluding each bargaining game. Their professional identities and, in some cases, their jobs are dependent upon the endurance of the ongoing bargaining relationship.

Successful Southern bargaining, as reflected in the cases of ACP and ASEAN, occurred when our four conditions were met. As our other cases demonstrate, when these conditions were not present, Southern states were unsuccessful in their bargaining efforts with Northern powers.

☐ *Win-Sets for Both Players*

ACP-EC. Through the Lomé accords, the ACP countries achieved a number of their short- and long-term goals in both trade and aid. The ACP countries hoped that Lomé I would provide an alternate set of trading arrangements to those in force under the existing GATT conventions. They negotiated for and partially received special trade concessions (some tariff and quota barriers were removed) regarding market access in the EC, as well as the right to export partially processed products where previously only primary products had been accepted. The ACP states won a significant, though short-term, goal with the establishment of the system for stabilization of export earnings (STABEX). STABEX was to stabilize prices of raw materials exported from Southern states. Under this system, whenever commodity earnings of any of the poorest twenty states fell by more than 2.5 percent, the Northern signatories would provide guaranteed loans to that Southern state. Guaranteed loans would also be provided to other Southern signatories if their earnings fell by more than 7.5 percent (Boardman et al. 1985). In addition, Systeme Mineral (SYSMIN) was established to offer financial compensation, similar to the STABEX agreement, to mineral exporters who suffered losses.

Although the ACP states were not unable to gain a reduction of agricultural tariffs, they did obtain preferential agricultural trade concessions over other third parties competing for EC markets. The EC also pledged to purchase 1.3 million tons of sugar from the ACP states annually, and special purchasing arrangements at set prices were established for sugar and beef exports from ACP states.

In Lomé I, the ACP states received substantial increases in foreign assistance to offset the burden of dramatic oil-price increases in 1974. During the Lomé II negotiations in 1980, the ACP states were again suffering from oil-price shocks. This time the ACP states won some additional aid concessions, but the aid was tied to certain structural adjustment restraints. The Southern states also fought successfully to have 10 percent of EC aid targeted at regional development programs. Lomé III (1985) provided $9.4 billion in soft loans (at low or no interest) from the European Investment Bank. In Lomé IV, although the ACP countries negotiated for new debt-reduction provisions, their debt to the EC at the time of the 1990 negotiations amounted to only 1.2 percent of their total debt-service costs (ACP-EEC 1989, 14 December). In addition to increased foreign aid and trade concessions, ACP states also received new programs of technical assistance from the EC.

The European Community also gained several short- and long-term policy objectives from the Lomé negotiations. The EC states hoped to establish and maintain common external commercial policies to non-EC states. Negotiating a common aid and trade program with a block of more than forty-four states was an efficient and cost-effective way for the EC to achieve both economic and political goals. Lomé also provided an international public relations victory for the EC states. In the early 1970s, the United States had been forced to close its gold window, had suffered a setback in Vietnam, and, by 1975 when Lomé I was negotiated, was embroiled in the Watergate crisis. The EC—France in particular—saw its negotiations with a large block of ACP countries as a way to demonstrate a resurgence of European leadership in the international system. Furthermore, Lomé I followed the expiration of the Yaoundé II accords in which the EC states had to redefine their relationships with the ACP countries, many of which had been former colonies. After Britain joined the European Community, the EC also had to decide how to manage its relations with the Commonwealth states. The Lomé negotiations provided a timely forum within which to accomplish many of these goals.

After the oil shocks of 1973, the Northern countries sought to secure their supply of raw materials and protect themselves from the cartelization of commodities in the Lomé negotiations. As one respondent noted:

Caribbean negotiator:
The era of "commodity power" meant that the EC was particularly keen to assure dependable sources of affordable raw material supplies. The continued success of subsequent [ACP-EC] agreements was largely due to a similar, but less keen, interest in such supplies but also to the cultural and political ties of metropolitan Europe and Africa.

In trade negotiations, the EC also felt that it had preserved its core advantage of no tariff and no nontariff barriers for European exporters. EC exporters had the advantage of insider marketing practices from many years of EC-ACP trade and were able to convince the ACP states to apply most-favored-nation status to all EC goods. In addition, European exporters stood to gain from the additional levels of EC aid to the ACP countries because much of that money would be spent for purchases in the EC.

Finally, the recently negotiated Lomé IV accords are unique in that they will be in force for ten years. The extended duration of these accords can be considered as a win-set for both Southern and Northern negotiators. The North wanted an accord of longer duration to defer the cost of repeated negotiations, and because it believed that the South had been unable to implement previously negotiated aid agreements within the five-year period before the commencement of new bargaining sessions. For the South, the ten-year duration was equally important. Lomé IV was negotiated at a time when the question of unification of Eastern and Western Europe as well as the harmonization of European policies in 1992 raised concerns among ACP states about the continued commitment by the EC to assist ACP states with development programs. The extension of the accord helped to preserve the benefits of their special relationship.

ASEAN–Northern states. The ASEAN group sought negotiations with the EC, Canada, the United States, and Australia as a remedy to its extreme dependency on Japan. In a limited way, the ASEAN group was able to diversify its dependence. ASEAN was successful in gaining the support of Western nations to encourage new investment by the North's private sector. It also won substantial increases in foreign aid from the United States, Canada, the EC, and during the 1980s, Australia. Like the ACP countries, the ASEAN group convinced Northern donors to fund regional programs as well as to provide bilateral aid. ASEAN also won technical assistance programs as part of its foreign aid package.

Japanese-ASEAN ties remained substantial. In the 1980s, although the Japanese had begun to assume an increasingly larger role in global affairs, regional concerns remained prominent. In addition to lessening some of its dependence on Japan, ASEAN gained a substantial increase in Japanese financial assistance.

Northern states' gains in negotiations with ASEAN in many ways replicate their gains from the Lomé accords. French nationals historically operated in ASEAN countries and stood to gain from aid and trade in the same way as their counterparts operating in ACP states. Moreover, by the late 1970s, Southeast Asia and particularly the ASEAN states remained the primary symbol of French interest and importance in Asia. West Germany was especially supportive because it saw ASEAN as a bulwark against the spread of communism in Asia. West German firms were also aggressively seeking new markets and stable sources of supply. And both Australia and New Zealand sought increased trade ties with the ASEAN states in an effort to promote a Pacific regional grouping that they believed would contribute to their economic expansion.

☐ *Limiting the Scope of the Agenda*

Both the ACP and ASEAN states sought a limited set of changes in their negotiations with Northern states. The ACP-EC negotiations contrasted sharply, for example, with the calls by the Group of 77 for a new international economic order. The ACP states were able to set priorities during the eighteen months of negotiating Lomé I. In Lomé II the ACP's negotiating agenda expanded and was less coordinated. As a result, as Ravenhill (1985b) has noted, there were fewer wins for the ACP. During Lomé II, however, when the ACP countries presented their priorities clearly, they were able to win concessions. ACP negotiators knew, for example, that they preferred the funding of regional aid programs over increases of bilateral aid and were successful, for the first time in the Lomé context, in achieving some regional financing. In Lomé III, by targeting specific areas of need, the ACP succeeded in winning EC support for development projects that took into account the role of women, ecology, and local cultural heritage preservation.

Certain active negotiators and individuals in the ACP Secretariat facilitated agreement on the subset of issues to be negotiated. It should be noted, however, that these priorities often reflected the primary concerns of African countries that compose the largest number of ACP states. This has been a complaint of some non-African states. As one Northern survey respondent noted: "The weight of the African bloc has been used at the expense of Pacific and Caribbean interests!"

The small size of the ASEAN group enhanced its ability to reach agreement on a set of priorities to be negotiated. Moreover, ASEAN is flexible enough to approach various Northern countries with alternative lists of projects and concerns that are likely to be of interest to each Northern state. Each ASEAN member is assigned primary responsibility for coordinating negotiations with a particular Northern country. This enables the ASEAN representative to find a subset of issues to be negotiated that is agreeable to both players.

☐ *Selective Targeting of Northern States*

Both the ACP and ASEAN groups recognize the gains that are derived from negotiating with particular Northern states with which they already enjoy a special relationship. As already noted, the original Lomé negotiations occurred, in part, because of the impending expiration of Yaoundé II's trade and aid provisions and because of the need for the United Kingdom to establish new relations with its Commonwealth states after joining the EEC. Most observers have acknowledged that historical ties played a role in providing Northern governments with domestic support for concluding negotiations successfully. The French support for ASEAN during the late 1970s stemmed largely from its historical ties to the region. The importance of ASEAN states to French policymakers was underscored in 1966 when President Charles de Gaulle proposed establishing a zone of neutrality in Southeast Asia as a counterbalance to the growing influence of communism. French ties to the region as well as stated German concerns encouraged the ASEAN group to wage a campaign to win European trade and aid concessions.

Support for ASEAN by the United States stemmed from its post–World War II efforts to contain the spread of communism in Southeast Asia. Throughout the Vietnam conflict, the ASEAN states remained strategically important to the United States. After the Bali meeting in June 1979 that addressed the issues of the Vietnamese invasion of Cambodia and the refugee crisis, the ASEAN group has again took on increased importance in U.S. strategic calculations. Throughout the 1980s, ASEAN used its renewed strategic importance in Washington to lobby vigorously for expanded trade and aid agreements.

As previously mentioned, ASEAN states have been so cognizant of the benefits of special relationships that each member is assigned to represent the group to a Northern state with which it already has a special relationship. The Philippines, for example, represents ASEAN to the United States and Canada, whereas Indonesia acts as ASEAN's primary contact with the EC.

☐ *Routinized Negotiations*

The ACP and ASEAN states have successfully routinized their bargaining sessions with Northern states. Both groups have regularly scheduled meetings with Northern countries. Between the Lomé I and Lomé IV accords, the ACP and EC states negotiated every five years and during the Lomé IV accords agreed to negotiate again in ten years. In ASEAN, each assigned liaison is responsible for maintaining periodic consultations with a particular Northern state.

Knowledge of future meetings provides an incentive for cooperative bargaining, as predicted in the scholarly literature on the "shadow of the future." As noted, many of our Lomé respondents commented on the existence of a "shadow of the past" in which veteran negotiators have a professional and personal interest in the maintenance of negotiations. Individuals from the EC Commission have been key supporters and proponents of continued European participation in the Lomé accords. In this way, the benefits of routinized negotiations have extended beyond the bargaining table and have contributed to domestic anticipation in Northern states for continued cooperation.

In sum, from our review of these cases of North-South bargaining, we conclude that win-sets for both bargainers, a limited set of issues to be negotiated, the selective targeting of Northern states, and routinized negotiations lead to successful Southern negotiations with the North. In the next section, we analyze the ongoing changes in the international economy to predict the likelihood of Southern success in future North-South bargaining.

■ The Changing International Political Economy

The distinctive features of the changing international political economy of the 1990s include the following:
1. An intensification of the debt crisis and the marginalization of Southern states;
2. An energized focus on Eastern Europe by Northern states;
3. A single market in the European Community in 1992;
4. A reorganization of the liberal international economic order into

regional blocs;
   5. An uncertain future of multilateral negotiations.

Theorists like Gilpin (1987) and Kindleberger (1986) and policy proponents of the Uruguay Round argue for policies to maintain a multilateral, liberal international economic order in the face of growing trends toward the formation of regional economic blocs in North America, Europe, and the Far East. The evolution of the international political economy in the 1990s into either regional blocs or an increasingly multilateral economic system will, we believe, have important implications for successful Southern bargaining with Northern states. The conditions we identified earlier for successful Southern bargaining are more likely to be present under an international economic system characterized by economic blocs than one lacking this feature (see Table 10.3).

Multilateral negotiations have historically been viewed as a failure in meeting the needs of Southern states. For example, Southern frustration with GATT's multilateral negotiations was a prime motivation for the South to negotiate the Lomé accords. As demonstrated by the Group of 77's effort to use the UN General Assembly, even when global negotiations have taken place in a sympathetic forum, they have yielded few gains for the South. In multilateral forums, Northern powers tend to dominate agenda setting and in essence control the issues that are openly debated. As a result, the specific concerns of the South are rarely addressed. In contrast, negotiations within or between blocs, like those between the ACP and the European Community, are more likely to address Southern concerns. As one respondent noted:

African Negotiator:
   The [ACP-EC] negotiations were considered successful in relation to the poor results achieved generally in the context of the North-South dialogue in other international fora and to the noncommittal nature of declarations and resolutions adopted in these fora.

Table 10.3 Characteristics of Bargaining in a Changing International Political Economy

Conditions	Economic Blocs	Multilateral Economic System
1. Win-sets for both North and South	Yes	No
2. Limited scope of agenda	Yes	No
3. Selective targeting	Yes	No
4. Routinized North-South negotiations	Yes	No

Negotiations among a large number of states minimizes the likelihood for trade-offs among particular actors. As the number of participants increases, each actor's relative influence and gain decreases. Moreover, despite the recent Cairns group example (in which Northern and Southern states together lobbied the EC for a reduction in agricultural tariffs), in most multilateral negotiations Northern actors have tended to group together to protect their interests. Under these conditions, Southern states are less able to take advantage of special relationships with particular Northern states. Furthermore, negotiations tend to be routinized among the Northern states in global forums, but Southern states rarely sit at the negotiating table and have been unable to routinize negotiations that address their primary concerns.

In contrast, the presence of economic blocs offers Southern states the opportunity to negotiate under favorable conditions. Northern bloc leaders are likely to engage in direct negotiations with the Southern members of their bloc. Sitting at the negotiating table increases the likelihood that Southern states will be able to influence the agenda and the outcomes of bloc negotiations. The scope of the demands debated is likely to be focused on issues of concern to this subset of players. In addition, because negotiations within blocs take place among a smaller number of players, the potential gain for each player is greater.

Blocs have generally formed among states with either geographical or historical ties that enable Southern states to capitalize on existing special relationships with the Northern states in the bloc. This facilitates selective targeting that can be used to Southern advantage. Furthermore, when negotiating with a bloc that includes a country with special ties, LDCs may be able to gain from the bloc as a whole. Finally, although routinized negotiations are not guaranteed, regularized consultation of all states is likely to occur for successful maintenance of the bloc.

■ Note

We gratefully acknowledge Alexandra Samuel, who assisted with the collection and presentation of foreign aid statistics.

11

The Need for an African Response

General Olusegun Obasanjo

By the end of 1992, the twelve member states of the European Community (EC) resolved to complete the creation of a single European market by removing all the remaining barriers to the free flow of goods and services within the EC. In other words, by the end of 1992, the European Common Market is supposed to become truly common. The EC Commission itself has described this impending development as a "quiet revolution." Quiet, it may be; revolution, it most assuredly is. An internal market of some 320 million people, with an annual GDP of $2.7 trillion, exports worth $680 billion, and imports of $708 billion—this, in brief outline, is the economic profile of the Europe after 1992. And as everyone has recognized, the completion of the single market will accentuate the EC's position as the world's leading trading bloc. How will this monumental development affect the sixteen member countries of the Economic Community of West African States (ECOWAS)?

Active interest in the magic date of 1992 has become something of a universal phenomenon. It is the urgent subject for discussion wherever policymakers and opinion formers are gathered together. That interest is also usually shot through with anxiety. Japan and the United States, among Europe's major trading rivals, were first off the mark to make public their anxieties about the implications of 1992 for their trade with the EC. Their respective governments and corporate worlds have since started working out responses to this impending change in the structure of the world's trading system and the composition of its economic powers.

Among many of the African, Caribbean, and Pacific (ACP) group of countries, linked to the European Community through the Lomé Convention, interest in 1992 has been no less feverish. At the beginning of October 1988, the West India Committee and the Caribbean Community (CARICOM) Secretariat organized a conference in London on the theme of "1992 and the Caribbean." The participants included a considerable number of Commonwealth Caribbean prime ministers, ministers, and senior officials as well as a distinguished group of over 200 people. The purpose of that meeting was to examine the implications of 1992 for the Caribbean region, to identify specific problem areas, and, after forming a consensus on issues of common concern, to investigate in depth practical ways in which these problems could be tackled.

Then in a week's time, in Brussels, representatives of the Preferential Trade Area (PTA) of East and Southern Africa in their turn met to consider the implications of 1992 for the fifteen member states of Eastern and Southern Africa. Sooner or later the Pacific too will be astir with similar initiatives. The seminar of the African Leadership Forum in Brussels in April 1989 is part of this worldwide reaction to the impending completion of the single European market (Obasanjo and d'Orville 1990).

And this is as it should be. At the level of generalities, no one can doubt that the completion of the internal European market in 1992 will present considerable opportunities in addition to strengthening further the international trading system. All of us who trade with Europe will be selling to a single unified market of some 320 million consumers. We will be dealing with a uniform set of standards and procedures and not twelve different sets of requirements. For warrant, we have the word of the EC Commission itself, and the thrust of that assurance is this:

- The post-1992 Europe will not be a fortress Europe but a partnership Europe.
- The 1992 benchmark will be of benefit to EC and non-EC countries alike because the completion of the single market will also give a major boost to the EC—a boost that will have favorable repercussions both inside and outside the EC.
- The 1992 integration will not mean protectionism because the EC has a fundamental stake in the existence of free and open international trade.
- Finally, the development of the EC's external economic policy in the transition to 1992 will take place in harmony with its existing international obligations, whether these be multilateral such as GATT or bilateral such as Lomé.

These are welcome assurances, but they do not go far enough and they certainly do not assuage all our anxieties. We in West Africa share with other ACP third parties a peculiar anxiety about 1992. The peculiarity of that anxiety arises from the fact that the present pattern of our exports to the European Community is determined by market regulation with its individual members. Such regulation must inevitably be vulnerable in an exercise aiming at the demolition of barriers and restrictions on trade. But there are also other reservations about the EC Commission's assurances.

First, they are all general. They apply to all of Europe's trading partners and to no one in particular. Second, there is no pretense that the repercussions of 1992 will be uniformly spread over all the EC's trading partners. In the nature of things, 1992 is bound to bestow affluence here and embarrassment there. How will the Europe after 1992 distribute its favors? In any case, even these general assurances will only hold good if, as the economists say, other things remain equal. The question is this: What will remain "equal" after 1992 and what will not?

I appreciate that the answers to some of these questions will emerge only later and under the pressure and stimulus of the actual events as the implications of 1992 unfold. But that is no reason for not raising them here. West Africa, like any other region, needs to be assured of a reasonable degree of predictability in its economic planning. Predictability is an indispensable key element of political activities and international relations in this age of global interdependence. And only by raising and answering the sorts of questions thrown up by the move to a single market in Europe will we be assured of a measure of provision into our economic future.

It is especially important that we in West Africa be as fully prepared for the impact of 1992 as possible. In spite of the vicissitudes of the commodity trade in recent years, the European Community remains West Africa's largest trading partner. No less than 70 percent of West Africa's principal exports—cocoa, timber, cotton, coffee, groundnuts, gold, and diamonds—goes to Europe. And it is from Europe that practically all West African countries derive the bulk of their imports of manufactured goods. In fact, so long-standing and so strong are the trading ties between the two regions that for virtually all West African countries, external trade is merely trade with Europe by another name. Related to this is the fact that a great deal of private investment in West Africa stems from countries of the European Community, principally Britain, France, and West Germany. We need to know—to the greatest extent the clarity of the crystal ball will allow—what 1992 will mean for these long-standing links and investment flows.

The ties born of trade and investment have been strengthened by those of aid. The European Community was the largest single source of foreign aid for fourteen of the sixteen member countries of ECOWAS in 1987. We would like to think that any increased prosperity accruing to the member countries of the EC as a result of 1992 will result in increased concessional aid flows to West Africa. Will we be right in so thinking?

In other respects, too, the evolution of the European Community has direct implications for the future evolution of our own West African group. Seven members of ECOWAS—Benin, Burkina Faso, Côte d'Ivoire, Mali, Niger, Senegal, and Togo—also form the West African Monetary Union (UMOA). They are united in a single currency zone with a common central bank and a single common currency, the CFA franc, which is linked to the French franc. How will the matter of this overseas franc be handled? Will it be taken into the European Monetary System, or will France help in the creation of a wider zone of convertibility within the framework of ECOWAS that will absorb the present seven members of WAMU?

I raise this question because by coincidence 1992 is also the year agreed upon by ECOWAS heads of government at Abuja in July 1987 for the monetary harmonization program to take effect. The program envisages a central bank, a common convertible West African currency, a common fiscal policy, a harmonized development strategy, and a liberalized trade policy. Currency harmonization is clearly indispensable to effect economic integration within West Africa. And in large measure our path to this objective has already been cleared by the fact that the economic recovery programs on which most member countries of ECOWAS have embarked have usually entailed substantial adjustments of exchange rates, thus bringing the exchange rates within the region into line with one another. There is an Implementation Committee mandate to negotiate this monetary harmonization within the region and we very much hope that the committee can count upon the support of our European and other partners in the principal multilateral financial institutions in the prosecution of its mandate.

But beyond the immediate gains we hope to be able to reap from 1992, we also look to the European example for inspiration in our efforts to build a thriving economic community in West Africa. ECOWAS was set up in May 1975 to pursue objectives very akin to those of the European Community. Like it, ECOWAS was to bring about economic union by stages through such measures as these:

- Elimination of customs duties;
- Abolition of administrative restrictions on trade;
- Establishment of a common customs tariff and a common commercial policy;
- Harmonization of economic and industrial policies, and
- Harmonization of the monetary policies of member states.

Fourteen years later, virtually all these objectives have still to be realized. None of the member countries has come anywhere near meeting the tariff-reduction deadlines that have already been revised and put back several times. The result is that there is still no preferential trade. And what exists by way of regional trade is minuscule—fluctuating around 4 percent of member countries' total exports. In any case, the bulk of this is made up of oil and oil products. Further, there is no harmonization of industrial policies. As for the free movement of people, the least said about that the better. It is not just that ECOWAS has advanced very little beyond what it was in 1975—the fear is that it is now in danger of moving backward. President Dawda Kairaba Jawara of the Gambia was only reflecting the true position when last year he said: "We move from the problematic to what is in danger of becoming the unattainable."

We are all familiar with the reasons for the tardy evolution of ECOWAS:

- All member countries are producers and exporters of primary commodities and thus there is little margin left for intraregional trade.
- There are marked disparities in the levels of economic development between the member states.
- For most ECOWAS countries, the major source of government revenue is tax; consequently, they are reluctant to accept a reduction in tax revenues arising from a lowering of tariff barriers.
- To the structural problems have been added those of a contingent nature associated with the fall in commodity prices and the debt overhang.

In addition, of course, we have the legacy of colonial partition and all that implies in terms of economic integration. All these and more are difficulties enough to influence the pace of regional integration in West Africa. But—and this is the point to grasp—these factors also cut the other way and should have been precisely the very reason impelling us to greater efforts at integration.

I agree that ultimately what is lacking to make the difference is the absence of the necessary political will. But frankly, I find this apparent lack of political will in the region even more surprising. ECOWAS was not founded in a fit of absent-mindedness on the part of West Africa's political leadership, and no country was dragooned into the treaty of Lagos of May 1975 and the subsequent protocols. Neither was it an external imposition on the region. The treaty, together with its protocols, remains an open covenant, openly arrived at and freely entered into. I should know because I had a hand in it.

When the region's heads of government said they signed the treaty "in faith," they meant it. And it was not a blind faith either. They knew and appreciated full well the practical benefits of effective economic cooperation. And if they were alive to the benefits of economic integration, they could hardly have been ignorant of the dangers of continued economic fragmentation.

It is often argued that in comparable contexts elsewhere in history, a perceived external threat has often served as the decisive factor to accelerate the pace of integration. But with deepening poverty and mounting external debt—and I should not need to go any further—what more awesome threats do we in West Africa need to concentrate our minds wonderfully?

Clearly, the situation calls for a new beginning to the whole question of economic integration in West Africa. One fruitful approach is to make it a people's cause. If the pressure from below is perceptible and sufficiently credible, resistance from above will be to no avail. It is one of the ways in which we can rekindle our flickering West African flame from the European torch. No doubt there are other approaches that will emerge in the course of our deliberations. The role of our intellectuals and other opinion formers in all this is self-evident.

One final thought: The charge requires us to examine the implications of 1992 for West Africa, but the spirit encompasses the rest of sub-Saharan Africa, if not the whole of the continent. I urge this flexibility for two main reasons. First, because most of the region's countries are also commodity producers for the most part, much of what is true of West Africa also holds good for the other countries of sub-Saharan Africa. Second, as a result of Europe's decision to complete its internal market in 1992, African finance ministers decided at their meeting in Malawi in March 1991 to bring forward the date for the creation of an African Monetary Union. It was therefore not only West Africa that was preparing for 1992; the whole of Africa hurryied to meet the challenge of that year.

I hope we can then draw up a possible blueprint for the consideration of ECOWAS governments, business organizations, and institutions of learning as they prepare for 1992—a blueprint we hope will register with the European Community. That program will have to be clear on a number of points: It will have to spell out in unambiguous terms what West Africa and indeed the rest of Africa expect from Europe as a result of 1992. High on that list of expectations is the need for increased official development aid (ODA), especially for the least developed of our countries, and the aid should aim to stimulate development. We also expect equal trade, increased direct investment, and the stabilization of commodity prices.

That is what we expect of Europe. What does Europe in turn expect of us beyond the creation of a hospitable environment for investment by such measures as guarantees on the security of investments, a favorable tax regime, and the ability to repatriate a reasonable proportion of accrued profits? We really do need to know, and we hope our European colleagues will be forthcoming on the issue.

Let us have no illusions. If Africa is to have a fair deal in these coming changes, it will need to have in place the necessary leverage—what U.S. political scientists often call countervailing power. Do we have such countervailing power? If not, how do we go about acquiring it?

We should not be disingenuous. The bald fact is that at present Africa does not have the leverage to deal on equal terms with its European and other trading partners. But we do have the constituent elements with which to forge that leverage.

Will we now under the pressure of developments from outside be spurred into accelerating our efforts at regional and ultimately continental economic integration? If we do not in our turn achieve meaningful economic integration, it is unrealistic to hope in our disunity to secure a square deal from our trading partners.

Bibliography

Aaby, Peter. 1978. "The State of Guinea-Bissau: African Socialism or Socialism in Africa?" *Scandinavian Institute of African Studies Research Report,* no. 45, p. 18.
ACP-EEC. 1989. *Press Release of the ACP-EEC Convention of Lomé.*
Adam, Heribert. 1990. "Eastern Europe and South African Socialism: Engaging Joe Slovo." *South Africa International,* vol. 21, no. 1 (July), pp. 29–45.
Adamishin, Anatoly. 1989. "Zum Zerwürfnis verurteilt?" *Neue Zeit,* no. 12, pp. 14–16.
Adedeji, Adebayo. 1987. "A Year After the Special Session." *Africa Report,* vol. 32, no. 6, pp. 20–23.
———. 1991. "The European Integration Process: Lessons for Africa." *The Courier* (January), Brussels, Commission of European Communities.
African Economic Digest. July 2, 1990. African National Congress (ANC) and Congress of South African Trade Unions (COSATU). 1990. "The Economy Beyond Apartheid." Proceedings of workshop in Harare, Zimbabwe, April-May 1990. Reprinted in *New Nation,* June 15–21, 1990, pp. 8–11.
Africa Research Bulletin. August–September 1985; June 1986; December 1987; January–April 1989.
Africa Research Bulletin (Economic Series). 1990. Vol. 27, no. 4 (May 31, 1990), p. 9932.
Agence Europe. March 10, 1989.
———. May 18, 1989.
Alagapa, Muthiah. 1987. *The National Security of Developing States: Lessons from Thailand.* Dover, Mass.: Auburn House.
Alnastawi, Abbas. 1985. *OPEC in a Changing World Economy.* Baltimore: Johns Hopkins University Press.
Aluko, Olajide. 1981. "African Response to External Intervention in Africa Since Angola." *African Affairs,* vol. 80, no. 319, pp. 159–180.
———. 1984. "Alliances Within the OAU." Pp. 67–84 in Yassin El-Ayouty and I. William Zartman, eds., *The OAU After Twenty Years.* New York: Praeger.
Amin, S. 1964. "The Class Struggle in Africa." *Revolution,* vol. 1, no. 9, p. 43.
ANC/COSATU. *See African Economic Digest.*
Anderson, K., and R. Tyers. 1984. "European Community Grain and Meat Policies: Effects on International Prices, Trade, and Welfare." *European Review of Agricultural Economics,* vol. 11, no. 4, pp. 367–394.

Andreyev, I. 1977. *The Non-Capitalist Way: Socialism and the Developing Countries.* Progress Publishers.
Arlinghaus, Bruce E. 1984. "Introduction." Pp. 1–6 in Bruce Arlinghaus, ed., *African Security Issues: Sovereignty, Stability, and Solidarity.* Boulder, Colo.: Westview.
Arms Control and Disarmament Agency (ACDA). 1990. *World Military Expenditures and Arms Transfers 1989.* Washington, D.C.: Government Printing Office.
Asante, S. K. B. 1984. "ECOWAS, the EEC, and the Lomé Convention." Pp. 171–197 in Domenico Mazzeo, ed., *African Regional Organizations.* London: Cambridge University Press.
Asoyan, Boris. 1989. "From Illusion to Realism." *Asia and Africa Today,* no. 5, pp. 32–34.
Axelrod, Robert. 1984. *The Evolution of Cooperation.* New York: Basic Books.
Ayoob, Mohammed. 1984. "Security in the Third World: The Worm About Turn." *International Affairs,* vol. 60 (Winter), pp. 41–51.

———. 1989. "The Third World in the System of States: Schizophrenia or Growing Pains?" *International Studies Quarterly,* vol. 33 (March), pp. 67–79.
Bach, Daniel. 1989. "Managing a Plural Society: The Boomerang Effects of Nigerian Federalism." *Journal of Commonwealth and Comparative Politics,* vol. 27, no. 2 (July), pp. 218–245.

———. 1992. "Pour une union monétaire euro-africaine," *Le Monde,* January 14.
Badiane, O. 1990. "The Role of Agriculture in Economic Development." Paper presented at the AGRICONA/IAAE Conference on Agricultural Restructuring in Southern Africa, Winhoek, July 20–27, 1990.
Baker, Pauline H. 1983. "Obstacles to Private Sector Activities in Africa." Unpublished paper prepared for the U.S. Department of State, Washington, D.C.
Bale, M. D., and E. Lutz. 1978. "Trade Restrictions and International Price Instability." *World Bank Staff Working Paper* no. 303, pp. 3–4.
Bayart, Jean Francois. 1989. *La Politique Africain de François Mitterrand.* Paris: Karthala.
BCEAO. 1987. "Politique Monetaire de la BCEAO et Incidences Sur Les Agents Economiques Depuis La Crise de 1974." *Banques et Monnaies,* no. 366 (December).
Bekolo-Ebe, Bruno. 1986. "La Devaluation du Franc Francais et les Economies de la ZF." *Presence Africaine,* no. 1378.
Bennell, Paul. 1990. "British Industrial Investment in Sub-Saharan Africa: Corporate Responses to Economic Crisis in the 1980s." *Development Policy Review,* vol. 8, pp. 155–177.
Bhatia, Rattan J. 1985. "The West African Monetary Union: An Analytical Review." *IMF Occasional Paper* no. 35.
Boardman, Robert. 1985. *Europe, Africa, and Lomé III.* New York: University Press of America.
Borchardt, Knut, and Christoph Buchheim. 1987. "Die Wirkung der Marshallplan-Hilfe in Schlüsselbranchen der Deutschen Wirtschaft." *Vierteljahreshefte für Zeitgeschichte,* vol. 35, no. 3, pp. 317–347.
Bozeman, Adda. 1976. *Conflict in Africa: Concepts and Realities.* Princeton: Princeton University Press.
Bratton, Michael. 1989. "Beyond the State: Civil Society and Associational Life in Africa." *World Politics,* vol. 61 (July), pp. 407–430.
Brown, R. 1986. "International Responses to Sudan's Economic Crises." *Development and Change,* vol. 17, pp. 489–511.
Brüne, Stefan. 1990a. "The EC Internal Market, Lomé IV, and the ACP Coun-

tries," *Intereconomics,* July-August, pp. 193–201.
———. 1990. "Zwischen Grandeur und Afrikapessimismus—Frankreichs Afrikapolitik im Zwiespalt." *Der Überblick,* vol. 26, no. 3, pp. 64–68.
Bryson, John M. 1988. *Strategic Planning for Public and Non-Profit Organizations: A Guide to Strengthening and Sustaining Organizational Achievements.* San Francisco: Jossey-Bass.
Buignes, Pierre, and Fabienne Ilzkovitz. 1988. *The Sectoral Impact of the Internal Market.* Report of the Directorate-General for Economic and Financial Affairs, Commission of the European Communities, Document II/335/88-EN.
Bukarambe, Bukar. 1983. "The Role and Impact of the OAU in the Management of African Conflicts." *Survival,* vol. 25, no. 2, pp. 50–58.
Burniaux, J. M., and J. Waelbroeck. 1985. "The Impact of the CAP on Developing Countries: A General Equilibrium Analysis." In C. Stevens, ed., *Pressure Groups, Politics, and Development.* London: Hodder and Stoughton.
Bustin, Edouard. 1987. "The Foreign Policy of the Republic of Zaire." *Annals,* vol. 489 (January), pp. 63–75.
Byron, Jessica. 1984. *Regional Security in Latin America and Africa: The OAS and OAU in the Light of Contemporary Issues.* Geneva: Program for Strategic and International Studies.
Cable, Vincent, and Bishnodat Persaud. 1987. "New Trends and Policy Problems in Foreign Investment: The Experience of Commonwealth Developing Countries." In V. Cable and B. Persaud, eds., *Developing with Foreign Investment.* London: Croom Helm.
Callaghy, Thomas M. 1987. "Between Scylla and Charybdis: The Foreign Economic Relations of Sub-Saharan African States." *Annals,* vol. 489 (January), pp. 148–163.
———. 1988. "Debt and Structural Adjustment in Africa: Realities and Possibilities." *Issue,* vol. 16, no. 2, pp. 11–18.
Campbell, Kurt M. 1986. *Soviet Policy Towards South Africa.* New York: St. Martin's.
Cantwell, John. 1989. "Foreign Multinationals and Industrial Development in Africa." *Discussion Papers in International Investment and Business Studies,* series B, vol. 2, no. 131 (August), University of Reading (England), Department of Economics.
Carey, R. H. 1990. "Prospects for Bilateral Concessional Assistance." Paper prepared for World Bank symposium, African External Finance in the 1980s. Paris: OECD (mimeo).
Carrington, E. 1990. "Many a Challenge for the ACPs." *The Courier,* vol. 120 (March–April), pp. 18–19.
Carter Center of Emory University. 1989. *Beyond Autocracy in Africa.* Working papers for the inaugural seminar of the Governance in Africa Program, February 17–18, 1989, Atlanta, Georgia.
Cassen, Robert, and Associates. 1986. *Does Aid Work?* Oxford: Oxford University Press.
Castaneda, Jorge G. 1990. "Latin America and the End of the Cold War." *World Policy Journal,* no. 3 (Summer), pp. 469–492.
CEC. *See* Commission of the European Communities.
Cecchini, Paolo. 1988. *The European Challenge 1992: The Benefits of a Single Market.* Aldershot, England: Wildwood House for the EC Commission.
Cervenka, Zdenek. 1977. *The Unfinished Quest for African Unity.* London: Hurst.
Chandavarkar, Anand G. 1987. "Developmental Role of Central Banks." *Finance and Development,* vol. 24 (December).

Chazan, Naomi. 1988. "Ideology, Policy, and the Crisis of Poverty: The African Case." *Jerusalem Journal of International Relations,* vol. 2 (December), pp. 1–27.
Chipman, John. 1989. *French Power in Africa.* Oxford: Basil Blackwell.
Church, C., and D. Keogh. 1991. *The Single Europe Act.* London: UACES.
Cockcroft, Laurence. 1990. *Africa's Way.* London: I. B. Taurus.
Cockcroft, Laurence, and Roger C. Riddell. 1990. "Foreign Direct Investment in Sub-Saharan Africa." Paper prepared for the World Bank symposium, *African External Finance in the 1990s.*
Commission of the European Communities (CEC). 1985. *Completing the Internal Market: White Paper from the Commission to the European Council.* Luxembourg: CEC.
———. 1990. *Lomé IV 1990–2000: Background, Innovations, Improvements.* Brussels: CEC.
Corden, Max W. 1972. "Monetary Integration." Princeton University International Finance Section, *Essays in International Finance* no. 93.
———. 1988. *Macroeconomic Adjustment in Developing Countries.* Washington, D.C.: International Monetary Fund.
Cosgrove, Carol. 1978. *From Association to Partnership.* London: Fainborough.
———. 1981. *A Framework for Development: The EEC and the ACP.* London: Fainborough.
Cosgrove, Carol, and Pierre-Henri Laurent. 1991. "EC Relations with the ACP States." In John Redmond, ed., *External Relations with the ACP States.* London: Fainborough.
Cot, Jean-Pierre. 1984. *A l'épreuve du pouvoir: Le tier-mondisme pour quoi faire?* Paris: Seuil.
The Courier. 1990. "Lomé IV" (September–October), Brussels, EC.
Crone, Donald. 1983. *The ASEAN States: Coping with Dependence.* New York: Praeger.
Crowder, Michael. 1987. "Whose Dream Was It Anyway? Twenty-five Years of African Independence." *African Affairs,* vol. 86, no. 342, pp. 7–24.
CTA Economic and Export Analysts Ltd. 1989. "EEC Trade Preferences and ACP Exports" (confidential report). Reading: CTA.
Culagovski, J., et al. 1990. "African Financing Needs in the 1990s." Paper prepared for World Bank symposium, African External Finance in the 1990s.
Dahrendorf, Rolf. 1990. "Transitions: Politics, Economics, and Liberty." *Washington Quarterly* (Summer) pp. 133–142.
Damis, John. 1984. "The OAU and Western Sahara." Pp. 273–296 in Yassin El-Ayouty and I. William Zartman, eds., *The OAU After Twenty Years.* New York: Praeger.
Dauderstädt, Michael. 1990. *Entwicklungspolitik '92 Abkehr von der Dritten Welt.* Bonn: Friedrich-Ebert-Stiftung, Reihe Eurokolleg 3.
Davenport, Michael. 1988. "European Community Trade Barriers to Tropical Agricultural Products." *ODI Working Paper* no. 27. London: Overseas Development Institute.
Davenport, M., and S. Page. 1991. *1992 and the Developing World.* London: Overseas Development Institute.
Davidson, Basil. 1987. "Thirty Years of Liberation Struggle." *Africa Today,* vol. 34, no. 4, pp. 5–16.
Davies, R. W. 1990. "Gorbachev's Socialism in Historical Perspective." *New Left Review,* no. 179, pp. 5–27.
Decraene, Philippe. 1985. "Le politique africaine de la France," in Marcel Daneau, ed., *Afrique: Enjeu des grandes puissances.* Quebec: Laval University.

Devarajan, Shantayanan, and Jaime de Melo. 1987a. "Evaluating Participation in African Monetary Unions: A Statistical Analysis." *World Bank Economic Review*, vol. 15, no. 4.
———. 1987b. "Evaluating Participation in African Monetary Unions: A Statistical Analysis of the CFA Zones." *World Development*, vol. 15, no. 4, pp. 483–496.
———. 1987c. "Adjustment with a Fixed Exchange Rate: Cameroon, Côte d'Ivoire, and Senegal." *World Economic Review*, vol. 2, no. 2.
Diallo, Siradou. 1989. "Deux Africains avec Lesquels il Faut Compter." *Jeune Afrique*, no. 1466 (February 8).
Dunning, John H. 1988. *Explaining International Production*. London: Unwin Hyman.
Dunning, John H., and J. Cantwell, eds. 1987. *The IRM Directory on International Investment and Production*. London: Macmillan; New York: New York University Press.
Economic Policy. October 1990.
Economist. January 23, 1988.
———. August 20, 1988.
———. February 4, 1989.
———. June 10, 1989.
———. June 17, 1989.
EDICESA News. 1990. Vol. 3, no. 9 (November).
EEC Bulletin. September 1990.
El-Badawi, I., and S. O'Connell. 1990. *Real Exchange Rate and Macroeconomic Adjustment in the CFA Zone*. Washington, D.C.: World Bank.
Elsenhans, Hartmut. 1981. "Abhängiger Kapitalimus oder bürokratische Entwicklungsgesellschaft, Versuch über den Staat." *Der Dritten Welt*.
Fabra, Paul. 1990. "Les Faux Semblants de la Zone Franc." *Le Monde* (March 13).
Faini, Riccardo, and Jaime de Melo. 1990. "Adjustment, Investment, and the Real Exchange Rate in Developing Countries." *Economic Policy*.
Faini, Riccardo, et al. 1990. "Growth-Oriented Adjustment Programs: A Statistical Analysis." *World Development*.
Financial Times. May 18, 1989.
———. June 7, 1989.
———. July 13, 1989.
———. June 7, 1990.
———. November 29, 1990.
———. December 12, 1990.
Fodor, Giorgio. 1984. "Why Did Europe Need the Marshall Plan?" *EUI Working Papers*, vol. 78, no. 6 (March 1984), p. 2.
Fuller, W., and G. Battese. 1974. "Estimation of Linear Models with Crossed Error Structure." *Journal of Econometrics*, vol. 2, pp. 67–78.
Gambari, Ibrahim. 1989. "The OAU and Africa's Changed Priorities." *TransAfrica Forum*, vol. 6, no. 2, pp. 3–14.
Garten, Jeffrey E. 1984. "Aid in the Eighties." *New York Times Magazine*, vol. 25, no. 3.
Garton Ash, Timothy. 1990. "Eastern Europe: Après le Déluge, Nous." *New York Review of Books*, vol. 16, no. 8, p. 51.
GATT (General Agreement on Tariffs and Trade). 1988. *International Trade 1987–88*. Vols. 1 and 2. Geneva: GATT.
Gavshon, Arthur. 1981. *Crisis in Africa: Battleground of East and West*. London: Pelican.
General Anzeiger. November 24, 1990.

Gilpin, Robert. 1987. *The Political Economy of International Relations*. Princeton: Princeton University Press.
Gittelman, Michelle. 1990. "Transnational Corporations in Europe 1992: Implications for Developing Countries." *CTC Reporter*, no. 29.
Goldin, I., and O. Knudsen, eds. 1990. *Agricultural Trade Liberalization: Implications for Developing Countries*. Washington, D.C.: OECD and World Bank.
Goldsbrough, David. 1985. "Foreign Private Investment in Developing Countries." *IMF Occasional Paper* no. 33.
Gordon, David F. 1987. "Anglophonic Variants: Kenya Versus Tanzania." *Annals*, vol. 489 (January), pp. 88–102.
Green, Reginald H. 1981. "Foreign Direct Investment and African Political Economy." In Adebayo Adedeji, ed., *Indigenization of African Economies*. New York: Africana.
Gromyko, Anatoli. 1989. "Adopt New Political Thinking in the Practice of International Relations." *Asia and Africa Today*, no. 4, pp. 51–54.
Group of Thirty. 1984. *Foreign Direct Investment, 1973–87*. New York: Group of Thirty.
Guillaumont, P., and S. Guillaumont. 1984. *Zone Franc et Developpement Africain*. Paris: Econometrica.
———. 1988a. "Participating in African Monetary Unions: An Alternative Evaluation." *World Development*, vol. 16, no. 5, pp. 569–576.
———. 1988b. *Stratégies de Developpement Comparées: Zone Franc et Hors Zone Franc*. Paris: Econometrica.
———. 1989a. "Africa's Franc Zone." *The Courier*, no. 117 (September 1989), Brussels, Commission of European Communities.
———. 1989b. "Implications of the European Monetary Unit (EMU) for African Countries." *Journal of Common Market Studies*, vol. 28, no. 2 (December).
———. 1991. *Franc Zone in Africa: Problems and Prospects*. France: Universite de Clermont (Centre d'Etudes et de Recherche sur les Developpement Internationale, CERDI).
Halliday, Fred. 1990. "The Ends of Cold War." *New Left Review*, no. 180 (March/April), pp. 5–24.
Handelsblatt. September 30, 1990.
Harrigan, J., and P. Mosley. 1990. *World Bank Policy-Based Lending, 1980–1987: An Evaluation*. Paper presented to EADI Oslo workshop, *Approaches and Methods in the Evaluation of Aid*. Manchester: Institute for Policy and Management.
Haynes, Jeff, et al. 1987. "Debt in Sub-Saharan Africa: The Local Politics of Stabilization." *African Affairs*, vol. 86, no. 344, pp. 343–366.
Heller, Peter S. 1975. "A Model of Public Fiscal Behavior in Developing Countries: Aid, Investment, and Taxation." *American Economic Review*, vol. 65, no. 3, pp. 429–445.
Helmboldt, Niles E., Tina West, and Benjamin H. Hardy, 1986. "Private Investment and African Economic Policy." In Robert J. Berg, ed., *Strategies for African Development*. Berkeley: University of California Press.
Henderson, George. 1987. "Qaddaffi's Waterloo." *Africa Report*, vol. 32, no. 5, pp. 20–23.
Herald Tribune. September 21, 1990.
Herbst, Jeffrey. 1990. "Migration, The Politics of Protest, and State Consolidation in Africa." *African Affairs*, vol. 89, no. 355 (April), pp. 183–203.
Hewitt, A. H. 1990. "British Policy Towards the European Development Fund." Paper presented to the conference, European Aid Policy: The Implication for

Trade, held at the University of Nottingham, September. London: ODI (mimeo).
Hirschman, Albert O. 1970. *Exit, Voice, and Loyalty.* Cambridge: Harvard University Press.
Hodd, Michael. 1987. "Africa: The IMF and the World Bank." *African Affairs,* vol. 86, no. 344, pp. 331–342.
Honohan, P. 1990. "Monetary Cooperation in the CFA Zone." *World Bank Working Paper* no. WPS 389.
Independent (London). May 4, 1989.
International Monetary Fund (IMF). 1990. *International Financial Statistics Yearbook.* Washington, D.C.: IMF.
Islam, Azizul, A., and Neema Majmudar. 1990. "Trends and Issues in FDI Laws in Least Developed Countries." *CTC Reporter,* no. 30.
Jacquemont, Pierre. 1989. "Exchange Rate Policy in Development: The Case of Africa." *The Courier,* no. 117 (September), Brussels, Commission of European Communities.
James, Franziska. 1987. "Habre's Hour of Glory." *Africa Report,* vol. 32, no. 5, pp. 20–23.
Johnson, D. G. 1991. *World Agriculture in Disarray,* 2nd ed. London: Macmillan.
Jordan, Pallo. 1990. "Crisis of Conscience in the SACP." *Southern African Political and Economic Magazine* (SAPEM) (June), pp. 28–34.
Kaldor, Mary. 1990. "After the Cold War." *New Left Review,* no. 180 (March/April), pp. 25–40.
Katz, Mark N. 1990. "Why Does the Cold War Continue in the Third World?" *Journal of Peace Research,* vol. 27, no. 4 (November), pp. 353–359.
Keller, Edmond J. 1987. "The Politics of State Survival: Continuity and Change in Ethiopian Foreign Policy." *Annals,* vol. 489 (January), pp. 76–87.
Killick, T. 1990. "The Developmental Effectiveness of Aid to Africa." Paper prepared for World Bank symposium, African External Finance in the 1980s. London: ODI (mimeo).
Kindleberger, Charles. 1986. *The World in Depression, 1929–39.* Berkeley: University of California Press.
Kiva, A. 1984. "Socialist-oriented Countries: Some Development Problems." *International Affairs* (Moscow), no. 10 (October), pp. 22–29.
———. 1989. "Developing Countries, Socialism, Capitalism." *International Affairs* (Moscow), no. 3, (March), pp. 54–63.
Kodjo, Edem. 1987. *Africa Tomorrow.* New York: Continuum.
Koester, U. 1982. "Policy Options for the Grain Economy of the European Community: Implications for Developing Countries." *International Food Policy Research Institute Research Report* no. 35.
———. 1990. "The Common Agricultural Policy: A Review of Its Operation and Effects on Developing Countries." *World Bank Research Observer.*
Koester, U., and M. D. Bale. 1984. "The Common Agricultural Policy of the European Community: A Blessing or a Curse for Developing Countries?" *World Bank Staff Working Paper* no. 630.
Koester, U., and P. M. Schmitz. 1982. "The EC Sugar Market Policy and Developing Countries." *European Review of Agricultural Economics.* vol. 9, pp. 183–204.
Koester, U., and S. Tangerman. 1987. *Agricultural Protectionism in the European Community.* Kiel: Christian-Albrechts-Universitat (Diskussionsbeitrage 60, Institut fur Agrarpolitik und Marklehre).
Koester, U., and H. Terwitte. 1988. *An Inventory of Disharmonies in EC Agricultural Policy Measures.* Kiel: Christian-Albrechts-Universitat (Dis-

kussionsbeitrage 62, Institut fur Agrarpolitik und Marklehre).
Kouamé, Patrice. 1988. *Intégration monétaire et croissance économique en l'Afrique de l'Ouest.* Abidjan: Les Nouvelles Africains.
KPMG. 1989. *Dealwatch.*
———. 1990. *Dealwatch.*
———. 1991. *Dealwatch.*
Krasner, Stephen. 1985. *Structural Conflict.* Berkeley: University of California Press.
Krell, Gert. 1990. "Europäische Revolution und globale Fundamentalkrise," in Entwicklungspolitik Dokumentation, a–f.
Kühne, Winrich. 1983. *Die Politik der Sowjetunion in Afrika, Bedingungen und Dynamik ihres ideologischen, ökonomischen und militärischen Engagements.* Baden:Baden.
———. 1988. "Update on Soviet Relations with Pretoria, the ANC, and the SACP." *CSIS Africa Notes,* no. 89 (September 1), pp. 1–8.
Laidi, Zaki. 1988. "Le déclassement international de l'Afrique." *Politique Etrangère,* vol. 53, no. 3, pp. 667–675.
Lancaster, Carol. 1990. "Reform or Else?" *Africa Report* (July–August), pp. 43–46.
Legum, Colin. 1980. "Foreign Intervention in Africa." *The Yearbook of World Affairs 1980.* London: Stevens and Sons.
Lindblom, Charles. 1980. *The Policy-Making Process.* Englewood Cliffs, N.J.: Prentice-Hall.
Lodge, Juliet. 1986. "The Single European Act," *Journal of Common Market Studies,* vol. 24, no. 3 (March), pp. 203–221.
———. 1987. "The Single European Act and the New Legislative Cooperation Procedure," *Journal of European Integration,* vol. 11, no. 1, pp. 5–28.
Lofchie, Michael, et al. 1982. "Food Deficits and Agricultural Policies in Tropical Africa." *Journal of Modern African Studies,* vol. 20, no. 1 (March), pp. 7–25.
Lowenkopf, Martin. 1989. "If the Cold War Is Over in Africa, Will the United States Still Care?" *CSIS Africa Notes,* no. 98 (May 30), p. 1.
Luckman, Robin. 1983. "Regional Security and Disarmament in Africa." *Alternatives,* vol. 2 (Fall), pp. 203–228.
Macedo, Jorge Braga de. "Collective Pegging to a Single Currency Union."
MacGaffey, Janet. 1989. "Perestroika Without Glasnost: The Need for a New Approach to the Real Economies of African Countries." Carter Center of Emory University, *Beyond Autocracy in Africa.* Working papers for the inaugural seminar of the Governance in Africa Program, February 17–18, 1989, Atlanta, Georgia.
Marchés Tropicaux. 1987. "Aux Défis du Financement de Developpement et du l'Integration Economique." no. 2948.
———. 1988. "L'UMOA Face Aux Defis du Financement." no. 2971.
Marsden, Keith, and Therese Belot. 1988. "Private Enterprise in Africa: Creating a Better Environment." *World Bank Discussion Papers.*
Martin, Guy. 1982. "Africa and the Ideology of Eur-Africa: Neo-Colonialism or Pan-Africanism." *Journal of Modern African Studies,* vol. 20, no. 2.
———. 1986. "Underdevelopment and Dependency in Francophone Africa." *Third World Quarterly,* vol. 8, no. 1 (April).
Le Matin, July 7, 1983.
Matthews, Alan. 1985. *The Common Agricultural Policy and the Less Developed Countries.* Dublin: Gill and Macmillan.
Matthews, Alan, and Dermot McAleese. 1990. "LDC Primary Exports to the EC: Prospects Post-1992." *Journal of Common Market Studies,* vol. 29 (December).

Mazrui, Ali. 1977. *African International Relations.* London: Heinemann.
Mazzeo, Domenico. 1984. "Conclusion: Problems and Prospects of Intra-African Cooperation." Pp. 225–242 in Domenico Mazzeo, ed., *African Regional Organizations.* London: Cambridge University Press.
Mbachu, Ozoemenam. 1990. "Capitalism, Socialism, and Democracy: A Nigerian Perspective." *Coexistence,* no. 27, pp. 187–197.
McFarlane, N. S. 1984. "Intervention and Security in Africa." *International Affairs,* 60 (Winter), pp. 52–71.
McNamara, Francis T. 1989. *France in Black Africa.* Washington: National Defense University Press.
McQueen, M., and C. Stevens. 1989. "Trade Preferences and Lomé IV." *Development Policy Review,* vol. 7, no. 3, pp. 239–250.
Meyers, B. D. 1974. "Intraregional Conflict Management by the OAU." *International Organization,* vol. 28, no. 3, pp. 345–373.
Mirsky, Georgy. 1987. "Newly Independent States: Ways of Development." *Asia and Africa Today,* no. 5 (September–October), pp. 53–59.
Mkandawire, Thandika. 1988. "Comments on Democracy and Political Instability." *Africa Development,* vol. 13, no. 3, pp. 77–82.
Molutsi, Patrick P., and John D. Holm. 1990. "Developing Democracy When Civil Society Is Weak: The Case of Botswana." *African Affairs,* vol. 89, no. 356 (July), pp. 323–340.
Monitor-Dienst (Africa). July 6, 1990.
———. December 6, 1990.
Moravcsik, Andrew. 1991. "Negotiating the Single European Act," *International Organization,* vol. 45, no. 1 (Winter), pp. 19–56.
Mosley, P. 1987. *Overseas Aid: Its Defence and Reform.* Brighton: Wheatsheaf.
———. 1990. "Increased Aid Flows and Human Resource Development in Africa." *Innocenti Occasional Papers* no. 5. Florence: UNICEF (International Child Development Centre).
Moss, Joanna. 1982. *The Lomé Conventions and Their Implications for the United States.* Boulder: Westview.
Moyes, A. 1988. "Common Ground: How Changes in the Common Agricultural Policy Affect the Third World." *OXFAM 1997.*
Mwaze, T. 1990. "Liberalization of Foreign-Exchange Rates." *Development Policy Review,* vol. 8.
Nana-Sinkam, Samuel C. 1989. "The Role and Structure of Banks." *The Courier,* no. 177 (September), Brussels, Commission of European Communities.
Ndegwa, Philip. 1989. "Increasing FDI in Africa." *CTC Reporter,* no. 27.
New York Times. April 28, 1989.
———. May 7, 1989.
Nicora, F. 1990. "Lomé IV: Processus, Phases et Structures de la Negociation." *Revue du Marche Commun,* vol. 337 (May), pp. 395–403.
Niegel, Meinhard. 1990. *Die Zeit* (May 4).
Nolutsungu, Sam. 1982. "African Interests and Soviet Power: The Local Context of Soviet Policy." *Soviet Studies,* vol. 24, no. 3, pp. 397–417.
Nyong'o, Peter Anyang. 1988. "Political Instability and the Prospects for Democracy in Africa." *Africa Development,* vol. 13, no. 1, pp. 84–95.
———, ed. 1987. *Popular Struggles for Democracy in Africa.* London: Zed.
Nzemen, Moise. 1989. "Tontines and Banking." *The Courier,* no. 177 (September), Brussels, Commission of European Communities.
Obasanjo, Olesegun, and Hans d'Orville. 1990. *The Impact of Europe in 1992 on West Africa.* New York: Taylor and Francis.
O'Connell, S. 1989. "Uniform Trade Taxes, Devaluation, and the Real Exchange

Rate: A Theoretical Analysis." *World Bank Working Paper* no. WPS 185.
OECD. *See* Organization for Economic Cooperation and Development.
Official Journal of the European Communities (OJEC). 1989. "Harmonised System Protocol," OJ387/89 (December 30).
―――. 1990. "Resolution on the Effects of the Single Market on ACP States," OJ C218/2 (September).
Ogunbadejo, Oye. 1988. "Nigeria and ECOWAS: From Vision to Reality." Pp. A124–A140 in Colin Legum, ed., *African Contemporary Record, Annual Survey and Documents, 1986–87.* New York: Africana.
OJEC. *See Official Journal of the European Communities.*
Onimode, Bade. 1989. *The IMF, the World Bank, and the African Debt: The Economic Impact.* London: Zed.
Organization for Economic Cooperation and Development. 1987. *National Policies and Agricultural Trade: Study on the European Community.* Paris: OECD.
―――. 1989a. *Development Cooperation in the 1990s, 1989 Report.* Paris: OECD.
―――. 1989b. *Financing and External Debt of Developing Countries.* Paris: OECD.
―――. 1989c. *Geographical Distribution of Financial Flows to Developing Countries.* Paris: OECD.
―――. 1990a. *Development Cooperation 1990 Report.* Paris: OECD.
―――. 1990b. *Financing and External Debt of Developing Countries: 1989 Survey.* Paris: OECD.
Osei-Hwedie, B. Z. 1983. "The Frontline States: Cooperation for the Liberation of Southern Africa." *Journal of African Studies,* vol. 10, no. 4, pp. 158–172.
Osterkamp, R., and A. J. Halbach. 1990. *Strukturanpassung in Entwicklungsländern und flankierende Massnahmen der Industrieländer sowie internationaler Einrichtungen.* London: München.
Overseas Development Institute (ODI). 1990. "Crisis in the Franc Zone." *ODI Briefing Paper.*
Parfitt, Trevor W., and Stephen P. Riley. 1989. *The African Debt Crisis.* London: Routledge.
Pisani, E. 1988. "Warning." *Lomé Briefing 2* (September).
Pittman, Dean. 1984. "The OAU and Chad." Pp. 297–326, in Yassin El-Ayouty and I. William Zartman, eds., *The OAU After Twenty Years.* New York: Praeger.
Pritchett, L. 1990. *The Merchandise Trade Balance and the Real Exchange Rate in LDCs.* Washington, D.C.: World Bank.
Quirk, Peter. 1987. "Floating Exchange Rates in Developing Countries: Experience with Auction and Interbank Rates." *IMF Occasional Paper* no. 54.
Ramirez-Rojas, C. L. 1989. "Monetary Substitution." *The Courier,* no. 177 (September), Brussels, Commission of European Communities.
Randal, Jonathan. 1990. "France Seen Reducing African Role." *Washington Post,* p. A21.
Ravenhill, John. 1985a. "The Future of EurAfrica." In Timothy Shaw and Olajide Aluko, eds., *Africa Projected: From Recession to Renaissance by the Year 2000?* London: Macmillan.
―――. 1985b. *Collective Clientelism: The Lomé Conventions and North-South Relations.* New York: Columbia University Press.
―――. 1987. "Negotiating the Lomé Conventions: A Little Is Preferable to Nothing." Pp. 213–258 in I. William Zartman, ed., *Positive Sum: Improving North-South Negotiations.* New Brunswick, N.J.: Transaction.
―――. 1990. "Reversing Africa's Economic Decline: No Easy Solutions." *World*

Policy Journal, vol. 7, no. 4 (Fall), pp. 703–732.
Riddell, R. C. 1987. *Foreign Aid Reconsidered.* London and Baltimore: James Currey and Johns Hopkins.
———. 1990b. "Côte d'Ivoire." Ch. 5 in R. C. Riddell.
Riddell, R. C., et al. 1990a. *Manufacturing Africa: Performance and Prospects of Seven Countries in Sub-Saharan Africa.* London and New York: James Currey and Heinemann.
Robbe, Martin. 1990. "Jahrhundertwende in Sicht: Versuch einer Standortbestimmung" (unpublished conference paper).
Rodrik, D. 1989. *The Welfare Economics of Debt Service.* Cambridge: Harvard University, JFK School of Government.
Rosenblatt, J. et al. 1988. "European Community: Principles and Consequences." *IMF Occasional Paper* no. 62.
SADCC. *See* Southern African Development Coordination Conference.
Sarris, Alexander H., and John Freebairn. 1983. "Endogenous Price Policies and International Wheat Prices." *American Journal of Agricultural Economics,* vol. 65, no. 2.
Schmidt, S. C., K. K. Frohberg, and D. L. Maxwell. 1987. "Implications of Grain Trade Liberalization in the European Community." *University of Illinois Agricultural Economics Research Report* no. 202.
Senghaas, Dieter. 1990. *Europa 2000: Ein Friedensplan.* Frankfurt: Suhrkamp Verlag.
Sesay, Amadu. 1986. "The OAU's Response to European Military Intervention in Africa." Pp. 153–182, in Amadu Sesay, ed., *Europe and Africa: From Partition to Dependence.* London: Croom Helm.
Shatalov, Sergei I. 1990. "Soviet Assistance to Africa: The New Realities." *CSIS Africa Notes,* no. 112 (May 22).
Shaw, Timothy, ed. 1982. *Alternative Futures for Africa.* Boulder: Westview.
Shaw, Timothy, and Olajide Aluko, eds. 1985. *Africa Projected: From Recession to Renaissance by the Year 2000?* London: Macmillan.
Shejnis, W. 1987. "Besonderheiten und Probleme des Kapitalismus in den Entwicklungsländern." *Sowjetwissenschaft, Gesellschaftswissenschaftliche Beiträge,* no. 4 (July/August), pp. 396–412.
Sklar, Richard L. 1988. "Beyond Capitalism and Socialism in Africa." *Journal of Modern African Studies,* vol. 26, no. 1, pp. 1–21.
Slovo, Joe. 1990. "Has Socialism Failed?" *South African Communist,* no. 121 (2d quarter), pp. 25–51.
Smirnov, Gleb V. 1989. "Economic Development of Socialist-Oriented African Countries." *Front File, IAIS Conference Special,* no. 17, vol. 3 (December), p. 6.
Southern African Development Coordination Conference (SADCC). 1990. *Annual Progress Report 1989–1990.* Reproduced and distributed by the Association of West European Parliamentarians for Action Against Apartheid (AWEPAAA), Amsterdam, September 1990.
Southern African Economist. 1990 (August–September).
Stadler, A. W. 1988. "A Contribution to the 'Conditions of Democracy Debate': A Working Paper." *International Affairs Bulletin,* vol. 12, no. 3, pp. 25ff.
The Star. September 15, 1990.
Stevens, Christopher. 1976. *The Soviet Union and Black Africa.* London: Macmillan.
———. 1990. "The Impact of Europe 1992 on the Maghreb and Sub-Saharan Africa." *Journal of Common Market Studies,* vol. 29 (December).
Stevens, Christopher, and Doeke Faber, eds. 1990. *The GATT Uruguay Round and Europe 1992.* Maastricht: Centre for European Development Coopera-

tion Management.

Stichele, M. V. 1990. "The Lost Spirit of Lomé," *Lomé Briefing Series* no. 14 (January–February). Brussels: Liaison Committee of Development NGOs to the European Communities.

Stremlau, J. 1977. *The International Politics of the Nigerian Civil War.* Princeton: Princeton University Press.

Suddeutesche Zeitung. July 23, 1990.

———. September 18, 1990.

———. November 20–21, 1990.

———. December 12, 1990.

Surry, Y., and G. Moschini. 1984. "Input Substitutability in the EC Compound Feed Industry." *European Review of Agricultural Economics,* vol. 11, no. 4.

Swampson, G. P., and R. H. Snape. 1980. "Effects of the EEC's Variable Import Levies." *Journal of Political Economy,* vol. 88, no. 5, pp. 1026–1040.

Tessler, Mark. 1986. "Explaining the Surprises of King Hassan II: The Linkage Between Domestic and Foreign Policy in Morocco." *UFSI Field Reports,* vol. 38, pp. 1–14.

Thompson, Edward. 1990. "The Ends of Cold War." *New Left Review,* no. 182 (July/August), pp. 139–150.

Thompson, W. Scott. 1969. *Ghana's Foreign Policy 1957–1966.* Princeton: Princeton University Press.

Tiewul, Sylvanus A. 1986. "TNCs in African Development: Some Policy Issues." *CTC Reporter,* no. 2.

Toepfer International. 1981. *The EEC Market Grain Regulation 1980/81.* Hamburg: Toepfer International.

Touval, S. 1982. *Politics of Independent Africa.* Cambridge, Mass.: Harvard University Press.

Tshiyembe, Mwayila. 1988. "De la Dialectique Binaire (En jeu/théâtre à la strategie africaine d'action collective maitrisée, la force militaire)." *Cahier de l'IPAG* (Travaux de recherches de l'Institut Panafrican de Géopolitique) no. 6 (October).

Tyers, R. 1990. "The Impact of Trade Liberalization on Domestic and International Price Instability." Pp. 41–76 in I. Goldin and O. Knudsen, eds., *Agricultural Trade Liberalization: Impacts for Developing Countries.* Washington, D.C.: OECD and World Bank.

United Nations. 1988. "Mid-Term Review of the Implementation of the United Nations Program of Action for African Economic Recovery and Development 1986–1990: Investment of Transnational Corporations in Africa." A/43/5—Add. 2.

United Nations Center on Transnational Corporations (UNCTC). 1985. *Transnational Corporations in World Development: Third Survey.* London: Graham and Trotman.

———. 1988. *Transnational Corporations in World Development: Trends and Prospects.* New York: UN.

———. 1990a. *Regional Economic Integration and Transnational Corporations in the 1990s: Europe 1992, North America, and Developing Countries.* United Nations publications, sales no. ST/CTC/Ser.A/15.

———. 1990b. "TNCs in the World Economy: Overall Trends of Foreign Direct Investment." *CTC Reporter,* no. 29.

———. 1990c. *A Regional Economic Integration and TNCs in the 1990s: Europe 1992.* New York: UNCTC.

———. 1991a. *European Integration and Foreign Direct Investment, 1957–1988: The Record Assessed.*

———. 1991b. *World Investment Report 1991: The Triad in Foreign Direct Investment.* United Nations Publication Sales No. E.91.11.A.12.
United Nations Economic and Social Council (UNESC). 1990. *Foreign Direct Investment in Africa and Strategies to Encourage Transnational Corporations to Respond Positively to the Improved Investment Climate.* New York, E/C/10/1990/9.
United Nations Industrial Development Organization (UNIDO). 1991. *Foreign Direct Investment Flows to Developing Countries: Recent Trends, Major Determinants, and Policy Implications.* Geneva: UNIDO.
U.S. Department of Commerce, International Trade Administration. 1988. *International Direct Investment: Global Trends and U.S. Role.* Washington, D.C.: Government Printing Office.
Valdes, A., and J. Zietz. 1990. "Examination of Proposals for Tariffication and Disciplines on Subsidies and Quantitative Controls Currently Under Negotiation." In A. Valdes and N. Islam, eds., *The GATT, Agriculture, and the Developing Countries.* Washington, D.C.: International Food Policy Research Institute.
Van Hooven, Eckart. 1991. "What Future for Europe?" *Euromoney* (January).
Vander Stichele, M., *See* Stichele, M. V.
Vinay, Bernard. 1980. *Zone Franc and Cooperation Monetaire.* Comoros: Ministere de Cooperation.
Volkov, Nikolai, and Vladimir Popov. 1989. "Has an Era of Neocolonialism Materialized?" *International Affairs,* no. 11, pp. 107–117.
Wallace, Cynthia Day. 1990. "Foreign Direct Investment in the Third World: U.S. Corporations and Government Policy." In Cynthia Day Wallace, ed., *Foreign Direct Investment in the 1990s: A New Climate in the Third World.* Dordrecht: Martinus Nijhoff.
Washington Post. January 26, 1989.
———. February 25, 1989.
———. April 30, 1989.
Weiland, Heribert. 1989. "Namibia auf dem Weg zur Unabhängigkeit." *Europa-Archiv,* no. 23, pp. 711–718.
West Africa. 1989. "CFA Under Threat." Vol. 3741 (May).
———. 1990. (Dieter Frisch article) February 26.
White, John A. 1991. *Military Expenditures in West African States: A Time Series Cross-Sectional Model* (working paper). Washington, D.C.: SAIS Program in African Studies.
Wickham, Peter. 1987. "The Choice of Exchange Rate Regimes in Developing Countries." *IMF Staff Paper.*
Widstrand, Carl Costa, ed. 1968. *African Boundary Problems.* Uppsala: Scandinavian Institute of African Studies.
World Bank. 1988. *Beyond Adjustment: Toward Sustainable Growth with Equity in Sub-Saharan Africa: Technical Report Part II.* Washington, D.C.: World Bank.
———. 1989a. *Sub-Saharan Africa: From Crisis to Sustainable Growth: a Long-Term Perspective Study.* Washington, D.C.: World Bank.
———. 1989b. *Africa's Adjustment and Growth in the 1980s: A Joint World Bank–UNDP Report.* Washington, D.C.: World Bank.
———. 1990. *World Development Report.* Washington, D.C.: World Bank.
Wright, Stephen. 1987. "Introduction." Pp. 1–13 in Stephen Wright, ed., *Africa in World Politics: Changing Perspectives.* London: Croom Helm.
Wubneh, Mulatu. 1990. "Foreign Direct Investment in Africa: Recent Trends and Prospects." Paper presented at the African Studies Association Meeting,

Baltimore, Maryland.

Yansane, Aguibou Y. 1978. "Some Problems of Monetary Dependency in French-Speaking African States." *Journal of African Studies* (Winter 1978–1979).

———. 1984. *Decolonization in West African States with a French Colonial Legacy, 1945–1980.* Cambridge, Mass.: Schenkman.

Zartman, I. William. 1967. "Africa as a Subordinate State System in International Relations." *International Organization,* vol. 21, no. 3, pp. 559–561.

———. 1971. *The Politics of Trade Negotiations Between Africa and the European Economic Community.* Princeton: Princeton University Press.

———. 1976. "Europe and Africa: Decolonization and Dependecy," *Foreign Affairs,* vol. 54, no. 2 (January), pp. 325–343.

———. 1984. "The OAU in the African State System: Interaction and Evaluation." Pp. 13–44 in Yassin El-Ayouty and I. William Zartman, eds., *The OAU After Twenty Years.* New York: Praeger.

———, ed. 1987. *Positive Sum: Improving North-South Negotiations.* New Brunswick, N.J.: Transaction.

———. 1989. *Ripe for Resolution: Conflict and Resolution in Africa.* New York: Oxford University Press.

Zolberg, Aristide. 1968. "Political Order in Changing Societies." *American Political Science Review,* vol. 23 (March), pp. 72–92.

Zysman, John, and Wayne Sandholtz. "1992: Recasting the European Bargain." *World Politics,* vol. 42, no. 1 (October), pp. 95–128.

About the Contributors

Ousmane Badiane is research fellow at the International Food Policy Research Institute, Washington, D.C. His work has focused on regional trade and integration among African countries. His latest work, *Agricultural Trade Pessimism in West African Countries and the Possible Role of Regional Markets*, is forthcoming in 1992.

Carol Cosgrove is an international consultant who advises the European Commission, the ACP Secretariat, the Commonwealth Secretariat, and many other international agencies and corporations on the European Community in the world economy. The is visiting professor at the College of Europe, Bruges, and at Tufts University. She is the author of seven books on the EC including, *Europe and Africa* (1977), *A Framework for Development* (1981), and *Trade from Aid* (1992).

Jaime de Melo is an economist in the research department at the World Bank and a visiting professor at the universities of Geneva and Clermont-Ferrand since 1989. His work is primarily in the field of commercial policy and macroeconomic stabilization in developing countries.

Shantayanan Devarajan is principal economist at the World Bank's Country Economics Department. He is on leave from the John F. Kennedy School of Government at Harvard University where he is an associate professor of public policy. His current research focuses on public expenditure in developing countries and problems of environmental degradation.

Persephone Economou is an economist currently on the staff of the Transnational Corporations and Management Division of the United Nations Department of Economic and Social Development. Her research interest include foreign direct investment trends and their impact on developing countries.

Michelle Gittelman is a doctoral candidate at the Wharton School in Philadelphia and holds a joint masters degree in business administration and international affairs from Columbia University. For three years she worked in the Transnational Corporations Management Division of the United Nations Department of Economic and Social Development. Her research has focused on European integration, foreign investment in the Triad, and multinational corporations.

Edmond Kwam Kouassi is a former vice dean and a current professor of law in the Law School, University of Benin, Togo. He formerly held the post of Togolese Ambassador to the United Nations. He is the author of a number of works on African international organizations.

Winrich Kühne is a senior research fellow and in charge of the Africa program of the German Research Institute for International Politics and Security of the Stiftung Wissenschaft und Politik (SWP) in Ebenhausen, Federal Republic of Germany. His work focuses on African affairs and Soviet policy toward the Third World.

General Olusegun Obasanjo was an officer of the Nigerian army, and chief of state of Nigeria from 1977–1978, coming to power on the assassination of General Murtala Mohammed. He launched the process to establish the Conference for Security, Stability, Development, and Cooperation in Africa (CSSDCA) and has been active as the founder of the African Leadership Forum, a consultative group of former heads of state and government.

John Ravenhill is senior fellow in the Department of International Relations, Research School of Pacific Studies, Australian National University. He previously taught at the University of Sydney and the University of Virginia. His books include *Politics and Society in Contemporary Africa* (with Chazan, Mortimer, Rothchild) and *Hemmed In: Responses to Africa's Economic Decline*.

Roger C. Riddell is research fellow of the Overseas Development Institute in London. He has been involved in a substantive study for the African Development Bank, Abidjan, on economic cooperation and integration in southern Africa. He has recently completed a book on the impact of non-governmental organizations on income-generating projects and is currently working on a study of the role of voluntary agencies in development in the 1990s.

Eve N. Sandberg is associate professor in the Politics Department of Oberlin College. She is editor of the forthcoming book, *Changing Politics of Non-Governmental Organizations and the African State*. Her other work has focused on structural adjustment programs, women in late industrializing states, and international donor influence in African domestic politics.

George E. Shambaugh IV is lecturer in the Department of Government at Smith College. He holds doctorate and masters degrees in international affairs and a masters degree in philosophy, all from Columbia University.

John White is a doctoral candidate in African studies at SAIS Johns Hopkins, Washington, D.C. He holds a masters in Public Management and Policy Analysis from Carnegie Mellon University.

Mulatu Wubneh is associate professor of planning and coordinator of the African Studies Program at East Carolina University at Greenville. He has written a number of articles on planning and economic development in Africa and is coauthor of *Ethiopia: Transition and Development in the Horn of Africa* (1988).

I. William Zartman is Jacob Blaustein Professor of Conflict Management and International Organization and director of African studies at The Johns Hopkins University Nitze School of Advanced International Studies. He is secretary-treasurer of the newly formed West African Research Association (WARA). He is author of *Ripe for Resolution: Conflict and Intervention in Africa* and many other books and articles on African affairs and international negotiation.

Index

Accord of Nonaggression and Assistance. *See* ANAD
ACP group, 41-61, 159, 176; access to EC markets, 42, 64, 90; bargaining strengths, 43, 56, 57, 59; competition from Latin America and Asia, 68; competitiveness in EC market, 69; debt-service ratio, 42; differential treatment, 48, 49; divisions within, 48, 59; economic decline, 46, 52, 56, 59; effect of European events, 63; exports to EC, 42, 90, 91; fear of Eastern Europe, 43, 63, 95, 108; negotiations with EC, 44, 161-165; preference-adjusted prices, 69; preferential tariffs in EC, 43, 90; promotion of service industries, 54; rum exports to EC, 67; stabilization of exports, 65; structural adjustment, 42, 44, 45, 46, 47, 50, 52-53, 59, 65; structural problems, 52; sugar exports to EC, 66; trade with EC, 53, 55, 63-73, 162, 163*fig*
Adamishin, Anatoly, 8, 11
Afghanistan, military intervention, 7, 8
Africa: banking, 105; decolonization, 1, 5, 27; dependencies, 5, 95; disengagement of Soviet Union, 8-12; disengagement of TNCs, 100-101; EC investment, 104*tab*; effect of CAP on economies, 78-79; effect of Gulf War on development, 72; European security roles, 27-40; extension of French monetary system, 4; foreign investment, 16, 95-119, 97*tab*; future of capitalism, 12-13; investment climate, 101; investment decline, 96; investment policies, 111-119; marginalization, 17; nonalignment, 2; per capita income, 1; political climate, 117; rural sector, 23; sub-Saharan, 139-158; trade arrangements with EC, 53, 55, 63-73, 90-93, 162, 163*fig*; transnational corporations in, 99-101; vulnerability to CAP, 77-78
African Financial Community, 121-137
African National Congress. *See* ANC
Africa Watch, 153
Agriculture: collectivization, 14; competition, 23, 60; dominant role, 78; EC imports, 81*tab*; exports, 86*fig*; liberalization, 80; markets, 75, 76; nationalization, 14; negotiation issues, 45; prices, 85*tab*; production, 14; protectionism, 75, 78-79; reform, 15, 87, 88, 89; role in developing countries, 75; trade, 53, 78, 81-85; wage gap with industry, 88; world prices, 83
Agrobusiness, 14
Ahidjo, Ahmadou, 29
Aid: to ACP group, 54, 55; automaticity, 43; commodity, 149; conditionality, 47, 60; declining, 23; dependencies, 5; development, 20, 23, 25n7, 39; diversion, 63, 147; to Eastern Europe, 21-23; EC to ACP group, 71-72; fatigue, 21; humanitarian, 22, 23; inflationary effects, 54;

203

linked to reform, 152; non-conditionality, 43; performance, 139-158; prospects, 139-158; relation to growth, 142-146, 157n9; to Sub-Saharan Africa, 139-158; tied to imports, 149, 157n17
Algeria, foreign investment, 98tab
Amin, Idi, 29, 32
ANAD (Accord of Nonaggression and Assistance), 33; defense protocols, 36; protection of natural resources, 34; security role, 34
ANC (African National Congress), 10; trade unions, 18; view on economy, 17
Angola: defense agreements, 32; economic growth, 12-13; famine, 14, 158n31; military interventions, 2, 3, 7, 9; mixed economy in, 17; oil production, 72
Apartheid, 11
Arms: exports, 38tab; imports, 36-39, 37tab; sales, 21; sources, 38, 40
ASEAN (Association of Southeast Asian Nations), 159, 174, 175, 176; negotiation success, 165-167
Association of Southeast Asian Nations. See ASEAN

Badiane, Ousmane, 75-94
Barbados, agriculture in, 66
Belgium: aid to Africa, 141; transnational corporations, 99-101
Benin: CEAO membership, 33; defense agreements, 28, 31; export earnings, 93tab; foreign investment, 98tab; investment policies, 112; Marxism in, 12; military intervention, 30; mixed economy in, 17; popular revolt, 19
Bokassa, Jean-Bedel, 29
Botswana: exports to EC, 65; foreign investment, 98tab; growth rate, 25n3; oil production, 103
Britain: aid to Africa, 54, 55, 158n34; imports from Commonwealth countries, 66; investment in Africa, 96, 100, 102; support for structural adjustment, 47; trade concessions, 45; transnational corporations, 99-101
Bureaucracy, 19; decreasing, 96
Burkina Faso: CEAO membership, 33; defense agreements, 28, 31; disengagement of TNCs, 101; export earnings, 93tab; foreign investment, 98tab; investment policies, 112
Burundi: defense agreements, 31; export earnings, 93tab; TNCs in, 110tab
Cameroon: defense agreements, 28, 31; export earnings, 93tab; foreign investment, 98tab; military intervention, 29; oil production, 72; TNCs in, 110tab
CAP (Common Agricultural Policy): and ACP exports, 65; African vulnerability, 77-78; effect on Africa, 5, 75-94, 78-79; effects on trade, 81-85; impact on welfare, 86-90; implications for international markets, 75, 77; and international price changes, 83tab; inward-looking policy, 75, 76, 77; liberalization, 78, 84, 85, 86, 87, 88; and market instability, 84; objectives, 76-77; price subsidies, 23; and price volatility, 83; relation to OECD, 80; tariff barriers, 50
Capital: accumulation, 13; foreign, 96; indigenous, 13; investment, 111; restructuring, 111; risk, 65, 101; transfer, 19, 22
Capitalism, future in Africa, 12-13
Carrington, Edwin, 45, 48, 61n6
CEAO (West African Economic Community), 33; defense protocols, 36
CEEAC (Economic Community of the Central African States), 4
Central African Republic: defense agreements, 28, 31; export earnings, 93tab; investment policies, 112
CFA Zone: adjustment in, 123-127; compte d'operations, 125, 126; growth rates, 123-127, 127-129; performance of members, 121-137
Chad: defense agreements, 28, 31, 32; export earnings, 93tab; military intervention, 29; opposition movements, 3
Cheysson, Claude, 47
Chissano, Joaquim, 8, 18
Collectivization, 14, 15
Colonialism, 11, 13, 20
Commodities: export, 42, 115; negotiation issues, 45; prices, 42, 46, 59,

183; processing for export, 104; protectionism, 91; world prices, 69
Common Agricultural Policy. *See* CAP
Communatí financìere africaine. *See* African Financial Community
Communaute Economique d' Estats de l'Afrique Centrale, 116
Communism: disintegration, 7, 63; South African, 10
Comores, export earnings, 93*tab*
Compensation, for loss of preferences, 49-50
Competition: ACP group, 42; in agriculture, 23; in arms market, 37; Cold War, 3; currency valuation in, 69; with Eastern Europe, 17, 69; East-West, 7; Soviet-African, 10-11; with Third World countries, 5; on world market, 16
Conflict: internal, 35; interregional, 115; management, 22; mediation, 35; regional, 7, 8; resolution, 4, 40
Congo: defense agreements, 28, 31; disengagement of TNCs, 101; economic growth, 12; Marxism in, 12; mixed economy in, 17; oil production, 12, 72; TNCs in, 110*tab*
Congo Conventions, 2
Congress of South African Trade Unions. *See* COSATU
Conseil de l'Entente, 28
Control, arms, 8
COSATU (Congress of South African Trade Unions), 17, 18
Cosgrove, Carole, 63-73
Crocker, Chester, 8
Currency: convertible, 182; devaluation, 96, 100, 116, 122, 135; European, 46, 64; inconvertibility, 71; overvaluation, 69, 70
Czechoslovakia, trade agreements, 11

Debt: ACP group, 42, 54; cancellation, 23, 39, 61*n7*; interest, 143; negotiation issues, 45; reductions, 164; relief, 50, 59, 69, 146; rescheduling, 157*n11*; service, 23, 42, 125; to GDP ratio, 125
Deby, Idriso, 30
Decolonization, 1, 5, 27
Defense agreements, 27-40; as colonial vestige, 32-33

de Klerk, F. W., 10
de Melo, Jaime, 121-137
Democratization, 23, 27; African, 72; Eastern European, 72; EC promotion, 53; pressures, 3, 4
Dependency, 1; on former metropole, 2-3; remaining, 5; reverse, 5; security, 3, 5, 27-40
Devarajan, Shantayaran, 121-137
Developing countries: arms exports, 37; capital flow to West, 23; distribution of wealth, 16; gap with North, 19; market vulnerability, 75; role of agriculture, 75
Development: aid, 20, 23, 25*n7*, 39, 141*tab*; dependencies, 5; economic, 72; noncapitalist, 12; rural, 143; women in, 164
Disarmament, 20-21
Distribution, unreliable, 69
Djibouti, defense agreements, 28, 31
Drought, 14, 115

ECA (Economic Commission for Africa), 20; on financial integration, 70
ECOMOG, 35
Economic: cooperation, 8; development, 72, 116; failure, 13, 14; growth in franc zone, 4; integration, 64; mismanagement, 13; reform, 96; restructuring, 115-118
Economic Commission for Africa. *See* ECA
Economic Community of the Central African States. *See* CEEAC
Economic Community of West African States. *See* ECOWAS
Economic Support Fund, 39
Economou, Persa, 95-119
Economy: centrally planned, 13, 14; global, 51; market, 7, 15-17, 18; mixed, 17-18; open, 78; political, 159-178; rural, 14; shadow, 15; social market, 15; subsistence, 14
ECOWAS (Economic Community of West African States), 4, 116, 179, 182, 183, 184; Community Armed Forces, 35; defense protocols, 36; Monitoring Group, 4; in PMA, 35
EDF (European Development Fund), 46, 50, 65, 144
EFTA (European Free Trade Association), membership in EC, 63

Egypt, foreign investment, 98*tab*
EMS (European Monetary System), 4; creation, 64
Engels, Friedrich, 14
Equatorial Guinea, in CFA, 121
Ethiopia, 3; defense agreements, 32; economic growth, 12-13; export earnings, 93*tab*; famine, 158*n31*; investment policies, 112; land reform, 15; Marxism in, 7; military intervention, 2, 3, 9-10; mixed economy in, 17
Ethnonationalism, 22
Europe, Eastern: collapse of communism, 63; competition with, 17, 69; diversion of aid from ACP group, 71-72, 148; economic problems, 21-23; emigration, 11; liberalizing economies, 43; multiparty systems, 40; reconstruction, 21-23
European Community (EC), 1; ACP group relations, 41-61; agricultural imports, 81tab, 90, 92*fig*; Agriculture Directorate, 44; aid to ACP group, 71-72; Common Agricultural Policy, 5, 75-94; common tariff reduction, 43; Council of Ministers, 45, 55, 56, 57, 58; debt cancellation policies, 23; Development Directorate, 44, 56, 57; domestic issues, 64; export role, 82; External Relations Directorate, 44; free access of African products, 51, 64; General System of Preferences, 5, 55, 67; industry restructuring, 109-111; internal markets, 81; intervention in domestic markets, 77; investment in Africa, 71-72, 104tab, 107; Japanese investment, 107; in Lomé conventions, 41-61, 58; Multi-Fibre Agreement, 67; national quotas, 68; North-South division, 45; and OECD interdependence, 84; protection for nontraditional imports, 67-69; restrictions, 4; Rome Treaty, 3, 4, 5; sugar import policies, 66; TNCs, 103tab, 109; trade with ACP group, 63-73, 90-93, 162, 163*fig*
European Development Fund. *See* EDF
European Free Trade Association. *See* EFTA
European Investment Bank, 50, 153

European Monetary Systems. *See* EMS
European Parliament, 44, 45, 52, 56
Exchange(s): Euro-African, 2; foreign, 72, 100; rates, 70, 135, 136*n3*
Exchange Rate Mechanism, 64
Expatriates, 3
Exploitation, 16
Export(s): ACP group, 42; agricultural, 86*fig*; barriers, 5; commodity, 42, 115; credits, 68; decrease in, 6; duty-free, 55; earnings, 91; earnings stabilization, 5; effect of CAP on, 5; fuel, 108; manufacturing, 42; nontraditional, 67-69; restitutions, 77, 84; stabilization, 65; subsidies, 80; supply-inelastic, 68-69; surplus, 80, 82; third-country, 81, 82
Eyedema, Gnassingbe, 30

Famine, 14, 21, 23, 115, 158*n31*; international response, 158*n31*
Fiji: agriculture, 66; exports to EC, 66
France: on aid to ACP group, 55; aid to Africa, 157*n23*; funding recommendations, 60*n5*; investment in Africa, 96, 100, 102; security role in Africa, 28-36; trade concessions, 46; transnational corporations, 99-101
Franc Zone, 4, 70-71; benefits to ACP group, 70; performance of members, 121-137
Frelimo, 8, 9

Gabon: defense agreements, 28, 31; military intervention, 29; oil production, 72, 103; TNCs in, 110*tab*
Gambia, export earnings, 93*tab*
General System of Preferences. *See* GSP
Germany: on aid to ACP group, 54, 55; aid to Africa, 141, 157*n22*; investment in Africa, 105; support for structural adjustment, 47; trade concessions, 45; transnational corporations, 99-101
Ghana: agricultural reform, 15; foreign investment, 98*tab*; investment policies, 112; structural adjustment programs, 144
Giscard d'Estaing, Valery, 29
Gittelman, Michelle, 95-119
Glasnost, 12

Gorbachev, Mikhail, 8, 10, 12, 20, 63
Government: authoritarian-bureaucratic, 13; centralist, 7; corruption, 100, 117; maladministration, 46; Marxist, 7; multiparty, 8, 19, 40, 72; one-party, 7, 19; state capitalist, 12
Grants, 47; and military expenditures, 39
Greece: in EMS, 64; opposition to trade concessions, 45
Gross national product, in developing countries, 16
Group of 77, 159, 174, 177; negotiating failure, 168
Growth: GDP, 126, 127tab, 134; per capita rates, 5; population, 16, 24; productivity, 16; rate in CFA Zone, 124*tab*; relation to aid, 142-146
GSP (General System of Preferences), 5; protection for ACP exports, 67
Guinea: CEAO membership, 33; investment policies, 112
Guinea-Bissau, export earnings, 93*tab*

Habré, Hissène, 30, 32, 33
Habyarimana, Juvenal, 30
Harmonization: monetary, 182; regulations, 43; standards, 5; of taxes, 69
Hungary, trade agreements, 11

Immigration: from Eastern Europe, 11, 22; problems, 34
"Imperialism as the Highest State of Capitalism" (Lenin), 11
Import(s): agricultural, 81*tab*; discrimination in, 81; displacement, 83; from Eastern Europe, 108; restriction, 80; strangulation, 46; substitution, 101, 102, 104
Income, per capita, 1, 16, 123
Industrialization, urban, 15
Industry, wage gap with agriculture, 88
Inflation, 136; effect on aid, 54
Infrastructure, 16; development, 119; Eastern European, 22, 71; in market economy, 18, 19; projects, 144; support, 164; upgrading, 107
Integration: financial, 70, 71; regional, 116
Inter-Governmental Agency on

Drought, 116
International Development Association, 140
International Monetary Fund: funding conditions, 50; obligation repayments, 52; structural adjustment programs, 42; on trade liberalization, 46
Intervention: criticism of, 32; foreign, 4; indirect, 31; military, 27, 32, 35; security, 3, 4; state, 17, 18, 76
Investment: in Africa, 16, 96, 111-119; decrease in, 6, 96; in Eastern Europe, 96; EC-ACP group, 63-73, 71-72; efficiency-seeking, 102; European Investment Bank, 50; foreign, 16, 22, 97*tab*; foreign direct in Africa, 95-119; French, 16; German, 16; guaranteed against loss, 96, 101; import-substituting, 101, 102, 106; joint-venture, 118; laws, 96, 113*tab*, 114, 117; long-term, 39; losses, 95; in manufacturing, 99, 104, 106; 103; market-seeking, 106; negotiation issues, 45; as neocolonialism, 96, 112; and political stability, 117; private, 71, 101, 117; rate of return, 100; rationalized, 101, 102, 105-106, 107; resource-based, 101-102, 105-106; sectoral distribution, 102-108; in services, 99, 103, 105; targeting, 118; trade-related, 105-106; transformation to grants, 50
Italy: on aid to ACP group, 55; opposition to trade concessions, 45; transnational corporations, 99-101
Ivory Coast: capitalism in, 12; CEAO membership, 33; defense agreements, 28, 31; disengagement of TNCs, 101; economic decline, 25*n3*; export earnings, 93*tab*; foreign investment, 98*tab*; structural adjustment programs, 144; TNCs in, 110*tab*

Japan: aid to Africa, 141; aid to ASEAN, 166*fig*; investment in Africa, 105; investment in EC, 107
Journiac, Réné, 29

Katanga province, 29
Kenya, 48; capitalism in, 12; exports

to EC, 65; foreign investment, 98*tab*; investment policies, 112; TNCs in, 110*tab*
Koffigoh, Joseph, 30
Kouassi, Edmond, 27-40
Kühne, Winrich, 7-25

Lesotho, export earnings, 93*tab*
Liberia: defense agreements, 32; opposition movements, 3; TNCs in, 110*tab*
Living standards: decline, 20; raising, 64
Loans, 47; as long-term investments, 39
Lomé conventions, 1, 5, 41-61, 144, 154; aid provisions, 64-65; duration, 52; EC discretionary power, 58; emphasis on infrastructure, 46; geographical extension, 51; negotiation process, 49-55; renegotiation, 57; special protocols, 65, 66, 67; total aid, 158*n*29; trade arrangements, 64-65, 90

Madagascar: defense agreements, 28, 31; export earnings, 93*tab*
Malawi: foreign investment, 98*tab*; TNCs in, 110*tab*
Mali: agricultural reform, 15; CEAO membership, 33; defense agreements, 31; export earnings, 93*tab*; foreign investment, 98*tab*
Manufacturing, ACP group, 42
Marginalization: of Africa, 17; resource, 17
Marin, Manuel, 44, 53, 54, 57
Market(s): access, 96, 162, 164; agricultural, 75, 76; black, 15, 38; common, 64; destabilization, 84; disturbances, 84; domestic, 76; economy, 7, 15-17, 18; foreign, 106; indispensability, 13-15; international, 84, 91; intervention, 76; negation, 13, 14; parallel, 15; preferential access, 2, 91; prices, 89; single European, 63, 64, 65-67, 68; stabilization, 85; vulnerability, 75; weapons, 37
Marxism, 19; African regimes, 2; effect on economy, 14; errors in, 12; failure, 25*n*5
Mauritania: CEAO membership, 33; defense agreements, 28, 31; military intervention, 29
Mauritius: agriculture, 66; exports to EC, 66
Mba, Leon, 29
Mengistu Haile Mariam, 9, 15, 32
Metropoles: dependence on, 2-3, 27; interest in former colonies, 57, 109; security withdrawal, 27
Military: arms sales, 21; assistance agreements, 28; balance of power, 8; expenditures, 25*n*8, 36-39, 115; foreign personnel in Africa, 3; interventions, 2, 3, 7, 8, 9, 10, 17, 18, 27, 29, 30, 32, 35; power, 8; retaliation, 29
Mining, negotiation issues, 45
Mitterrand, François, 30
Moi, Daniel Arap, 48
Morocco, foreign investment, 98*tab*
Movimento Popular de Libertaçao de Angola. *See* MPLA
Mozambique: defense agreements, 32; economic growth, 12-13; famine, 14, 158*n*31; military intervention, 8, 9; mixed economy in, 17; Soviet aid, 25*n*7; trade unions, 18
MPLA (Movimento Popular de Libertaçao de Angola), 9
Multilateralization, 3; of dependencies, 5; global, 5
Museveni, Yoweri, 32

Namibia: end of conflict, 8; independence, 7; UN role, 8
Nationalization, 15, 17; agriculture, 14; trade, 14
Negotiations: failures, 167-169; North-South, 159-178; successful, 160-167
Neocolonialism, 11, 96
Neoimperialism, 11
Netherlands: on aid to ACP group, 54; investment in Africa, 105; support for structural adjustment, 47; trade concessions, 45; transnational corporations, 99-101
NGOs (nongovernmental organizations), 56, 149; foreign-based, 144
Niger: CEAO membership, 33; defense agreements, 28, 31; export earnings, 93*tab*; investment policies, 112
Nigeria: foreign investment, 98*tab*; investment policies, 112; oil produc-

tion, 72, 103; TNCs in, 110*tab*
Noninterference policy, 53
North-South: negotiations, 159-178; relations, 16

OAU (Organization of African Unity), 20, 32, 33
Obasanjo, Olusegun, 179-185
OECD (Organization for Economic Cooperation and Development), 141, 142; agricultural reform, 87, 88; data on investments, 96; Development Assistance Committee, 99, 140; and EC interdependence, 84; relation to CAP, 80; trade liberalization, 90*tab*
Oil: in ACP group, 42, 72; exporting countries, 98; prices, 42, 105; production, 167-168
Olympio, Sylvanus, 29
OPEC (Organization of Petroleum Exporting Countries), 159; negotiating failure, 167-168
Organization for Economic Cooperation and Development. *See* OECD
Organization of African Unity. *See* OAU
Organization of Petroleum Exporting Countries. *See* OPEC
Organizations, nongovernmental. *See* NGOs

Pact of Mutual Assistance in Defense Matters. *See* PMA
Patronism, 13
"Peace Accords for Angola," 9
Peace dividend, 20-21, 72
Perestroika, 8
Pisani, Edgar, 47
Planning: macroeconomic, 17; role in market economy, 18
PMA (Pact of Mutual Assistance in Defense Matters), 35, 36
Poland: bureaucracy in, 19; trade agreements, 11
Polisario, 29
Population, 45; agricultural, 76; expatriate, 3; growth, 14, 16, 24
Portugal: agricultural processing, 66; competition with ACP group, 60; in EMS, 64; opposition to trade concessions, 45
Poverty, 14, 24, 115

Power: military, 8; purchasing, 116
Preferential Trade Area. *See* PTA
Price(s): agricultural, 83, 85*tab*; commodity, 43, 46, 59, 183; controls, 100; distortions, 91; fluctuations, 77; instability, 69, 90; international changes, 83*tab*; international commodity, 42; intervention, 77; market, 89; oil, 42, 70, 105; preference-adjusted, 69; support, 76; volatility, 83, 85
Privatization, of state enterprises, 112, 116
Production: adjusting domestic, 84; costs, 107; domestic, 42; import-replacing, 102; for local markets, 102; support, 77
Productivity: growth, 16; price-reducing increases, 81
PTA (Preferential Trade Area), 4

Rates: convertibility, 4; exchange, 70, 125, 126, 135, 136*n3*; fixed, 4; investment, 126; per capita growth, 5
Ravenhill, John, 41-61
Reagan, Ronald, 8
Reform: agricultural, 15, 87, 88; economic, 96; land, 15; linked to aid, 152
Refugees, 115; negotiation issues, 45
Relations: EC-ACP group, 41-61; North-South, 16; rural-urban, 14; Washington-Moscow, 8
Renamo, 9
Resources: allocation, 13; diversion to arms acquisition, 40; marginalization, 17; protection, 34; transfer, 20
Riddell, Roger, 139-158
Rights, human, 13, 23, 33, 40, 44, 45, 53, 58, 152, 153, 155
Romania, trade agreements, 11
Rome Treaty, 3, 4, 5
Rural development, 143
Rwanda: defense agreements, 31; export earnings, 93*tab*; military forces, 3-4; military intervention, 30

SADDC (South African Development Coordination Conference), 18; economic planning, 23
Saint Lucia, agriculture, 66
Sandberg, Eve, 159-178
Sector, private, 17; inefficiency, 13;

support for, 155
Sector, rural, 13; African, 23; subsistence economy, 14
Security: collective, 4, 31, 33, 36; dependencies, 5, 27-40; economic, 55-56; European roles, 27-40; interventions, 4; of trade access, 55
Senegal: CEAO membership, 33; defense agreements, 28, 31; disengagement of TNCs, 101; export earnings, 93*tab*; investment policies, 112; TNCs in, 110*tab*
Shambaugh, George, 159-178
Shultz, George, 8
Sierra Leone, export earnings, 93*tab*
Single Europe Act of 1985, 1, 44, 64
Smuggling, 15
Social: antagonism, 16; market, 15; retrogression, 12; stability, 65; stratification, 16
Somalia: defense agreements, 32; investment policies, 112
South Africa: arms exports, 38; Eastern European immigration, 11; Soviet Union and, 10-11; trade agreements, 11; trade unions, 18
South African Development Coordination Conference. *See* SADDC
Soviet Union: attempted coup, 7, 10; disengagement from Africa, 8-12; interest in Africa, 2, 10; relations with U. S., 8
Spain: agricultural processing, 66; competition with ACP group, 60; opposition to trade concessions, 45
STABEX, 5, 45, 47, 76, 90; eligibility, 154; expansion, 72; grants, 50; objectives, 91; stabilization of ACP exports, 65; transfers, 61*n5*
Stability: of agricultural markets, 84; decrease, 84; Eastern European, 22; metropole fostered, 31; political, 117; social, 65
Standard of living, CAP objectives, 76
State: intervention, 17, 18, 76; technocratic role, 19; transformation of, 18-19
Sterling zone, 4
Structural adjustment, 16, 46, 47, 116; ACP group, 42, 65; assistance, 59, 69; in CFA countries, 122; EC involvement, 50, 52, 54, 58; financing, 44; funding, 50; lending, 151; linked to aid, 144, 151; negotiation issues, 45; and STABEX transfers, 52-53
Subsidies: agricultural, 23; removal, 23; surplus exports, 80
Sudan: export earnings, 93*tab*; famine, 158*n31*; foreign investment, 98*tab*
Swaziland: export earnings, 93*tab*; exports to EC, 65
SYSMIN, 5, 42, 45, 50; stabilization of ACP exports, 65

Tanzania: agricultural reform, 15; export earnings, 93*tab*; investment policies, 112
Tariff: barriers, 50, 102, 173; preferences, 42; protection, 46
Taxes: harmonization within EC, 69; inflation, 122, 134; luxury, 69; producer, 77; revenue, 69, 183; seigniorage, 125; on tropical products, 69
Taylor, Charles, 35
Technology: accelerated innovation, 16; access to foreign, 96
Third World: allies of, 20; competition in, 5
TNCs (transnational corporations), 99-101, 102, 103tab, 109; disengagement from Africa, 100-101; joint-ventures with, 118; viewed as exploiters, 117
Togo: CEAO membership, 33; defense agreements, 28, 31; export earnings, 93*tab*; investment policies, 112; military forces, 3-4; military intervention, 30; structural adjustment programs, 144
Trade: access, 44, 46; agricultural, 78, 81-85; barriers, 23, 76, 102, 162; concessions, 42, 45; declines, 162; deficits, 6; dependence for food consumption, 78; disruptions, 63; diversification, 42; diversion, 63; EC-ACP group, 63-73; effect of CAP, 81-85; informal, 15; liberalization, 86, 89fig, 90tab, 96; nationalization, 14; negotiation issues, 45; pessimism, 80; preferences, 55; reciprocity, 68; regional, 106, 116, 182; terms, 6; uncertainty, 91
Transnational corporations. *See* TNCs
Trinidad and Tobago, oil production, 72
Tunisia, foreign investment, 98*tab*

Uganda, 29, 32; export earnings, 93*tab*; foreign investment, 98*tab*
UNCTAD (United Nations Conference on Trade and Development), 48, 59; on differential treatment, 49
Uniao Nacional para a Independência Total de Angola. *See* UNITA
Unions, trade: autonomy, 18; independent, 17
UNITA (Uniao Nacional para a Independência Total de Angola), 9
United Kingdom. *See* Britain
United Nations: Angola Verification Mission, 9; Conference on Trade and Development. *See* UNCTAD; Economic Commission for Africa, 4; interventions, 4; Multilateral Investment Guarantee Agency, 96; role in Namibia, 8
United States: foreign investment, 96; interest in Africa, 2; investment in Africa, 101, 105, 119*n1*; relations with Soviet Union, 8; transnational corporations, 99-101
Uruguay Round of GATT, 43, 44, 51, 60, 68, 69, 72, 75, 78, 177

War: Chado-Libyan, 30; Cold, 2, 3, 17; Gulf, 22, 72; Liberian civil, 4; national liberation, 8; regional, 35
Wealth, uneven distribution, 16
West African Economic Community. *See* CEAO
White, John, 27-40
Women: in development, 164; role of, 45
World Bank, 3, 16, 23, 115, 142; capacity-building initiatives, 152; funding conditions, 50; Multilateral Investment Guarantee Agency, 96; obligation repayments, 52; structural adjustment programs, 42; on trade liberalization, 46
Wubnuh, Mulatu, 95-119

Yaoundé conventions, 5, 58, 90
Youlou, Fulbert, 29
Yugoslavia, trade agreements, 11

Zaire: capitalism in, 12; defense agreements, 31, 32; foreign investment, 98*tab*; military forces, 3-4; military intervention, 29, 30; TNCs in, 110*tab*; unofficial sector, 15
Zambia: foreign investment, 98*tab*; oil production, 103; structural adjustment programs, 144; TNCs in, 110*tab*
Zartman, I. William, 1-6
Zimbabwe: agricultural reform, 15; exports to EC, 65; independence, 27; mixed economy in, 17; oil production, 103; structural adjustment programs, 144; TNCs in, 110*tab*

About the Book

With the 1992 state of European unification and the fourth Lomé Agreement, signed in 1990, Europe and Africa are entering a new phase in their postcolonial relations. Europe is turning inward to consolidate its integration; Africa is pulling away, retaining only an increased aid commitment from its former colonial metropole. This book examines the consequences of these two tendencies and looks forward throughout the 1990s to identify likely trends in matters related to security, trade, investment, aid, the Franc zone, and other ongoing negotiations between the countries of Europe and sub-Saharan Africa.

The SAIS African Studies Library

Tunisia: The Political Economy of Reform, edited by I. William Zartman

Ghana: The Political Economy of Recovery, edited by Donald Rothchild

Europe and Africa: The New Phase, edited by I. William Zartman

Botswana: The Political Economy of Democratic Development, edited by Stephen John Stedman